GOTHIC ITALY

Crime, Science, and Literature after Unification, 1861–1914

Gothic Italy

Crime, Science, and Literature after Unification, 1861–1914

STEFANO SERAFINI

UNIVERSITY OF TORONTO PRESS
Toronto Buffalo London

© University of Toronto Press 2024
Toronto Buffalo London
utorontopress.com
Printed in the USA

ISBN 978-1-4875-5863-5 (cloth)   ISBN 978-1-4875-5865-9 (EPUB)
                                 ISBN 978-1-4875-5864-2 (PDF)
Toronto Italian Studies

Library and Archives Canada Cataloguing in Publication

Title: Gothic Italy : crime, science, and literature after unification, 1861–1914 /
    Stefano Serafini.
Names: Serafini, Stefano, author
Series: Toronto Italian studies.
Description: Series statement: Toronto Italian studies | Includes bibliographical
    references and index.
Identifiers: Canadiana (print) 20240445678 | Canadiana (ebook)
    20240445694 | ISBN 9781487558635 (cloth) | ISBN 9781487558642 (PDF) |
    ISBN 9781487558659 (EPUB)
Subjects: LCSH: Italian literature – 19th century – History and criticism. |
    LCSH: Italian literature – 20th century – History and criticism. |
    LCSH: Crime in literature. | LCSH: Science in literature.
Classification: LCC PQ4085 .S47 2024 | DDC 850.9/3556 – dc23

Cover design: Val Cooke
Cover images: Cover of issue 15 of *I grandi processi illustrati*, 20 December
1896. Courtesy of the Ministry of Culture. National Library of Florence;
iStock.com/Olga_Z

We wish to acknowledge the land on which the University of Toronto
Press operates. This land is the traditional territory of the Wendat, the
Anishnaabeg, the Haudenosaunee, the Métis, and the Mississaugas of the
Credit First Nation.

This book has been published with funds from Cariparo Foundation
"Starting Package" managed by Dipartimento di Scienze Storiche,
Geografiche e dell'Antichità of the University of Padova.

University of Toronto Press acknowledges the financial support of the
Government of Canada, the Canada Council for the Arts, and the Ontario Arts
Council, an agency of the Government of Ontario, for its publishing activities.

   Canada Council   Conseil des Arts
        for the Arts   du Canada

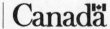

Contents

Acknowledgments vii

Introduction 3
1 Gothic Cities 20
2 Gothic Minds 57
3 Gothic Bodies 90
Conclusion 126

Notes 135
Bibliography 167
Index 191

Acknowledgments

This book would simply not exist without Giuliana Pieri and Abigail Lee Six: they believed in me when no one else did and I will never forget it. I owe much to a number of great scholars and friends who read and critiqued my work, listened to my rambling thoughts, and offered me overwhelming support: Maurizio Ascari, Guido Bartolini, Fabio Camilletti, Claudia Dellacasa, Marco Malvestio, and Nicolò Palazzetti. I would also like to thank the anonymous readers at the University of Toronto Press, who commented on the first draft of this book with attention and care, and those who helped me revise and improve my manuscript throughout its path to publication: Mark Thompson, Luca Somigli, Anna Finozzi, Fabrizio Foni, Elena Past, and Nicoletta Pireddu. My gratitude, finally, to the Modern Humanities Research Association, whose award was crucial to the completion of this manuscript.

The book's introduction contains ideas and concepts that previously appeared in the introduction and the chapter "Gothic Criminology" of the volume *Italian Gothic: An Edinburgh Companion* (Edinburgh University Press, 2023), which I co-edited with Marco Malvestio. Earlier reflections on Gothic cities (chapter 1 of this book) can be found in the chapter "Early Developments, 1861–1914" in *Italian Gothic* and in the article "Gotico e misteri nell'Italia post-unitaria," *Transalpina* 25 (2022): 87–100, https://doi.org/10.4000/transalpina.3773.

This book was conceived and written in London, where my heart is and will always be.

GOTHIC ITALY

Introduction

To a nineteenth-century external observer, Italy appeared to be a truly Gothic place. Over the course of the previous two centuries, foreign authors, commentators, and travellers had crystallized the image of Italy as a multiform, dark site of premodern survivals, plagued by superstition, Catholic obscurantism, and irrationalism, as well as degeneration, violence, corruption, and sexual deviance. The fragmented Italian territory was the favourite geographical and historical setting of British Gothic novelists such as Horace Walpole and Ann Radcliffe, who famously depicted it as a place dominated by chaos, excess, and brutality and ruled by both a feudal and despotic nobility and a corrupt and dissolute Catholic clergy.[1] Gothic Italy was not, as Kenneth Churchill has argued, simply "an imaginary Italy."[2] Although Radcliffe never travelled to the country, Walpole visited it with Thomas Gray between 1739 and 1741, and both the moral background of his novel *The Castle of Otranto* (1764) and its landscape, characterized by labyrinthine castles, claustrophobic churches, and desolate ruins, derived partly from his own Italian experience.[3]

The Gothicization of Italy was not merely the result of Gothic imagination. In his unfinished *Journey to Italy*, detailing a journey he undertook in 1775, the young French Count de Sade depicted Italian cities as places of moral depravity and sexual transgression: "Incest and adultery, and in general all crimes of impurity, are not in Florence among the number of reserved sins," Sade notes, while in Rome and Naples violence is "the only response to a discussion."[4] In 1781, the British traveller and commentator John Moore used an explicitly Gothic image to describe his impression of Venice: Who, he wonders, would not prefer to "live in a convenient, comfortable house, which could stand only a few centuries, than in a gloomy Gothic fabric, which would last to the day of judgment?"[5] Pam Perkins observes that, in this passage, the natural assumption "is to see the 'convenient, comfortable house' as a smugly self-satisfied image of the English constitution ... Modernity, comfort, and adaptability are opposed to darkly gloomy splendour, with the English supposedly on the side of light and progress."[6]

There is, as Perkins insists, an indissoluble relationship between the different, apparently opposite, representations of Italy in travel writing and in the Gothic novel: in the "British literary context, the traveller's Italy and Gothic Italy are impossible to disentangle completely."[7] This image did not fade in the following century. In Anglo-Irish Gothic stories, such as Charles Maturin's *The Fatal Revenge or the Family of Montorio* (1807), the anonymous novelette *The Castle of Savina, or the Irishman in Italy: A Tale* (c. 1807), or Joseph Sheridan Le Fanu's short stories "Spalatro: From the Notes of Fra Giacomo" (1843) and "Borrhomeo the Astrologer: A Monkish Tale" (1862), Italy continued to be represented as dangerous and Italians as savage, uncontrollable, and corrupt.[8] "There are no fixed times for the administration of justice, or its execution, in this unaccountable country," Charles Dickens laconically comments in his 1846 *Pictures from Italy*.[9]

Yet, to most Italians, Gothic Italy sounded, and continues to sound, like a contradiction in terms. The Gothic, as defined by Fred Botting, is a multifaceted, hybrid, and destabilizing mode that constantly transgresses boundaries and subverts accepted paradigms of realism, rationality, and morality.[10] The Gothic gives positive value to disorder and chaos, to violent emotions and forbidden desires, in open opposition to the harmony, equilibrium, and moderation of neoclassicism and the Enlightenment. From a critical perspective, it is a deviant, ambiguous form that resists systematic theorization and defies established, natural assumptions. For David Punter, what lies at the heart of the Gothic is its "ambivalence," its inherently conflictual nature, and its power to function as an instrument of both critique and repression.[11] The Gothic explores the dark, disturbing side of individuals, cultures, and societies to interrogate socially dictated and institutionally entrenched attitudes and laws relating to gender, class, race, and power. The Gothic allows the uncontrollable emergence of what modern societies seek to control and repress, including racial struggles, female sexuality, gender instability, the occult, class conflict, and the agency of nature. The power of the Gothic, as Jerrold E. Hogle puts it, stems precisely from "the way it helps us to address and disguise some of the most important desires, quandaries, and sources of anxiety, from the most internal and mental to the widely social and cultural"; it forces its readers to "confront what is psychologically buried in individuals or groups, including their fears of the mental unconscious itself and the desires from the past now buried in that forgotten location."[12]

Essentially, the Gothic is excess, instability, ambiguity, abjection, contamination, and mobility. Italian-speaking culture, in contrast, has nearly always viewed itself as innately "rational," rooting its identity, Fabio Camilletti and Alessandra Aloisi explain, "in the worship of aesthetic 'measure,' the refusal of superstition, and philosophical/ theological rigour."[13] Since the beginning of the Restoration period, Camilletti argues, every "Nordic" influence on Italian culture has faced ostracism that had no equivalent in other European countries; such radical opposition, which combined climatic and anthropological considerations with a refusal to contaminate the premises of classic aesthetics, contributed to a repudiation of the literary paradigms of Northern Europe by Italian Romanticism.[14] Widespread scepticism, for instance, characterized the debate on Romanticism that took place in the literary journal *Il conciliatore* at the beginning of the nineteenth century. Morena Corradi reminds us that the article "Poesia romantica dall'Oriente" (dated 26 November 1818), which focuses on Romantic poetry from the Orient, mocks Romanticism's "bizzarre invenzioni" (bizarre inventions) and discredits "l'apparizione degli spettri dei morti" (the apparition of the ghosts of the dead) as "le superstizioni del volgo" (superstitions of the common people).[15] In the often cited letter "Sul romanticismo" sent by Alessandro Manzoni to the Marquis d'Azeglio in 1823, the author expresses disdain for literary manifestations of Gothic writing,[16] famously defining them as "non so qual guazzabuglio di streghe, di spettri, un disordine sistematico, una ricerca stravagante, una abiura in termini del senso comune" (an unimaginable muddle of witches, spectres, a systemic disorder, an extravagant research, and an abjuration of common sense). These are examples of literary creation that, for Manzoni, "si sarebbe avuta molta ragione di rifiutare, e di dimenticare, se fosse stato proposto da alcuno" (one would have much reason to refute and forget, had it ever in fact been proposed by anyone).[17]

During the Classicist-Romantic quarrel that inflamed the literary scene between approximately 1816 and 1827 – one of the defining moments in Italian cultural history, when the conflict between rationalism and irrationalism, measure and excess, modernity and Gothicism assumed a recognizable shape – the Italian cultural establishment sought to ostracize, negate, and reject what Aloisi and Camilletti call "the potentially dangerous drives of 'Northern' forms of knowledge and discursive practices."[18] The Gothic, however, did not dissolve. The Italian refusal of and resistance to the Gothic, as Camilletti has recently argued, led to complex and oblique forms of incorporation and rearticulation.[19] In fact, the Classicist-Romantic quarrel did not result in the firm establishment of one movement or the other but rather gradually faded, generating the paradoxical coexistence of two antithetical historical forces.[20] Instead of recognizing the unstable nature of this relationship, nineteenth-century critics and commentators – the case of the Neapolitan politician and historian Francesco De Sanctis is emblematic – praised Italian literature's ability to reconcile national tradition and foreign influences, with the result that the Romantic/Gothic dimension of its cultural heritage was gradually dispelled.

Over time, modern Italian literature's profoundly Gothic, transgressive, and popular lineage has been overshadowed and its genealogical tree progressively cleansed of seemingly disreputable genetic connections with narratives imbued with violence, horror, and the supernatural. Complex, hybrid forms of writing that cross national, textual, and generic boundaries and constantly move between high and popular culture have been either dismissed as essentially alien to Italian sensibilities or purified using the filters of rationality, restraint, irony, and classical measure.[21]

The history of late nineteenth-century Italy, however, is tinged with the Gothic. After formal unification in 1861, the governing elites focused on the promotion of modern social values, fighting against those forces (premodern beliefs, Catholicism, superstitions) and forms of deviance that both intellectuals and scientists saw as a serious obstacle to the secularization of the country, the civilization of the population, and the normalization of the body politic. What was considered Gothic – the supernatural, the diseased and the contaminated, the criminal, the excessive, and the abject – was exorcised, rejected, metaphorically expelled, and relocated to those interstitial spaces that were deemed safe because they were subjected to disciplinary control and the medical gaze: courtrooms, prisons, mental institutions, rooms or theatres hosting séances, experiments in magnetism or other apparently supernatural occurrences, the most remote and less civilized areas of the country, and the poorest and most violent neighbourhoods of the cities. The Gothic, then, was never successfully repressed but rather assumed different forms and infiltrated new spaces.

Between 1861 and the outbreak of the First World War in 1914, the building of the new nation took place against a backdrop of political turmoil, social tension, and turbulent processes of industrialization and urbanization that contributed to the perceived dramatic rise in violent crime. Crime quickly became, in the eyes of both administrators and commentators, the principal reason for the country's backwardness, chronic instability, and inability to pursue the path of modernity. My contention is that the Gothic, proliferating across different literary, sociocultural, and scientific spaces, permeated and influenced the project of Italian nation-building, casting a dark and pervasive shadow on Italian history. *Gothic Italy* explores the nuances, contradictions, and implications of the conflict between what the Gothic embodies in post-unification Italy (transgression, mayhem, the occult) and the values that a supposedly secular, modern country tries to uphold and promote (law, moral and social order, rationality). This book analyses a variety of literary works concerned with crime in conversation with medical, legal, sociological, and police texts that tapped into fears relating to contagion, race, and class fluidity, deviant minds and abnormal sexuality, female transgression, male performativity, and the instability of the new body politic. By tracing how writers, scientists, and thinkers engaged with these issues, *Gothic Italy* unveils the mutual network of exchanges that informed national discourses about crime and shaped the unificatory process during a historical moment that was crucial to the development of modern attitudes towards normality and deviance, which continued to circulate widely in the years to come and still resonate disturbingly in contemporary society.

Gothic Italy

In the aftermath of national unification, Italy was still a project whose content and forms were vague and often contradictory. The establishment of a unified nation in a territory with an exceptionally diverse history proved extremely complicated. Many divisive factors – linguistic, regional, religious – resulted in liberal hegemony being weak from the beginning and generated anxieties and discontent. One of the most pressing problems faced by the ruling class was crime, particularly in its common, rather than political, manifestations.[22] It was seen as the principal cause of the country's backwardness, while also providing a compelling explanation for the country's inability to compete internationally, especially with other European nations. Not only did official administrators have to fight the phenomenon of brigandage – which plagued Southern Italy in the 1860s and 1870s, forcing the government to declare a state of emergency in many regions and to allow military intervention – they also had to deal with the apparently exponential increase, particularly noticeable in the largest and most developed cities, of various forms of violent crimes, which represented, notes Paul Garfinkel, "both an immediate danger and a long-term threat to the Liberal state-building project."[23]

In reality, as Mary Gibson has shown in her landmark work on crime in modern Italy, the situation, as reconstructed by criminal statistics, was not bleak enough to cause such major alarm over immorality and disorder among specialists and government officials.[24] This perception was a consequence of the major expansion of the Italian population, which grew by 40 per cent between 1861 and 1911 in spite of emigration, leading to an increase in the number of outcasts and outsiders, which gave both bourgeois residents and administrators the impression of a dramatic rise in criminal activity.[25] Against this background of mayhem and uncertainty, it is unsurprising that crime came to occupy a central place in the politics of the new state. The Italian government urgently demanded new and reliable measures to prevent what was seen as a rising tide of criminals from undermining an already precarious sociopolitical order. The main aim was the identification of those individuals deemed dangerous so they could be neutralized and excluded from civil society. The emergence of positivist medical theories and technologies that promised the correct identification of deviants through a study of their bodies and minds represented a dramatic turning point in the long-lasting battle against crime.

The figure who systematized and popularized such theories, in Italy and beyond, was the physician, anthropologist, and criminologist Cesare Lombroso,[26] the founder of the Italian school of positivist criminology and one of the most influential thinkers of the nineteenth century.[27] His theories and those of his colleagues and followers found fertile terrain in the politics and social policies of the new state. Silvana Patriarca has argued that the unificatory process exacerbated cultural debates on "the current state of decline and deficiency of the Italians,"[28] solidifying the perception of the country's atavistic backwardness and struggle with modernity, and the explanation for the country's violent-crime problem was believed to be, as Garfinkel notes, in the "moral character" of the Italians.[29] In such a moment, the ability to scientifically distinguish between healthy social subjects capable of improvement who might be re-included in the bourgeois social order and those biologically inferior social subjects who would never be compatible with modern societies gave positivists a major status and strong credibility among government officials and administrators. Discriminating between the "us" of a community and the dangerous "other" excluded by it served to protect the body politic from within and to lay the foundation for the modernization of a country that, in the eyes of its administrators, appeared to be truly Gothic – underdeveloped, degenerated, and sick.

The centrality that medical knowledge acquired in the second half of the nineteenth century, as theorists of biopolitics such as Roberto Esposito have pointed out, contributed to transforming the issue of public health, understood in its widest sense as the welfare of the nation, into "the pivot around which the entire economic, administrative, and political affairs of the state revolved."[30] Lombroso, as the embodiment of medical authority, was tasked with finding a remedy for Italy's sickness and lack of civilization. It is emblematic that in 1871, one of the first acts of the newly formed Società italiana di antropologia e di etnologia was to charge Lombroso and three other scientists – the anthropologists Paolo Mantegazza and Arturo Zannetti and the physiologist Moritz Schiff – with mapping the anatomical and physical character of the Italian population. The objective, as David Horn puts it, was to trace "the progress and state of health of the Italian nation" and to develop "both an evolutionary history and a geography of crime."[31] The realization of this project implied the ability "to make dangerous difference visible at the level of the body," so that "the larger body of Italy might be defended against risks" and "made modern."[32] The way to achieve this, paradoxically, was to embrace, rather than confront, the Gothic.

Gothic Science

Born in 1835 into a Jewish family in Verona, in Northern Italy, Lombroso graduated in medicine from the University of Pavia in 1858. From the beginning of his medical training in the 1850s, he was influenced by an exceptional variety of schools of thought, including German materialism, Italian pre-Darwinian evolutionist theory, physiognomy, phrenology, and anthropometry.[33] Other crucial influences include the research of 1860s and 1870s British criminologists – such as the psychiatrist Henry Maudsley, the prison physician David Nicolson, and the prison director James Bruce Thomson, who all advanced atavistic or constitutional and hereditary explanations of criminality[34] – and the work of evolutionists such as Herbert Spencer, Ernst Haeckel, and, of course, Charles Darwin.

Lombroso's theory of the principally biological foundations of crime gradually grew out of his research conducted on human subjects in the prisons and insane asylums of Pavia, Pesaro, and Reggio Emilia between 1863 and 1872. Building on what he regarded as a groundbreaking revelation – the discovery, during the examination of a brigand's skull in 1871, of a certain impression, the median occipital fossa, which he also found on the skulls of inferior animals, especially rodents – Lombroso contended that the phenomenon of delinquency is the product of atavism, that is, arrested development at a more primitive mental stage. Criminals' natural predisposition to deviant behaviour, for Lombroso, is explained by their alleged reversion to a subhuman type of man, characterized by physical features reminiscent of primitive people, including jug ears, thin beards, pronounced sinuses, protruding chins, and broad cheekbones.[35] Gibson suggests that Lombroso, who had read *The Origin of Species* (1859) before the publication of its Italian translation in 1864, "drew on the popularity and prestige of Charles Darwin to build an evolutionary scaffold that ranked certain groups as more successful in the struggle for existence than others."[36] He combined both "the Darwinian theory of the descent of man from animals" and "monogenism, or the single ancestry of all humans," to argue that the most complex white species represented the final, perfected stage of human evolution from a physical, moral, and psychological perspective, thus placing the other, less developed races at the bottom of the evolutionary ladder.[37] What distinguishes Lombroso's criminological thinking is the belief that criminals naturally predisposed to deviant behaviour are savages, members of the non-white races. European, white criminals, for Lombroso, are throwbacks on the evolutionary scale, as they exhibit physical, moral, and psychological features that he believed were anomalies for the white race but normal for lower, less civilized races. This theory was first popularized when it appeared in the first edition of *L'uomo delinquente* in 1876, the same year Lombroso was appointed Chair of Legal Medicine and Public Hygiene at the University of Turin and formed the nucleus of his positivist school.

The composite nature of the school was exceptional. Lombroso's followers were not only medical doctors but also criminal lawyers and penal jurists, psychiatrists, anthropologists, and sociologists who shared a positivist approach to the study of deviance, based on the assumption that the collection of data was instrumental in determining general laws. This methodology served to break the link between responsibility and practices of punishment originally established by Cesare Beccaria, the founder of what would later be called the classical school of legal thought. In his *Dei delitti e delle pene* (1764), Beccaria held that crime constitutes an expression of free will and that individuals should be held responsible for their actions and punished according to the severity of their crime. Rejecting Beccaria's belief in free will, positivists contended that human behaviour, including its deviant manifestations, was determined by a variety of different factors, predominantly biological but also psychological, environmental, and social. Positivists took a comprehensive approach to the analysis of crime, evaluating deviants' physical and mental features, personal and family medical histories, emotional development, ethnicity, environment and upbringing, and social factors. They shifted the focus from the crime to the criminal, arguing that the degree of punishment must correspond not to the seriousness of the criminal act but the dangerousness of the perpetrator, a quality that, according to them, could be diagnosed by scrutinizing the body and mind of the subject in search of physical and psychological abnormalities.

The popularity of Lombroso also derived from his extraordinary ability to mobilize and attract people, both from within and outside the academe. His journal, the *Archivio di psichiatria, scienze penali ed antropologia criminale*, founded in 1880, was truly interdisciplinary, situated at the intersection of anthropology, psychiatry, medicine, jurisprudence, sociology, psychology, and pedagogy, and had a readership much greater than the mere scientific community. He and his disciples published a wealth of articles in journals and magazines aimed at the general educated public, including the *Gazzetta Letteraria*, *Il Fanfulla*, and *La Lettura*, while also producing numerous scientific studies exploring literary and artistic texts within the frame of criminology. The popularization of positivist theories of deviance contributed to the reconceptualization of crime as an attack on the integrity of the social body, with criminals being evaluated according to the danger they posed to the health and well-being of the population.[38]

These controversial positions, however, did not remain unchallenged. Penal jurists, penal reformers, lawyers, and legal experts, such as Enrico Pessina, Pietro Ellero, Francesco Carrara, and Luigi Lucchini, whose approach to crime and punishment was rooted in Beccaria's theses, emphasized the importance of legal responsibility and were thus troubled by the rejection of free will and the positivist doctrine of social defence. They saw positive criminology's medicalization of crime as a significant invasion of the legal domain by non-legal discourses through the construction of what Michel Foucault defines as the "dangerous individual," who is no longer subject to the concept of responsibility but, rather, is identified as a "potential source of acts" based on "what he is by nature, according to his constitution, character traits, or his pathological variables."[39] Criticism of Lombroso's school came not only from the legal sphere but also from sociologists such as Napoleone Colajanni, who, despite adopting a broadly positivist approach, minimized the role of biology and purported to trace the aetiology of crime primarily to social, moral, institutional, and environmental factors.[40]

The debate on the criminogenic factors underlying criminal behaviour that dominated the late nineteenth and the early twentieth centuries was far more nuanced than had been acknowledged until very recently. While members of the positivist school, including Lombroso himself, gradually moved towards a multi-causal approach that included social conditions such as poverty, alcoholism, and unemployment in the production of crime, along with the individual's inherited biological and psychological constitution, penal jurists and exponents of the classical school came to accept that external conditions acted together with constitutional ones to determine deviant behaviour. The positions of different scientists and schools of thought often overlapped, and medical knowledge assumed an increasingly influential status. By the end of the century, as Nicole Rafter sums up, "the understanding of criminality as a medical problem became dominant and almost automatic, an assumption more than a proposition."[41]

Remarkably, despite widespread criticism, Lombroso had an extraordinary influence on numerous aspects of post-unification Italian culture. Although positivist criminology had a relatively minor impact on the development of Italian criminal law – most of its propositions failed to be incorporated in the 1889 criminal code, the first criminal code of the unified country – its principles penetrated the state and governmental levels and the everyday workings of the criminal justice system, that is, the police, the prisons, the hospitals, the mental facilities, and the courts. Moreover, they penetrated the realm of culture, infiltrating literature and popular publishing. I contend that Lombroso's science aroused so much interest, attracting and repulsing at the same time, because it was imbued with Gothicism and was thus able to capture common prejudices and manipulate widespread anxieties.

Lombroso's criminology is deeply Gothic in its methods, applications, and implications.[42] Andrew Smith identifies a "Gothicised presence" inhabiting late nineteenth-century criminological theories that "rely on images of perversion, atavism and forms of monstrosity."[43] The concept of atavism is strongly infused with the Gothic because it highlights the disturbing power of the past to reappear and influence the present. In *The Descent of Man* (1871), Darwin writes that through "the principle of reversion" in hereditary processes, "a long-lost structure is called back into existence,"[44] which, Stephan Karschay points out, "makes the evolutionary past readable in the present."[45] The idea of the atavistic criminal tapped into widespread fears of degeneration that characterized the post-Darwinian Western world, both giving shape to and providing scientific validation for a purely Gothic figure, a throwback to an earlier evolutionary era that was physically and mentally abnormal.[46] Lombroso's criminal bodies can be compared to what Kelly Hurley, in her landmark work on fin de siècle Gothic writing, identifies as the ab-human, that is, Gothic liminal bodies that occupy the ambiguous space between the human and the beast, the civilized and the primitive.[47] These bodies, which threaten the integrity of human identity, are the product not of uncanny supernatural forces but rather of scientifically explicable processes.[48] It is thus the duty of criminologists and diagnosticians such as Lombroso to provide the necessary tools to identify and categorize these elements of horror and abnormality. His theories, then, destabilized accepted boundaries and traditional assumptions about human identity and sexuality, converting what Nicole Rafter and Per Ystehede call "Gothic anxieties" – such as the spectre of degeneration, the bestiality within humans, and the divided nature of the self – into "scientific concerns."[49]

Besides the creation of the born, atavistic criminal, Lombroso's criminology itself seems like a Gothic labyrinth of often contradictory principles with no central reference point. Throughout his long career, Lombroso constantly revised his theses, especially in response to widespread criticism. He examined, measured, and experimented on the physical bodies of inmates in Italian prisons, while also studying their artefacts (graffiti, sculptures, and tattoos); he performed autopsies on dead criminals and analysed bones of ancient peoples preserved in archaeological museums. All of this work provided the data that filled his books, particularly *L'uomo delinquente*. The revisions of this treatise were produced at intervals of various lengths over a period of twenty years, with the second published in 1878, the third in 1884, the fourth in 1889, and the last in 1896; each was longer, broader in scope, and invariably more complicated and confused than the last. The first volume consists of only 255 pages, while the last edition consists of four volumes, totalling nearly 2,000 pages. By comparing the different versions of this work, we can see how Lombroso accumulates, rather than revising. The result is a Gothic, labyrinthine text, full of contradictions, inconsistencies, and errors. In the first volume, Lombroso's approach is still very narrow, as he groups all lawbreakers in the same category, which is then compared to the insane and other groups of deviant subjects. In the following editions, he identified different categories of criminals (the habitual or born criminal, the morally insane criminal, the criminal by passion, the epileptic, the occasional criminal), and he observed that crimes were caused by multiple factors, including social factors, thus extending the range of causes beyond atavism. However, he was unable to explain the interrelations between the immediate causes of crime; as time went on, he put forward different ultimate causes – moral insanity, epilepsy, degeneration – without satisfactorily articulating their relationship to atavism. The infinite possible combinations of measurable signs of criminal behaviour eventually frustrated the effort to construct specifically recognizable types of criminals. Criminologists, in Horn's words, "made everyone potentially (if not equally) dangerous,"[50] ultimately painting a Gothic picture of generalized and fundamentally incomprehensible deviance that threatens the rationality of our world and fuels, instead of assuaging, social fears and anxieties.

Moreover, although Lombroso was not the first thinker to scientifically address the question of the supernatural, he was certainly the one who most persistently explored the nature of occult phenomena and their relation to crime, encouraging a large number of successors and collaborators to follow the same path.[51] In these years, criminological research delved into previously unexplored territories, investigating the controversial effects of the latest medical and technological discoveries. Lombroso and his disciples worked on a rich variety of unusual and seemingly supernatural phenomena, including cases of mesmerism, thought transference, spiritualism, premonitions, and haunted houses, revealing how even research into that which is beyond the realm of matter served to probe the boundaries between normality and abnormality, health and sickness, the known and the unknown.[52] The Gothic dimension of Lombroso's science ultimately has the effect of demonizing a vast and indiscriminate range of cultural others – not only criminals but all "deviant" figures at the margins of the social body – onto whom Italians could project their fears and concerns about a deeply fragmented, profoundly Gothic country.

Fin de siècle science and literature drew on a common repertoire of ideas that originated in the Gothic imaginary. Lombroso's research on crime as a pathological re-emergence of primitive, animalistic habits was shaped by Gothic narratives and simultaneously encouraged and legitimized the creation of literary figures of monstrosity – from Dracula to Mr. Hyde – that leave the spatially and temporally remote locales of early Gothic fiction to threaten the realm of the contemporary reader, infiltrating the new urban landscape and penetrating the bourgeois domestic world. This mutual interaction between Gothic and scientific narratives contributed to changing the location of the monstrous. As Botting has explained, whereas in late eighteenth-century Gothic literature, horrors tended to be external to the human form – ghosts and evil monks who threatened the protagonists from outside – in the nineteenth century, the horrors became internal and the perversions that menaced Gothic figures came from inside their own degenerating minds.[53]

In Italy, the discourses on criminality produced by positivist criminology engendered a multifarious response in the field of Gothic fiction. Italian authors, from Francesco Mastriani and Giulio Piccini to Matilde Serao, Carolina Invernizio, Luigi Capuana, and Gabriele D'Annunzio, variously experimented with the narrative possibilities afforded by the latest scientific discoveries, the scope and diversity of which proved malleable and ambiguous enough to provide such authors with new models and themes. The narratives produced by these authors had a major impact on both their wider readership and criminological thinking, largely due to their popularity. The boundaries between scientific and cultural imaginaries were particularly porous, and thus the exchanges between criminology and Gothic literature were anything but unidirectional. Ideas and images of criminality worked their way, with fascinating fluidity, across generic and disciplinary boundaries, ultimately shaping how modern Italians reflected on and conceptualized the origins of evil. At a moment in which the technological and commercial means of satisfying the public appetite for lurid and sensational stories were rapidly expanding, Gothic narratives concerned with crime and transgression became a significant arena where social preoccupations, anxieties, and conflicts were culturally explored. However, most of these stories have resisted rigorous analysis or have had their Gothic potential deactivated. After all, in a territory that openly refused Nordic literary forms, and in which generic modes of fiction seem never to possess a subversive character, there is no place for the Gothic.

Gothic Literature

Italianists have long struggled to even acknowledge the existence of the Gothic mode in Italian literature.[54] Monica Farnetti, for instance, has identified "la natura sostanzialmente parodica e citazionale – quando non meramente esornativa – del gotico italiano" (the substantially parodic and "citational" – when not merely decorative – nature of the Italian Gothic), which essentially failed to make an impact in the long nineteenth century.[55] The term *gotico* is hardly found in Italian literary criticism and is often utilized in its restrictive, eighteenth-century sense. In Francesco Orlando's posthumous *Il soprannaturale letterario*, which consists of a series of lectures from 1984 onwards, the word "Gothic" appears only ten times, mostly as an adjective used to describe the works of Ann Radcliffe.[56] More importantly, since 1977, when Tzvetan Todorov's seminal volume *Introduction à la littérature fantastique* (1970) was translated into Italian, it has often been used as a synonym of *fantastico* to define a homogeneous group of literary texts.[57] In the 1980s, the work of writers and scholars such as Italo Calvino, Enrico Ghidetti, and Gianfranco Contini contributed to the canon of the *fantastico* by denying much of its irrational, excessive, and popular character in order to emphasize its rational, deliberately ironic, and markedly elitist nature. Calvino dismisses the fantastic in the nineteenth century as a "campo veramente 'minore'" (very "marginal" domain) characterized by "il controllo della ragione sull'ispirazione istintiva o inconscia" (reason's control of instinctive or unconscious inspiration) and "disciplina stilistica" (stylistic discipline).[58] Quite surprisingly, in Calvino's view, the only notable nineteenth-century Italian authors of fantastic tales are Giacomo Leopardi, with his *Operette morali* (1827), and Carlo Collodi, with his *Le avventure di Pinocchio* (1881–3).[59] Enrico Ghidetti and Leonardo Lattarulo have also denied the existence of Gothic fictions during the nineteenth century, arguing that, unlike in the rest of Europe, explorations of Gothic themes and devices in Italy were conducted exclusively by Decadent artists at the beginning of the twentieth century.[60] Gianfranco Contini, in the 1988 reprint of his *Italia magica* (which originally appeared in France in 1946), writes about the fantastic exclusively as an ironic genre, practised by "umoristi e balordi" (humourists and buffoons), which borders on surrealism and humour.[61] Giuseppe Lo Castro, in a 2007 collective volume on the Italian fantastic, follows in the footsteps of Calvino and Ghidetti, pointing out that "la maggior parte degli scrittori italiani che hanno subito il fascino del fantastico si confrontano comunque con una istanza irriducibilmente logico-razionale, che tende a confinare il potenziale perturbante in ambienti ristretti e in situazioni-limite" (the vast majority of Italian writers who have been fascinated by the fantastic are faced with an irreducibly logical-rational demand that tends to restrict the uncanny to narrow environments and liminal situations).[62]

Fabio Camilletti and Fabrizio Foni were among the first to highlight how such Italian theorizations of the Gothic/fantastic as an exclusively "'alto,' intellettualistico e razionale" (high, intellectual, and rational) form of writing are historically problematic and critically inadequate, as they marginalize the "contaminazione con altri codici e la cultura 'popolare,' il manieristico e l'irrazionale" (contamination with other modes and popular culture, the manneristic, and the irrational).[63] Scholars have lost sight of the complexity of the Gothic, its hybrid nature, and its tendency to combine high and low culture. One of the most prominent and influential theorists of the Italian Gothic/fantastic is Remo Ceserani, who has consistently ignored developments in international Gothic studies in order to promote a relatively outdated critical paradigm rooted in the Italian tradition of literary criticism. In the pioneering and significant *The Italian Gothic and Fantastic: Encounters and Rewritings of Narrative Traditions* (2007), edited by Francesca Billiani and Gigliola Sulis, the theoretical coordinates of the book are provided by Ceserani, who argues that the difference between the Gothic and the fantastic resides in their very essence. The Gothic is a genre that "constructed its tradition for the most part using the model of the romance (and, if necessary, combining it with elements of the fable or fairy tale, the extraordinary and the horrific)." The fantastic, on the other hand, is a "new, unmistakably modern literary mode which is also found in texts belonging to different genres, even those characterized by the clearest mimetic realism."[64] Not only does Ceserani privilege the fantastic over the Gothic, but he also uses the term "Gothic" in its restrictive sense, dismissing its manifestations in the Italian context. These equivocal statements are ostensibly contrasted by the way in which the Gothic mode has been theorized and studied in Anglo-American scholarship since the 1990s. Nonetheless, this theoretical approach has created, as Stefano Lazzarin writes, an "amalgama di abbagliante prestigio" (amalgam of dazzling prestige) that continues to go largely undisputed in Italian literary criticism.[65]

However, over the past few years, and particularly in the English-speaking world of Italian studies, something seems to have changed. The recent publication of *Italian Gothic: An Edinburgh Companion*, which I co-edited with Marco Malvestio, the first in the Edinburgh Companions to the Gothic series to focus on a non-English-speaking culture, has both challenged the dominant Anglo-centric paradigm and revitalized debates on the Gothic in Italian culture. It has offered the first systematic theorization of the Italian Gothic by tracking its historical trajectory, examining how it infiltrated various media (including poetry, cinema, comics, and music), and probing some of its major themes, from the female Gothic to Gothic criminology and the ecogothic. This monograph, then, does not exist in a vacuum. However, instead of trying to examine and define the Italian Gothic, the volume embarks on a descent into a grim, subversively Gothic Italy that has long remained occult. I will not only focus on texts that have been labelled as strictly Gothic and stories that appear, from the outside, to belong to the Gothic tradition; I will also consider texts that either contain Gothic elements or engage with what the Gothic embodies – the contaminated, the transgressive, the deviant, and the monstrous. This book focuses on the interaction and interplay between crime, science, and the Gothic. That said, I will not read literary and scientific texts as if the former were essentially fictional reformulations or rearticulations of discourses that developed in the scientific realm. As Robert Mighall cautions in his fundamental *A Geography of Victorian Gothic Fiction* (1999), different agents, from novelists to criminologists, "have different professional and epistemological agendas and obligations"; thus, "to subsume all utterances produced at a given time into a monolithic cultural 'context' suppresses these important differences."[66] In the following pages, then, I will explore the complex and manifold relationship between Gothic literature and (Gothicized) discourses pertaining to the spheres of medicine, criminal law, sociology, religion, politics, and the occult, tracing a series of underlying ideological implications, with the aim of reconstructing the debates and discourses relating to crime that informed the formation of the modern Italian state.

The book is divided into three large chapters: "Gothic Cities," "Gothic Minds," and "Gothic Bodies." The first chapter starts from the premise that, in the aftermath of Italy's unification, the ruling class was concerned by the power of the uncivilized lower classes to infect society with their dangerous tastes and morals, especially in the largest cities, where the growing slums were increasingly identified as sites of crime and degeneration and the proximity between diverse social classes became a reality. This chapter thus explores the dynamics underlying the medical and sociocultural construction of individuals as dangerous by reading a variety of post-unification urban novels by authors such as Francesco Mastriani, Giulio Piccini, and Matilde Serao, among others, in conversation with the work of criminologists, sociologists, police delegates, inspectors, and examining magistrates. Italian writers were strongly preoccupied with the developing urbanization of the modern city, and the Gothic arose largely as an acknowledgment of this disquiet. Through the analysis of three specific Gothic motifs – the city as labyrinth; the representation of the lower classes in terms of racial otherness; and the connection between smell, disease, and contagion – I reveal how the modern Italian city was constructed as a Gothic body with a frighteningly real propensity for physical disease that led to social and moral disorder.

Chapters 2 and 3 consider how contemporary medical and legal research on the nature of criminal behaviour filtered into the literary sphere. Both chapters capture and explore the ambiguous or ambivalent nature of the Gothic, which tends to reinforce and recirculate deeprooted ideas and theories concerning male and female criminality (with the first markedly associated with the mind and the second with the body), while simultaneously manipulating or subverting dominant perceptions and assumptions. Chapter 2, "Gothic Minds," analyses male-focused, transgressor-centred stories in which deviance is represented as an outward manifestation of the internal workings of the criminal's mind. The first part looks at the crime-confession pattern in Emilio De Marchi's *Il cappello del prete* (1887) and Luigi Capuana's *Il marchese di Roccaverdina* (1901), two novels that conceal anxieties about preternatural forces and biological roots of transgression beneath a superficial association between free will, responsibility, and punishment. The second part explores the figure of the sexual monster within the context of emerging sexology by examining how, in Giuseppe Bevione's short story "L'ossessione rossa" (1906), the issue of homosexuality is pathologized and articulated through the connection between disease and crime.

Chapter 3, "Gothic Bodies," investigates how gendered, Gothicized research on female criminal behaviour in modern Italy foregrounded corporeal imagery and biology, producing and disseminating ideas that associate markedly female forms of transgression such as prostitution and infanticide with monstrosity and alterity. The first part examines literary women who challenge the patriarchal, sociocultural, and legal boundaries intended to circumscribe and control them within a historical moment characterized by anxieties about women's emancipation and an interest in the punitive classification of female sexuality. I focus on texts that have received little or no critical attention by authors such as Carolina Invernizio and Francesco Mastriani, examining the medical, legal, and sociocultural contexts from which these confrontational fictional women emerged, thus demonstrating the constant interaction and interplay between scientific and (Gothicized) cultural discourses. The second part examines a series of texts concerned with vampires, including D'Annunzio's *L'innocente* (1892), Daniele Oberto Marrama's "Il dottor Nero" (1904), and Luigi Capuana's "Un vampiro" (1904), to probe how the theme of (male) vampirism is absorbed into Gothic fiction with the effect of ambiguously exposing specifically Italian fears and anxieties about post-unification politics, male performativity, and female sexuality.

As in Dario Argento's *Profondo rosso* (1975), one of the greatest films in the history of Italian *giallo* cinema, in which the protagonist (the pianist-turned-detective David Hemmings) scrapes off a mural in an abandoned villa to discover a walled-up drawing room that reveals a tragic story of murder, mayhem, and madness, this book tries to bring to the surface that which was (historically) occulted and has been (critically) repressed. Behind its facade of positivist rationality, restraint, and classical measure, a truly Gothic Italy did exist, and its ghosts continue to haunt us all.

1 Gothic Cities

The Italian nation-building process was a sociocultural normalization project. It entailed the identification of all those phenomena regarded as socially and culturally deviant and the consequent application of legal and police measures in an attempt to curb them. This process served to legitimize the new political order, both domestically and internationally, while simultaneously allowing Italy to be included within the larger imperialist, industrial, and more civilized European context. The main form of social deviance, crime, figured prominently in the political agendas of Italian leaders and official administrators. As Garfinkel points out, crime was viewed by the ruling class as "the defining feature of Italian lawlessness, if not the country's 'incontestable' primacy in comparison with 'civilized' Europe."[1] Statistics seemed to clearly point to a sharp growth in habitual delinquency or recidivism, particularly in the South and in the largest cities, where the proximity and more frequent interaction between criminals and indigents generated social tension.[2] Increasing immigration from rural areas and the invasive and uneven processes of urbanization significantly contributed to the overcrowding, impoverishment, and degradation of some of the cities' most populated areas, which gradually became prolific breeding grounds for criminal and other antisocial activities. For the first time, a considerable number of urban areas, which had, until that time, remained the exclusive prerogative of the middle and upper classes, experienced a significant influx of a more diverse group of people, including indigents who needed charitable assistance but also repeat offenders such as vagrants, beggars, and prostitutes, who relied on illicit means to survive and were prosecuted under the criminal codes of the unified country.[3]

Physicians, jurists, criminologists, and sociologists saw the rise in urban criminality as a threat to public health and society and a considerable challenge to the prison system, and they sought to understand why specific individuals proved so resistant to correction and deterrence. According to Luigi Lacchè, the problem of recidivism helped draw attention to the existence of a recognizable social group of lawbreakers: from the early 1870s, discussions and theorizations about the potential perilousness of this great multitude of subversives, who came to be known as the "dangerous classes," started to proliferate.[4] This all-encompassing label was used to categorize perpetrators of very different unlawful acts that frequently occurred in cities, such as murder, vagrancy, prostitution, robbery, and larceny. In the widely read *La polizia e le classi pericolose della società* (1871), a lengthy manual that addresses the problem of public security in post-unification Italy, the lawyer and provincial police chief of Bologna Giovanni Bolis identifies as dangerous those individuals who live at the expense of the honest working class. He observes,

> le classi pericolose della società sono formate da tutti quegli individui che essendo sprovvisti dei mezzi necessari di sussistenza, vivono nell'ozio e nel vagabondaggio a spese degli altri cittadini; calpestando la legge suprema dell'uomo che è quella del lavoro, essi costituiscono un pericolo permanente all'ordine sociale.

> (the dangerous classes are those made up of those individuals who, lacking the necessary means of subsistence, live as idlers and vagrants at the expense of other citizens; by trampling on the supreme law of man, which is that of work, they constitute a permanent threat to social order.)[5]

The backwardness of these individuals constituted a menace to the process of state-building and the creation of a homogeneous, normal population. Their antisocial behaviour was seen as a public order issue that always legitimized, reproduced, and strengthened the social order. From a medical perspective, the problem of why normal, responsible citizens abided by the law while others kept violating social norms and rules was particularly urgent. To explain this, many doctors and other specialists used, variously and often inconsistently, the notion of race. Race is a historically problematic category that is better understood, as scholars such as Aliza Wong have argued, as a subset of the larger category of ethnocentrism, if by ethnocentrism we mean the construction of essentialized differences between socially and culturally defined groups.[6] Historians have increasingly pointed to the ways in which the science of race was integral to the politics of post-unification Italy.[7] For Michele Nani, the idea of otherness played a major role in the representation and construction of the new nation,[8] with the exclusion or inclusion of subjects becoming, as Gaia Giuliani maintains, "a tool for defining the borders of modern national citizenship through the social and political status they were gradually assigned."[9] The process of state-building thus required the identification of the country's weaknesses and anomalies, which were located in parts of Italy seen as "other," remote, uncivilized, and hence disposable because they were further from the European core, including the South and the poorest and most troubled areas of the country. According to Lacchè, Italians elaborated a theory of inferiority of the lower, dangerous classes that was both biological and historical;[10] it is telling, to use Francesco Benigno's words, that this social group was defined simultaneously as "class" and "caste" to underline its impermeability and the hereditary nature of its inferiority.[11]

As Foucault claims in his work on biopower and biopolitics, biopower maintains the best life chances for the biological entity of the population by identifying and eliminating threats to its survival.[12] To do this securitizing work, biopolitics required a criterion for determining the relative biological value of the features of the population. For Foucault, the idea of "race" – or better, "the distinction among races, the hierarchy of races" – becomes the primary "way of fragmenting the field of the biological that power controls," of singling out which of the population's characteristics were beneficial to its growth and which threatened its survival.[13] Consequently, it would be best to eliminate the latter: "The death of the bad race, of the inferior race (or the degenerate, or the abnormal) is something that will make life in general healthier: healthier and purer."[14] What is called scientific racism thus provides the ideology that enables the identification, exclusion, or elimination of the "menacing other" so that the life of the population can improve. The fundamental implication is that "the discourse of race struggle" becomes the discourse of "power itself," a "centered, centralized, and centralizing power" that allows "the race that holds power" to "define the norm ... against those who pose a threat to the biological heritage." This is what historically spawns "all those biological-racist discourses of degeneracy, but also all those institutions within the social body which make the discourse of race struggle function as a principle of exclusion and segregation and, ultimately, as a way of normalizing society."[15] In this sense, biological theory, Foucault insists, became "a real way of thinking" about the relations between different phenomena, including "criminality, ... madness and mental illness, [and] the history of societies with their different classes."[16] The language of biology and heredity was widely used – even by those who did not fully adhere to the precepts of positivist criminology, as I suggest in the introduction – to explain why the vicious and harmful population that constitutes the underbelly of the modern city was biologically inferior and fundamentally different from normative, working citizens. Drawing on surveys, statistics, and case studies, many scientists and commentators effectively supported an evolutionary and racialized paradigm that defines this different sociocultural group, with its own language, customs, and traditions, as truly other, excluded from the benefits of civilization and immersed in a realm of moral degradation that inevitably leads to criminality.

Within this variegated cultural and scientific climate, it comes as no surprise that discourses regarding the existence, characteristics, recognizability, and potential perilousness of the dangerous classes transcended disciplinary boundaries and generated an unprecedented response in various fields, including social and documentary literature, urban fiction, and police writing. Police writing is a cultural sphere that has remained little explored by scholars, who have mostly concentrated on how specialists grappled with aberrant behaviour. This is surprising considering the variety of theorizations produced by law enforcement officers on the subject of dangerous individuals. An early example is *Delle persone sospette in Italia* (1874), written by the examining magistrate of Bologna Giorgio Curcio. Focusing on the legal aspects of the subject, Curcio draws attention to the anomalies of the Italian judicial system, including the lack of a unified criminal code, the dehumanizing nature of the penitentiary and the disastrous conditions of the Italian prisons, and, more generally, "un sistema di prevenzione ... che non è che fonte di reati" (a system of prevention ... that is nothing but a source of crime).[17] In the manual *Sorveglianti e sorvegliati* (1876), police inspector Paolo Locatelli examines the customs, characteristics, and ways of working of various offenders roaming the streets of the cities, from vagrants to idlers, gamblers, and prostitutes, as well as offering readers the psychological and practical guidance for dealing with the phenomenon of urban criminality. Likewise, in his *Polizia e delinquenza in Italia* (1887), police delegate Giuseppe Alongi argues for the importance of police forces in the urban world, discussing the various approaches adopted by police officers to understand, prevent, contain, and repress criminality, especially in its manifestations within the fastest-growing cities. These texts are written with a view to improving the reputation of the police in the eyes of the public: "Figlio della Polizia, non potevo restare insensibile alle continue ed acrimoniose accuse a cui vien fatta segno" (as a son of a police officer, I could not remain insensitive to the constant and acrimonious accusations directed at the police), Alongi writes.[18] Unlike specialists, law enforcement officers were not particularly interested in trying to grasp the origins or nature of urban delinquency among the lower classes; instead, they were more concerned with the practicalities of the everyday experience on the streets. This is reflected in the complicated relationship between police writing and contemporary medical science, as shown by the superficiality of officers' discussions of the constituents of crime, which do not rely on scientific sources but rather conflate diverse views on the subject without clearly explaining their interaction. Locatelli, for instance, problematically merges various factors, including social ones such as lack of education and biological ones such as natural tendencies, in his consideration of the key causes of transgression: "Nei delinquenti difettava l'educazione e l'istruzione ... erano stati trascinati al mal fare, oltreché dalle prave tendenze naturali, anche dalla bramosia sfrenata dei godimenti materiali" (delinquents lack basic education ... they turn to crime because of their natural tendencies, but it is also the result of their unrestrained desire for material pleasures).[19] Police officers also express divergent attitudes towards medicine and its application to police work. While, for instance, Alongi advocates "leggi preventive ispirate ai dettami della scienza positiva" (preventive laws inspired by the precepts of positivist science),[20] Locatelli is more sceptical and does little to conceal his distaste for specialists: "La psichiatria poggia su elementi sintomatici e induttivi, e non di assoluta certezza" (psychiatry is founded on symptomatic and inductive, rather than certain, elements), he points out, and only "casi rarissimi e specialissimi" (extremely rare and special cases) require the "esclusiva competenza dei medici alienisti" (exclusive competence of alienists).[21]

The landscape in which debates regarding the dangerous classes developed was thus a complex and contested terrain, in which multiple agents intervened and contributed their own version of knowledge. Lacchè suggests that the interaction between police officers, urban travellers, and novelists was crucial to the circulation and popularization of Gothicized discourses of criminality within ostensibly non-scientific domains: "Il potente immaginario letterario e le inchieste sociali 'sul campo'" (the powerful literary imaginary and the social investigations in the field), he observes, "sono la base per *costruire* ... i nuovi 'discorsi' destinati a intrecciarsi ... con le pratiche di polizia e di prevenzione" (are the basis for *constructing* ... new discourses destined to intertwine with ... police and preventive practices).[22] It is for this reason that, in the following pages, I offer a larger and more nuanced picture of the dynamics underlying the medical and sociocultural construction of dangerous individuals in post-unification Italy by reading the urban novels and social investigations of authors and journalists such as Francesco Mastriani,[23] Matilde

Serao,[24] Lodovico Corio,[25] Paolo Valera,[26] and Giulio Piccini[27] in conversation with the work of criminologists and sociologists but also police delegates, inspectors, and examining magistrates.

I have singled out portrayals of Milan, Florence, and Naples in a variety of late nineteenth-century urban novels and social investigations that, notwithstanding their ideological and aesthetical differences, relate to the process of state-building through the exploration of the city-crime nexus and its implications for the social question. All the authors, as we will see, attack the government for not taking action to remedy the city's ills and seek to propose ways of addressing the problem of dangerous individuals. The first section draws attention to the sociopolitical engagement of Italian authors by delineating the complex yet often ambivalent modalities through which they denounce the dismal effects of a corrupt system upon the poor, who were forced to live side by side with a criminal population in filthy and insanitary housing in the underbelly of the city or in the poorly constructed neighbourhoods that rapidly grew outside the old city centres. What distinguishes these texts is their attempt to hybridize seemingly incompatible elements, such as objectivity, scientific detachment, crude realism, and the Gothic, to convey a stronger political message, although the outcome is rather ambiguous. Hence, the second section investigates how the deployment of specific Gothic motifs – the metaphor of the city as labyrinth, the representation of the lower classes in terms of otherness, and the connection between smell and disease – eventually undermines the realistic and polemic character of the texts, while also weakening the authors' political message.[28] I contend that the ideological framework underlying Italian literature's portrayal of low and criminal life paradoxically serves the interests of politics, unwittingly reinforcing the ideas disseminated by the ruling class and further marginalizing a vast, indiscriminate range of cultural others. At the same time, I suggest that the interaction between scientists, novelists, urban travellers, and police officers in the three decades after unification shaped future scientific research on the dangerous classes. The language, ideas, case studies, narrative techniques, and devices used by these authors had a major impact on later analyses of the anthropology of the lower classes, influencing how scientists and commentators addressed the subject in the years to come.

Dangerous Individuals

The association between the city and crime represents one of the constitutive features of nineteenth-century Gothic literature. Outside of Italy, discussions of the dangerous classes took place throughout the first half of the century, inspiring some of the most famous novels of the period, including Eugène Sue's *Les Mystères de Paris* (1842–3), whose publication and immediate translation gave rise to an array of adaptations, imitations, and rewritings that have been categorized under the labels city mysteries or urban mysteries.[29] Many Italian authors were ready to capitalize on the widespread success of this literary trend, which quickly took hold in Italy, and played on the threatening dimension of the urban environment, constructing a varied lowlife topography of urban terrors.[30] The literary form of Italian urban mysteries has remained deeply undertheorized and understudied due to the lack of homogeneity between the texts, their ambivalent ideology, and their fundamental distance from the original foreign models.[31] In this chapter, I consider texts that have occasionally been included in surveys of Italian urban mysteries. Nonetheless, my intention is not to mark borders or create critical pigeonholes. Instead, I endeavour to trace connections between very different texts, mainly published when the genre had already become unfashionable (that is, between the early 1860s and the mid-1880s), in concomitance with the beginning of a slow, contested process of state-building that generated new tensions in urban Italy.[32] In terms of literary sources, this chapter focuses primarily, though not exclusively, on Mastriani's *I vermi: Studi storici su le classi pericolose in Napoli* (1863–4) and *I misteri di Napoli: Studi storico sociali* (1869–70); Corio's *La plebe di Milano* (1876–7), which was published in a single volume as *Milano in ombra: Abissi plebei* (1885); Valera's *Milano sconosciuta* (1878–9); Piccini's *Firenze sotterranea* (1884); and Serao's *Il ventre di Napoli* (1884).

This body of work is neither homogeneous nor without internal conflicts. These texts present many dissimilarities, most of which relate to the diverse urban structures of cities such as Naples, Florence, and Milan. Nineteenth-century Naples was one of the most populous and contradictory cities in Europe, characterized by the utmost wealth and extreme poverty, with a frightening, obscure underbelly that closely recalled those of London and Paris.[33] Shortly after unification, Naples was troubled by a serious emigration problem, gross economic mismanagement, brigandage, and organized crime, as well as a grave housing problem and class division, which created ideal conditions for social unrest.[34] Moreover, urbanization without a real increase in industrialization, as well as the outbreak of repeated cholera epidemics, aggravated the social discomfort.

Unlike Naples, Milan and Florence did not possess such a dichotomic character, nor did they have a teeming, dark underbelly. Instead, it was the growing city centre that made these cities a source of anxiety and ambivalence for residents, as well as for journalists, travellers, and writers of fiction. These city centres experienced an influx of lower and working classes into urban spaces that had, up until that point, been the domain of the affluent bourgeoisie. The problem of immigrants – both new industrial workers and outcasts from rural areas who did not have stable employment – was perceived as central in Florence. After having undergone an enormous urban renewal when it was the capital of the Kingdom of Italy between 1865 and 1871, Florence was completely neglected by the government when the country's centre of gravity moved to Rome, provoking a series of social problems.[35] Immigration also constituted a pressing issue in Milan, the country's wealthiest commercial city and the first in Italy to become an industrial city towards the end of the century. The pressure of immigration grew significantly over the decades and increasingly troubled Milanese residents, destabilizing an already precarious balance.[36] Although in the decades that followed the unification, as Simona Mori has noted, "neither the economy nor society underwent any sudden and dramatic changes that resulted in a noticeable and continuous growth in crime," large segments of the community felt more and more uneasy about law and order, nourishing the collective perception of a significant social crisis.[37] For northern cities like Milan and Florence, then, the progressive coalescence of immigrants from rural areas, many of whom had no employment at all and survived on charity or illegal activities, and the urban population heightened the already precarious conditions in the city centres.[38] For a large part of the community, the connection between poverty, moral corruption, and crime became stronger, and both the moderate liberals and the rising bourgeoisie felt increasingly insecure and called for a tougher policy to curb lawbreaking. Ultimately, notwithstanding the differences between these three Italian cities, what links them is the growing proximity between delinquents and indigents within the poorest districts of the urban fabric and the problematic implications of this for the moral development of the entire country.

These connections allow a fruitful comparative analysis of a wide range of different, often conflicting, sources. A first major element to consider is the issue of class in relation to crime. In the cultural and legal process of the definition and categorization of dangerous individuals, class played a major role, as people were classified as deviants insofar as they did not conform to what the middle class viewed as important to society. As Susan Ashley remarks, in the 1870s and 1880s, the middle class embraced the various branches of positivism, including criminology, sociology, and anthropology, as a weapon of class warfare: "In their strictures against lawbreaking, vagabondage, and idleness, lawmakers mainly targeted the lower classes."[39] In administrators' view, "it made no sense to prosecute the idle rich since they did not endanger others, but they were of two minds about those without means who nonetheless intended to avoid working."[40] It was thus poverty, in particular, that explained why rates of violent crimes were higher in the most degraded areas of the country. Curcio, in discussing why the number of criminals was constantly on the rise, affirmed that in the 1861 census "non meno di 315,343 individui vennero dichiarati poveri" (no less than 315,343 individuals were below the threshold of poverty), a statistic that seems to account for the presence of approximately 400,000 dangerous individuals throughout the peninsula.[41] In police writing, the relation between poverty and criminality was framed as nearly mutual. Bolis posits an explicit connection between indigence, inactivity, and criminal behaviour: "Le classi povere e inoperose ... furono sempre e saranno il semenzajo più produttivo di tutte le specie di malfattori, essendochè il delitto diventa per esse quasi una necessità di esistenza." (The poor and inactive classes ... were and will always be the best breeding ground for all kinds of criminals, since wrongdoing becomes for them almost a basic necessity.)[42] Locatelli similarly observes that although "la tendenza all'oziosità e al vagabondaggio ... non è istintiva come la tendenza al delinquere" (the tendency towards laziness and vagrancy ... is not innate like criminal behaviour), there is "assoluta certezza che l'ozioso e il vagabondo, non provveduto di rendite di qualsiasi natura, è costretto a ricorrere al delitto ... per sopperire ai suoi bisogni più stringenti e primitivi" (absolute certainty that the idle and the vagrant, not having any form of income, are compelled to resort to murder ... in order to fulfil their most urgent and primitive needs).[43]

A combination of morbid fascination with and profound anxiety about the dangerous classes may explain why, despite the variety of criminal activities carried out by wealthy and apparently honest individuals, police officers, urban travellers, and novelists focus nearly exclusively on lowlife crime. In *I vermi*, Mastriani admits early on that his intention is to shed more light on those people, called "vermi sociali" (social worms), that "si danno a vivere d'illeciti guadagni" (live on illegal earnings) and roam the slums of the new metropolis.[44] Corio, in *Milano in ombra*, attempts to study the "falange plebea" (army of plebeians) formed by "vagabondi, giuntatori, paltonieri, ... pitocchi, [che] si mescolano insieme" (vagrants, swindlers, mendicants, ... beggars that are mixed up with each other).[45] It is precisely within this "specie di formicaio" (sort of ants' nest), as Curcio defines it, or "specie pericolosa" (dangerous species), as Alongi puts it, that "si trovano i malfattori più incorreggibili" (the most incorrigible delinquents can be found).[46] Echoing the problematic words of theorists, Corio discusses the dangerous classes as if they were a measurable and empirically classifiable entity; as he asserts, it "costituisce una società nella società" (forms a society within society), with "lingua propria, con mestieri speciali, e con una certa gerarchia" (its own language, special trades, and a precise hierarchy).[47] The existence of this social phenomenon seems both natural and inescapable.

Another noteworthy element is the factual, nearly journalistic dimension of the urban narratives. Just like scientists and police officers, who employed empirical methods, including statistics, tests, and case studies, to legitimize their claims, Italian authors continually assert the actuality of their accounts and in several cases reference statistics and newspaper sources to verify their claims.[48] In *I vermi*, a book that illustrates the social and moral decay of 1850s and 1860s Neapolitan society, plagued by ignorance, dire poverty, and idleness, Mastriani immediately cautions that "io non iscrivo un romanzo" (I am not writing a novel).[49] Similarly, through a number of striking real-life case studies, Valera, in his reportage *Milano sconosciuta*, explores the "luoghi più orridi e spaventevoli" (the most horrid and appalling locales) of Milan without the fear "di sprofondarci nei bassi fondi sociali per studiare, rovistare, scandagliare nelle più intime latebre quell'elemento cinicamente detto impuro, che galleggia nelle grandi metropoli" (of precipitating into the lowest social depths to study, rummage through, and plumb the darkest recesses of that element which we cynically call the impure and which floats around the great metropolises).[50] Serao's *Il ventre di Napoli*, which describes the inhabitants of three districts of Naples – Porto, Vicaria, and Mercato – just after a major epidemic of cholera in the city, constitutes a "breve studio di verità e di dolore" (a brief study of truth and sorrow) and an "opera incompleta di cronista, non di scrittore" (incomplete work of a journalist, not a novelist) that serves "per ricordare a chi deve: non abbandonate Napoli" (to remind those concerned: do not abandon Naples).[51] In *Firenze sotterranea*, which depicts the degenerated conditions of both the centre and the periphery of Florence in the early 1880s, Piccini claims to have written "un documento di storia" (a historical document) and concludes by pointing out, "Io vi ho detto il vero: ora, voi giudicate!" (I told the truth: now you judge!)[52]

The divergences between these writers – the radically anti-bourgeois and anti-positivist political stance of Valera, the markedly socialist-humanitarian world view held by Mastriani and Serao, and the positivism of those two bourgeois observers of urban reality, Corio and Piccini – should not obfuscate their overarching goal. All of them appropriate realism in service of a larger social reform agenda that aimed to redress poverty by uncovering the effects of class difference on the production of deviance. A third element of connection, then, is precisely their main objective, which is raising awareness of the condition of the lower classes and calling for social reforms. This seems to be the same objective as that of many police delegates. "Scopo del mio lavoro" (The goal of my work), Locatelli remarks, is the "viva e sincera aspirazione al miglioramento delle classi più numerose e neglette della società" (real and sincere aspiration to improve the largest and most neglected social classes).[53] Using the plural, and thereby acting as the spokesperson for a larger group of intellectuals, Corio claims that "non scriviamo a provocare la corruzione, ma ad eccitare in chi può e in chi deve il desiderio e la volontà di porre rimedio a questi orrori" (we do not write to cause corruption, but to arouse the desire and the will to redress these horrors in those who can and must).[54] This objective is translated into texts that are meant to be oppositional, challenging, and strongly anti-authoritarian. According to both novelists and police delegates, the ruling class deliberately and culpably ignored the most wretched populations living in the city. For Curcio, the wealthy and the respectable – which he significantly calls "uomini d'ingegno e di cuore" (men of talent and heart) – have a moral duty to "occuparsi del miglioramento delle nostre infime plebi" (work on the improvement of our plebians).[55] Piccini points the finger at "coloro che ... si dichiarano tutori del consorzio civile" (those who ... declare themselves to be guardians of civil society) and "lo spensierato crudele egoismo delle classi, che si dicono da sé, superiori" (the carefree, cruel egotism of the classes that call themselves higher).[56] Valera critiques those snobbish bourgeois who disparage the lower classes and their "rozzezza selvaggia" (savage coarseness), and he de-responsibilizes the poor for their hopeless social condition: "Che cosa volete esigere da una plebe cresciuta in mezzo alla prostituzione e al carcere, in mezzo alle turpitudini ed ai digiuni?" (What could you ask of plebeians who grew up in prostitution and prison, in depravity and hunger?)[57] The unfairness of the Italian law must thus be counteracted by protecting the poor against the ruling class's abuse of power: "Proteggeremo sempre coloro i quali non furono che il bersaglio di leggi che essi non hanno mai conosciuto." (We shall always protect those who were nothing more than the target of laws that were unknown to them.)[58]

This confrontational dimension is mirrored in the way authors frequently and directly address those tasked with the administration of the state, who are seen as incapable of dealing with the vast array of problems with which the cities were afflicted. In *I vermi*, Mastriani repeatedly addresses the "autorità competenti" (competent authorities) and denounces the fact that "gli uomini governativi che hanno nelle mani le redini della pubblica amministrazione non iscesero giammai negli antri dove languisce di freddo e di fame la carne umana" (men who govern and hold the reins of the public administration have never descended into the caves where human flesh languishes in cold and hunger).[59] In *Il ventre di Napoli*, Serao targets the Italian prime minister Agostino Depretis in the famous invective at the beginning of the book, launching a forthright attack on the government for not taking action to fight the devastating cholera epidemic in August 1884: "Voi non lo conoscevate, onorevole Depretis, il ventre di Napoli. Avevate torto, poiché voi siete il governo e il governo deve sapere tutto." (You did not know, honourable Depretis, the underbelly of Naples. And you were wrong, because you are the government, and the government must know everything.)[60]

The repeated polemics against the government for its inability to address social questions are, however, profoundly undermined by the fact that these authors lack serious initiative and offer very few ideas for how to remedy the problems of the city, with virtually the only concrete solution being the forced separation between the deserving poor and the actual lawbreakers. Piccini remarks, "Innanzi a tutto bisogna pensare a separare i poveri, gl'infelici, dai furfanti" (first and foremost we need to separate the poor and the unfortunate from the criminals).[61] It is significant, and problematic, that theorists of the dangerous classes were simultaneously putting forward the same propositions. Locatelli points out that petty criminals and common delinquents cannot be compared to murderers and robbers on account of their different biological and psychological constitution: the latter, he argues, "non devono essere giudicati alla stessa stregua dei ladri comuni, dei truffatori e dei falsari. Per diventar grassatore, occorre veramente una nequizia d'animo, che ordinariamente i ladri comuni, i truffatori e i falsari non hanno." (Cannot be judged according to the same categories of common thieves, swindlers, or forgers. To become a robber it is necessary to have an inherent wickedness that, ordinarily, common thieves, swindlers, and forgers do not have.)[62] Curcio also starts from the premise that real offenders are "perversi e bestiali" (perverse and savage) and "non appartengono a quella classe di proletari che vivono senza tetto, alla ventura, luridi e cenciosi [nelle] grandi città" (do not belong to that class of proletariats who are homeless, filthy, and ragged, and roam the largest cities).[63] According to him, then, the police need to divide this population into "colpevoli e birbanti, in infelici e disgraziati" (criminals and scoundrels, unfortunate and wretched).[64]

Notwithstanding the authors' polemical and realistic intentions, there are several contradictions between the writers' objectives and their textual realization. The lack of significant critical literature on the subject means that Italian scholars have principally drawn attention to the stylistic aspects of urban literature. The language employed by Piccini, for instance, has been defined by the linguist Massimo Arcangeli as "turgida e legnosa ... irrealistica ... assurda, ben lontana anche da quella di tanti medi scrittori 'realisti' contemporanei" (pompous and rigid ... unrealistic ... absurd, far even from the language used by many coeval mediocre realist writers).[65] For Antonio Palermo, Mastriani's style borders on the "antinaturalismo più oltranzoso" (most extreme antinaturalism) and his complicated lexicon – Mastriani uses different linguistic registers to represent life in diverse social environments – often lacks verisimilitude.[66] Giovanna Rosa has pointed out that, notwithstanding their very different ideological stances, Valera and Corio frequently employ narrative strategies and stylistic techniques belonging to sensational and melodramatic writing that ultimately undermine the texts' realistic dimension.[67] More generally, the magniloquent, emphatic, and often contrived language that Italian writers adopt stimulates a repulsive reaction in the bourgeois reader. Piccini, for instance, repeatedly underscores that he is narrating "cose che a me stesso non sarebber parse credibili, se non le avessi vedute!" (things that I personally would never have thought credible if I had not seen them!).[68] A novel like Mastriani's *I misteri di Napoli* – a reconstruction of Neapolitan society between 1846 and 1862 that vividly conveys the lives of decadent aristocrats, in this case the wealthy Massa-Vitelli family of landowners, as well as underworld criminals and the virtuous poor – emphasizes the fears and horrors of city life to highlight that the terrible actuality of the urban reality is worse than fiction. The language is crude and somatic, particularly when horrific effects are deployed to convey the horror of living in the city slums.

It is unsurprising that these authors were criticized at the time for works sometimes perceived as mere fictional accounts of imaginary threats, narrated in a gratuitously sensationalistic manner. Giuseppe Conti, for instance, the author of *Firenze vecchia: Storia, cronaca aneddotica, costumi, 1799–1859* (1899), another sociological enquiry into the heart of Florence, covertly accuses Piccini of having invented most of his *Firenze sotterranea*: "I grandi delitti inventati per fare effetto e far perdere i sonni; le paurose tragedie, i sanguinosi drammi, descritti e raccontati come cose vere e naturali accaduti in quel luogo, salvo rare eccezioni, non sono mai esistiti se non nella fantasia di chi li ha scritti." (The great crimes conceived to shock and to make people lose sleep; the frightening tragedies and bloody dramas, described and narrated as if they were real and natural events that occurred in that place: with rare exceptions, such events never happened, except in the imagination of those who wrote them.)[69] Even Valera, in the later *Gli scamiciati*

(1881), strongly critiques those writers who claim to have "vissuto ai fianchi della plebe" (lived in proximity to plebeians) when authoring sociological studies of the conditions of the lower classes. He continues: "Bisogna aver vissuto con lei; aver riposato sullo stesso capezzale di granito o di paglia, aver indossato gli stessi cenci" (One has to have lived among them, to have slept on the same bed of stone or straw, to have worn the same rags). Writers cannot say anything about these "rogues" other than "menzogne, buaggini, asinerie; non si possono scrivere che romanzi" (lies, stupidities, and inanities: they can only write fictional novels).[70]

The ambiguous nature of these novels was not, however, the result merely of impassioned participation and sensationalism at the expense of realism. In fact, their supposedly denunciatory and reformatory purpose is in striking contrast with the textual representations of poverty, crime, the slums, and their inhabitants. It is remarkable that, notwithstanding the areas of prosperity and wealth in late nineteenth-century Italian cities such as Naples, Milan, and Florence, novelists remained firmly focused on the depressed conditions of impoverished, dreadful districts that formed a breeding ground for delinquents of every kind. Portrayals of the city in nineteenth-century Italian mysteries or urban novels very often collapse into depictions of lower-class spaces. Italian writers are strongly concerned with the urbanization of the modern city, and the Gothic is largely an acknowledgment of such disquiet. In the following sections, I explore some of the contact zones connecting Gothic modes and late nineteenth-century writing about criminality, the underclasses, the city, and the slums.[71] By depicting inner-city districts made up of storerooms, basement tenements, narrow and winding alleys, secret passages, hidden doorways, subterranean chambers, and small squares, Italian writers plunge the reader into an enclosed, claustrophobic, and ultimately Gothicized fictional space from which it seems impossible to escape.

Labyrinths

In the urban Gothic, as Jamieson Ridenhour suggests, "the cityscape replaces the classic Gothic edifice, or rather multiplies it."[72] The labyrinthine nature of the criminal underworld constitutes an obsessive concern in many of these texts. Mastriani employs the labyrinth in a figurative sense to convey the meandering character of his *I misteri di Napoli*, taking the reader through a "laberinto di fatti" (labyrinth of events), an expression that the Neapolitan author most likely borrowed from *The Mysteries of London* (1844–8), in which G.W. Reynolds famously wrote, "The reader who follows us through the mazes of our narrative has yet to be introduced to many strange places."[73]

The metaphor of the labyrinth is widely used in nineteenth-century popular fiction to depict Naples and its "innumeri arterie, le strade e i vicoli, che l'intersecano in ogni verso" (countless arterial roads, streets, and alleys which intersect it every which way).[74] Mastriani, in his early novel *La cieca di Sorrento* (1852), portrays a poor district of Naples as a "laberinto d'infiniti viottoli, ronchi e stradelle non più larghe d'un distender di braccia, … attraversando le quali si ha sempre una certa sospensione di animo, come quando si visita un carcere o un ospedale" (a labyrinth of infinite lanes, terraced plots and paths no wider than an extended arm, … walking along them, one has that same feeling of being kept on tenterhooks as when one visits a prison or a hospital).[75] The parallels between a poor neighbourhood and both the prison and the asylum, which evoke crime and madness but also inescapability, are not coincidental. Mastriani uses the labyrinth metaphor to introduce the first horrific image in the novel: a young medical student dismembering a corpse. This scene incidentally serves to address the problem of the trade in dead bodies, a plague in nineteenth-century Europe that encouraged many criminals to kill in order to sell the corpses for dissection in medical schools. It simultaneously contributes to the creation of a sinister and markedly Gothic atmosphere: "Ma cosa fa quell'uomo da costa del tavolo … che cosa è gittato su quel tavolo? Cielo! Una testa! Una testa umana! Ed il sangue è tuttavia rappreso sulla parte svelta dal tronco! Ed un coltello è nelle mani di colui!" (But what is that man doing next to the table … what is that lying on the table? Heavens! A head! A human head! And the blood is still clotting on the part of the torso that has been torn off! And there is a knife in that man's hand!)[76]

The unhealthy, overcrowded, and densely packed districts of Naples, particularly those suffering from the highest rates of poverty in the city, are at the centre of Serao's *Il ventre di Napoli*, in which the metaphor of the labyrinth becomes a way to establish the city as the modern urban equivalent of the Gothic mansion: remote, impenetrable, and dangerous. The claustrophobic narrowness of the alleys is cause for alarm and confusion, and "the secrecy of the labyrinth," Richard Maxwell points out, always "signifies crime."[77] Serao claims that "i napoletani istessi … non conoscono *tutti* i quartieri bassi" (the Neapolitans themselves … do not know *all* the lowest neighbourhoods), hinting at the unfamiliarity, inaccessibility, and unknowability of certain areas of the city, where crime spreads like a wildfire.[78] In describing the old Via dei Mercanti, she emphasizes its convoluted character and uses words associated with the labyrinth: "Sarà larga quattro metri, tanto che le carrozze non vi possono passare, ed è sinuosa, si torce come un budello." (It is about four metres wide, so that carriages cannot pass, and winding: it twists like an intestine.)[79] A small, dark, and gloomy neighbourhood called Tentella is vividly portrayed as "un intrico quasi verminoso di vicoletti e vicolucci, nerastri, ove la meridiana mai discende, ove mai il sole penetra" (an almost verminous tangle of blackened back streets and alleyways which midday passes by, which the sun never reaches).[80] In *Il ventre di Napoli*, the urban landscape is depicted as desolate and disturbing. The slums constitute a space suited only to despair and are portrayed as a modern ruin, atrophied and abandoned, reflecting fears about the future of the city space and its uncontrollability.

While the slums of Naples seem to be confined, mostly separated from the rest of the city, suggesting that an ordered and knowable city exists beyond these circumscribed regions, Piccini's Florence is even more disturbing. In *Firenze sotterranea*, Piccini explores both geographically secluded areas of the city – for instance, the infamous neighbourhood of San Frediano, the "quartiere dei ladri, dei malviventi oltr'Arno" (neighbourhoods of the delinquents beyond the Arno), where the houses are hollowed out and customized by criminals and which is extremely difficult for an outsider to penetrate – and the city centre, for example, the area of the Ghetto.[81] The Ghetto is portrayed as one of the most dangerous districts of the city. These neighbourhoods are depicted as intricate, maze-like, and terrifying to both the outsider and the police, who find it very difficult to chase criminals within that "laberinto di ragnaie, di serpai, di ortaglie, di corti, di capannacce" (labyrinth of spider webs, snake pits, vegetable gardens, courtyards, and run-down shacks).[82] Piccini's *L'assassinio nel vicolo della luna* (1883), which fictionalizes and dramatizes the locales and characters of the coeval *Firenze sotterranea*, is largely set in the Ghetto, "un luogo de' più orridi e sozzi di Firenze" (one of the most horrid and filthy locales of Florence), in which it is almost impossible not to get lost:[83]

> L'andito lungo, indescrivibile, ha, ad ogni svoltata, tre, quattro, cinque rami di scale, che salgono in direzioni differenti: è un vero laberinto, un luogo che pare edificato a bella posta per servire a tetre e misteriose imprese. Gli abitanti primitivi del Ghetto, lo chiamavano: l'*andron bujo*.
>
> (At each turn, the indescribably long corridor branches off into three, four, or even five stairways, ascending in different directions: a veritable labyrinth, a place that seems to have been intentionally built to serve dismal, mysterious ends. The early inhabitants of the Ghetto called it the *dark entrance*.)[84]

Maxwell writes that, in the new metropolis of the urban mysteries, "the visitor who is not a native may well feel mystified."[85] The innocent individual as much as the policeman faces grave peril in these areas. In *L'assassinio nel vicolo della luna*, two old and scared parents leave their house at night in search of their missing daughter Antonietta and inevitably get lost "nei laberinti di quelle straduzze" (in the labyrinth of those small streets), which gives rise to a sensation of total ineluctability: "In quei momenti il cieco sentiva più che mai tutto il peso della sua terribile sventura." (In those moments, the blind man felt more than ever the weight of his great misfortune.)[86]

The labyrinth makes the city seem distorted, strange, and unfamiliar. Sigmund Freud experienced the feeling of what he calls the uncanny – the sudden reappearance of that which is deeply and internally familiar in seemingly unfamiliar forms – when he became lost one summer afternoon in one of the labyrinthine districts of an Italian provincial town:

> I hastened to leave the narrow street at the next turning. But after having wandered about for a time without enquiring my way, I suddenly found myself back in the same street ... I hurried away once more, only to arrive by another *détour* at the same place yet a third time. Now, however, a feeling overcame me which I can only describe as uncanny.[87]

In exploring the uncanniness of the experience, Freud observes that the labyrinthine streets cause an involuntary but obsessive repetitive movement which "forces upon us the idea of something fateful and inescapable."[88] Although the old couple in Piccini's novel finally manage to exit the maze, the two move in a compulsive way through streets that become progressively narrower, deeper, and darker. These passages of the novel are infused with images that evoke claustrophobia and sensory and psychological confusion and that contribute to conjuring up a nightmarish, labyrinthine city in which there is little hope of escaping the evil that lies at its centre. People find themselves entrapped and hedged in by the perils lurking in the urban labyrinth, which always suggests secrets, fears, and anxieties and hints at the presence of monsters prowling around the buildings. It is precisely the labyrinthine coils of a dark urban district – "ogni strada era al buio, o quasi, illuminata soltanto da uno o due fanali, e da fanali a olio, a riverbero, con sottili lumicini" (every street was dark, or nearly so, illuminated only by the dim reflected light of one or two lanterns and oil lamps) – that engulf Antonietta's lover, the painter Roberto Gandi, who is brutally attacked and almost murdered, triggering the investigation that dominates the second half of the story.[89]

Italian authors create a disorientating, alienating, and ultimately uncanny city that transforms the purposeful walker into a helpless victim, a version of the Gothic heroine trapped in a dark and threatening environment. In these texts, the uncanniness of the city, in the words of Anthony Vidler, "finally became public."[90] These places are essentially defamiliarized – "lungo le mura di San Rocco ... vi credereste a mille miglia da Firenze!" (within the walls of San Rocco ... you would believe yourself to be far away from Florence!), Piccini writes in *Firenze sotterranea* – bolstering the strangeness of the environment and its inhabitants, as remote as the castles and monasteries of the Gothic landscape, and establishing a fundamental distance between the civilized and the barbarous, the observer and the observed.[91] Whereas respectable people are physically and psychologically entrapped in the labyrinth, become hopelessly lost, and are preyed upon by the various criminals they encounter, delinquents negotiate the city's mazes with ease. The vagrant and criminal Pilato, one of the most famous characters in Mastriani's *I misteri di Napoli*, is perfectly familiar with the topography of the slums, while Lucertolo, the detective protagonist of *L'assassinio nel vicolo della luna*, who is, at least in this first adventure, inextricably linked to the criminal underworld, can easily navigate the narrow lanes and filthy alleys of the centre of Florence. Knowledge of the underworld ultimately betrays evilness and bespeaks crime. This may explain the obsessive recurrence of the metaphor of the maze in these texts, reflecting bourgeois anxiety about uncontrolled immigration and increasing urbanization, but it may also suggest a specifically middle-class desire to reaffirm those class hierarchies that were becoming increasingly blurred in the growing cities.

Otherness

In these texts, both the lowlife locales and the people who inhabit them are themselves Gothic objects of horror. As Ann Williams has famously argued, the "Gothic systematically represents 'otherness.'"[92] In a state that rewards employment, stability, and conformity and condemns any form of cultural and social transgression, the figure of the vagrant constitutes a major menace to the values and world views of the middle class. Ashley suggests that the connection between vagrancy and criminality "was obvious to the public."[93] It does not come as a surprise, then, that the vagrant figures prominently in these texts and is often described in a racialized paradigm imbued with medical language. In the late nineteenth century, biological factors gained favour as the cause of what experts labelled as professional or habitual vagrancy. In Lombroso's view, vagrants possess physical and psychological traits reminiscent of those of born criminals: in his analysis of the French criminal and vagrant Joseph Gleydson Vacher, Lombroso notes, on the basis of the man's photos, that he exhibits physical and constitutional features also found in the born criminal, the sadist, and the epileptic, including "un'esagerazione nel volume degli zigomi e della mandibola" (an exaggeration of the volume of the cheekbones and the mandible), the "atrofia degli organi riproduttori" (atrophy of the reproductive organs), and "la sua strana agilità scimmiesca e della possibilità di percorrere 50 o 60 miglia senza stancarsi" (his strange ape-like agility and his ability to walk for 50 or 60 miles without getting tired).[94] Lombroso's statement validated Locatelli's position on vagrancy: Locatelli had previously argued that vagrants possess "una speciale conformazione muscolare, che li rende poco atti alla fatica, benché, in apparenza, perfettamente sani e robusti" (a specific muscular conformation that makes them unsuitable for fatigue, although they appear to be perfectly healthy and strong).[95]

The most important Italian study on vagrancy, written by the sociologists and legal experts Eugenio Florian and Guido Cavaglieri and published in two volumes in 1897 and 1900, pathologized habitual or professional vagrancy.[96] The authors posit "una viva rassomiglianza, quasi una identità, fra il caratteristico motivo psicologico del vagabondaggio e quello della delinquenza" (a strong resemblance, almost an exact likeness, between the psychological profiles of habitual vagrants and hardened criminals),[97] while also identifying a "piena rassomiglianza" (total resemblance) between the "carattere psicologico" (psychological character) of both vagrants and prostitutes: "L'abito psicologico in esse abituale sono la pigrizia, l'ozio, l'odio e l'orrore per ogni sorta di lavoro metodico e continuato, l'apatia più assoluta." (The psychological characteristics of prostitutes include laziness, idleness, a hatred and horror of any kind of methodical and continued work, the most absolute apathy.)[98] From a psychological perspective, Florian and Cavaglieri see vagrants as suffering from what they, borrowing from the work of the positivist criminologist Paolo Riccardi, refer to as a form of "atavismo psichico" (psychic atavism) that, in the case of vagrants, compels them to regress to a more primitive, nomadic state.[99] There is

> l'identità od almeno la rassomiglianza grande fra la psicologia caratteristica dei vagabondi e le prime fasi della evoluzione psichica, quale si riscontra nei popoli e negli individui. Ne deriva che i vagabondi, dal punto di vista psicologico, rappresenterebbero alcunché di primitivo, di arretrato, quasi a dire un arresto di sviluppo. Di qui è sorta una notevole teoria, la quale del vagabondaggio e della mendicità offre una spiegazione atavistica.

(the sameness of, or at least a great resemblance between, the psychology typical of vagrants and the early phases of psychic evolution as it occurs in populations and individuals. Consequently, vagrants, from a psychological standpoint, represent something primitive, backward, almost an arrested development. This has given rise to a remarkable theory, which offers an atavistic explanation for vagrancy and mendicancy.)[100]

This popular, racially charged explanation for deviant behaviour, particularly vagrancy and prostitution, is a symptom of that larger historical process that Foucault calls the "recasting of the theme of racial confrontations ... [within] the theory of evolutionism and the struggle for existence," which contributed to the consolidation of "modern biologico-social racism" and "modern political power."[101] Kyla Schuller argues, "As opposed to earlier understandings of human difference in which races were unequivocally distinct entities with diverse origins and were thus fundamentally at odds with one another, evolutionary perspectives conceived of racial difference as ... the lingering prehistory of the individual body."[102] To be racialized in biopower, then, is "not to be figured in as an innately distinct species ... but to be located within the past of civilization itself."[103] As a consequence, socially and culturally marginalized subjects now represent "the past of [the] race."[104]

We see confirmed here the unstable nature of racial discourse, which, in the words of Ann Laura Stoler, is "neither always a tool of the state nor always mobilized against it" but is rather diffused "over a broad field." The power of racial discourse, which circulates widely while simultaneously generating "sites of dispersion," is that it "accrues its force not because it is a scientifically validated discourse but [because] it is saturated with sentimentalisms that increase its appeal."[105] The popularization of discourses regarding dangerous individuals is largely the result of such Gothic representations of them as internally abject, degenerate, and racially inferior savages that constitute a threatening antithesis to the Italian national character and populate areas of the country unredeemed by civilization. In literary texts, the dangerous class is portrayed as an utterly impoverished, demoralized, alienated, and morally degenerated class and, as such, it emerges as far more dangerous than the real mass of criminals who roamed the streets of the cities, which mostly consisted of petty delinquents. The case of Mastriani is indicative of both the ambiguity and the power of racial discourses on otherness. Although he did not endorse positivist criminology's positions on the irremediable nature of born criminality – in fact, he thought physiological tendencies could be counteracted and corrected by social and moral improvement – he frequently draws on biological imagery to depict his deviant characters (this is a distinctive element of his narrative I will briefly touch upon again in chapter 3). For instance, the vagrant Pilato, a protagonist of *I misteri di Napoli*, is described as a born criminal in a strictly Lombrosian vein:

> Su [di lui] la scienza antropologica è chiamata a fare gravissimi studi. Negazione assoluta e vivente dell'anima, egli odiava per istinto tutto ciò che è bello nel mondo morale e nel fisico. E questo odio si traduceva in un istinto feroce, come quello che si desta nelle belve affamate. Egli strangolava *per diletto*, per antipatia invincibile, per bisogno irresistibile.
>
> (Anthropological science needs to carry out very serious studies on [him]. As the absolute living negation of the soul, he instinctively hated everything beautiful in the moral and physical world. And this hatred was transformed into a ferocious instinct, like that which is awakened in hungry beasts. He strangled people *for pleasure*, motivated by unconquerable aversion and irresistible need.)[106]

The character of Carolina, a prostitute introduced by Mastriani in *I vermi*, is similarly portrayed as belonging to a specific, physically and morally recognizable and inherently hopeless, category of deviants: "Riuniva nella sua persona tutt'i caratteri fisici e morali che costituiscono il tipo della prostituta, caratteri che si verificano in 90 individui su 100 di questa disgraziata specie." (She possessed all the physical and moral traits that are characteristic of the prostitute type, traits that are present in 90 out of 100 individuals who belong to this wretched species.)[107] Similarly, there is a strong ambiguity in Serao's portrayal of the underclasses, in which a paternalistic view is conflated with racialized discourses. While she criticizes those who treat the poor as an inferior population with physically identifiable traits – "la gente che abita in questi quattro quartieri popolari ... non è una gente bestiale, selvaggia, oziosa ... non è dunque una razza inferiore ... non merita la sorte che le cose gl'impongono" (the inhabitants of these areas ... are not bestial, savage, lazy ... they are not an inferior race ... they do not deserve the fate that is imposed on them) – she affirms that she has, in the same districts, personally encountered dangerous people, including prostitutes, vagrants, and beggars, "sul cui viso la delinquenza è impressa e la cui espressione non mente" (on whose face delinquency is impressed and whose facial expression does not lie).[108] Valera often resorts to the paradigm of the unspeakable to convey the otherness of these individuals – "vi sono bruttezze che sfuggono ad ogni manifestazione" (there are kinds of ugliness that elude every representation) and "la penna talvolta rifugge dal narrare certe turpitudini" (the pen sometimes spurns the narration of such turpitudes) – while Corio emphasizes their physical monstrosity, as can be seen in this description of an old female beggar: "Il viso di lei crespo, gli occhi infossati, aveva le ossa zigomatiche sporgenti, il naso adunco, il mento aguzzo e prominente, il colorito terreo, tutto insomma contribuiva a renderla orribile, mostruosa." (The wrinkled face, sunken eyes, protruding cheekbones, hooked nose, prominent, pointed chin, and ashen colour – all these features combined to make her look horrible, monstrous.)[109] The body is a transparent window to morality: as Corio claims after having met the dwellers of a particularly filthy inn, "i fisionomisti potrebbero quivi far studi di non lieve importanza" (physiognomists could carry out studies of no small importance here).[110]

This obsession with the body reflects the anxieties and disordered state of the nation. As David Forgacs highlights, in the social investigation of late nineteenth-century Italy, "the lower classes are imagined by middle-class or lower-middle class authors as bodies, both individual and collective, and in relation to other bodies: the city, society, and the state."[111] The bodies of the socially undesirable – not only the urban poor but also people from the South and women, Forgacs has shown – were perceived as diseased waste that endangered the integrity of the idealized nation, whose coordinates were reflected in the normative frame of the middle-class man.[112] In the texts I have analysed here, the slums represent the wounds of the social body on which parasites feed. The authors' outcasts bear evident physical marks of otherness and monstrosity. Even authors like Mastriani, Serao, and Valera, who do not endorse the deterministic implications of Lombrosian criminology, eventually validate the functioning of science as a means of containing and controlling otherness and reinforce an evolutionary and racialized view of wrongdoing. In Piccini's novel *I ladri di cadaveri* (1884), which revolves around the investigation of a macabre double murder that occurs in the periphery of Florence, the culprit is clearly described as an aberration of nature, "un bruto, senza intelligenza e con appetiti di sangue da sbramare" (a brainless, bloodthirsty beast).[113] Here, the narrator claims to have personally researched criminal archives and found clear evidence of the hereditary nature of crime: "È noto che in certe famiglie, pur troppo, il crimine, la disposizione a delinquere sono ereditarii. Io, studiando negli archivi certi processi ho rintracciato sino alla quarta e quinta generazione la propaggine di certi ladri e delinquenti." (It is well known that in certain families, unfortunately, crime and a predisposition to delinquency are hereditary. Researching certain trials in the archives,

I came across four to five generations of certain thieves and criminals in some families.)[114] Piccini's words echo the coeval analyses of the sociologist Scipio Sighele, who, in 1890, produced a study of Artena, a small village in the province of Rome that he called "un paese di delinquenti nati" (a town of born delinquents), "un'oasi selvaggia" (a savage oasis) in the middle of a civil population where the number of crimes was so exceptional that it could only be explained by the laws of heredity.[115]

Notwithstanding their reformatory intentions, then, Italian writers somewhat ambivalently further proto-biological deterministic explanations of moral inferiority and the solidification of prejudices about innate class differences. Unsurprisingly, this is more accentuated in the works of Piccini and Corio, who apply a strong orientalizing gaze in depicting the underclasses. Following Sue, who, in *Les Mystères de Paris*, relates "some episodes from the lives of *French* savages who are as far removed from civilizations as the Indians Cooper so vividly depicts," Piccini uses the label "selvaggi d'Europa" (European savages) to describe "gente che prova della legge le pene e non il beneficio … gente dannata dalla ingiustizia, o dalla imprevidenza di chi dovrebbe pensare a educarla" (people who receive the punishments and not the benefits of the law … people condemned by injustice or by the shortsightedness of those who should educate them).[116] Corio likewise draws a parallel between the indigents of Milan and some of the most remote populations of the world:

> Riguardo ad ignoranza e ad abbiettezza la feccia plebea di qualsiasi grande città può dare dei punti ai Papuas, agli Akka ed agli Esquimesi. E la marmaglia pullula e brulica in ogni grande città, eppure gli onesti cittadini non la curano, perché non la vedono quasi mai, e appena ne ricordano talvolta con disprezzo il nome.

> (Regarding ignorance and baseness, the plebeian dregs of any large city can claim superiority over Papuans, the Hakka people, and Eskimos. The rabble teems and proliferates in every big city. Yet even so, respectable citizens do not concern themselves with such people because they rarely see them, and on the rare occasion they remember their name, they do so with disdain.)[117]

The inhabitants of the slums are exoticized as foreign or savage threats to Italy from within. They appear, in Foucault's words, both "very close and quite alien, a perpetual threat to everyday life, but extremely distant in its origin and motives, both everyday and exotic in the milieu in which it takes place."[118]

In the eyes of specialists, this indistinct mass of dangerous individuals is fundamentally hopeless. The case of the jurist and sociologist Michele Angelo Vaccaro, whose work, he admits, "si discosta dalla vecchia scuola giuridica, quanto da quella detta positiva" (differs from that of both the old school of legal thought and the new positivist school), is particularly illustrative.[119] In his *Genesi e funzioni delle leggi penali* (1889), in the chapter devoted to the figure of the criminal, Vaccaro analyses the lives of those who deviate from the social norm in terms of a major struggle, a constant battle in which only the fittest and toughest are able to avoid either physical demise or falling into crime, such as vagrancy and murder: "Il delitto, socialmente considerato, non è altro ... che una conseguenza dell'inadattamento alle speciali condizioni in cui la lotta per l'esistenza conduce gli uomini" (crime, considered from a social perspective, is nothing other ... than the consequence of the inability to adapt to the special conditions of the struggle for life). It is only natural, Vaccaro insists, that those who have "lottato con la miseria e cogli stenti" (fought against misery and the difficulties of life) eventually manifest "segni di degenerazione" (signs of degeneration) because of atavism, arrested development, or congenital or acquired diseases. On this point, Vaccaro concludes, "i dati dell'antropologia si armonizzano al pari con quelli della sociologia, e si corroborano a vicenda" (the data of anthropology and sociology harmonize with and corroborate each other).[120]

The problem, Vaccaro continues, is that in this "lotta per l'esistenza" (struggle for life), the poor and weak individuals who live at the margins of the social body "non periscono tutti" (do not necessarily die). Many of them actually survive, "portando scolpiti nel loro organismo i segni più manifesti della loro debolezza" (retaining in their organism the clearest signs of their weakness). The battle for life, then, produces multiple signs of degeneration that are passed from parents to children, creating over time "una disgraziata falange di degenerati" (an unhappy class of degenerates), among whom Vaccaro includes "i pazzi, i criminali, i mendicanti" (the insane, criminals, and beggars).[121] These classes of degenerates are seen as a threat to public health and society and hence need to be discouraged from reproducing. Ideally, they would be eliminated. Vaccaro disturbingly suggests that elimination is unfeasible not because it is ethically aberrant but simply because it would be fundamentally useless: given the significance of poverty in the production of crime, "ben presto nascerebbero nuovi degenerati, e quindi la necessità di nuove eliminazioni" (sooner or later new degenerates would be born and this would make new eliminations necessary).[122] However, he adds, if conditions were better, the "final" solution would represent a path worth taking: "Se le cause che conducono alla degenerazione fossero del tutto cessate, si potrebbe dire: eliminiamo una buona volta i degenerati che vi sono, al fine di ottenere che la famiglia umana rimanga soltanto composta di elementi sani, produttivi e buoni." (If the causes that lead to degeneration were completely stopped, we could say: let us eliminate once and for all every degenerate who is left so as to ensure that humanity remains exclusively made up of healthy, productive, and good subjects.)[123]

Such discourses concerning the application of eugenic measures to improve the human race started circulating in Italy at least from the 1880s and intensified in the period leading up to and following the First World War. This is evidenced, as Francesco Cassata has shown, by the many articles dealing with eugenics in the *Archivio di psichiatria, scienze penali ed antropologia criminale*, which, from its inception in 1880, informed readers of the legislative initiatives relating to sterilization and castration introduced in the United States and Europe.[124] Many Italian criminologists and psychiatrists received such developments in eugenics favourably. Pasquale Penta, a major figure in Italian criminology and sexology, argued in his *Pazzia e società* (1893) that degenerates of any kind, whether disabled or mentally unstable, should be legally prevented from marrying and reproducing: "Impedite ... che i pazzi, i semipazzi, gli imbecilli, gli epilettici, i delinquenti, i nevrastenici, gli strani, gli eccentrici, i nevropatici, i tisici, i diabetici, i sifilitici, e tutti gli altri già mentovati si sposino: e avrete già fatto un gran bene." (Forbid ... the insane, the quasi-insane, the imbecile, the epileptic, the delinquent, the neurasthenic, the weird, the eccentric, the neuropathic, the phthisic, the diabetic, the syphilitic, and all those abovementioned from marrying: and you would do great good.)[125] Enrico Morselli, professor of psychiatry at the University of Turin and one of the most important Italian eugenicists of the time, would later endorse the position of the "più competenti eugenisti" (most competent eugenicists), who were demanding "l'inibizione del matrimonio agli individui ereditari" (the prohibition of marriage to individuals with hereditary defects) and insisting on the importance "di adottare mezzi energici per arrestare la decadenza fisica della razza e il pervertimento delle sue qualità intellettuali e morali" (of adopting energetic means, such as the sterilization of degenerates, to arrest the physical deterioration of the race and the perversion of its intellectual and moral qualities).[126] Discourses on race, degeneration, and exclusion or elimination are inextricably intertwined. Degenerates, it turns out, are potentially contagious.

Infection

The image of the labyrinth and the portrayal of the underclasses as truly other constitute deliberate attempts to organize a dichotomous city, in which the distance between the horrible and the horrified, the respectable and the outcast, is constantly buttressed. By employing the metaphor of the underbelly, through which social investigators descend into hell, the city is imagined as a sick body where the utterly evil underworld must be gutted and sanitized in order to make it safe. Despite their original intentions, then, the authors considered here fail to draw a clear line between delinquents and indigents. The underclasses are depicted as an illness, a parasite infecting the middle and upper classes, thus codifying the poor as a foreign entity, alien to the real Italians. Criminality ultimately seems indistinguishable from poverty, the historical and sociopolitical causes of which are transmuted into an essential nature no longer amenable to reform and change. In such an essentialist and fatalistic view, the poor are Gothicized and replace the vicious aristocrats as the quintessentially Gothic villains, causing the status of evilness to move to the opposite end of the social scale: both are equally alien and hence frightening to the bourgeois readership.

The emphasis on stench and filth, and the narrator's response to them, represents a further example of the Gothicization of the underworld and its inhabitants. As Mighall explains, while early Gothic fiction was not notable for paying attention to smells, as the horrors were principally associated with sight and touch, the late nineteenth-century Gothic became more fastidious about smell.[127] In his seminal *The Foul and the Fragrant* (1982), Alain Corbin defines this process as the "redefinition of the intolerable" and explains how the bourgeoisie reinforced class difference by emphasizing the smell and dirtiness of the lower orders, defined as "the great unwashed," a distinction that had not been in place in the premodern era.[128] In the long nineteenth century, European anxieties about smell and impurity were the product of colonial expansion and the rise of democracy, which, for the first time, placed the heteronormative self (European, colonizer, civilized, and upper or middle class) in troubling and dangerous proximity to the deviant other (non-European, colonized, and working class or poor). William Ian Miller writes in his political analysis of disgust that democracy itself erected social and cultural boundaries that, if transgressed by the lower classes, would make them immediately recognizable; the upper classes' dominant response to the violation of such boundaries was disgust: "The stench of the low seems to bear a direct relation to the anxiety they generate in the high. When out of place they smell; when safely in place they do not."[129]

Bad smells are omnipresent in the novels analysed here. The metaphors of mud, darkness, germination, swarms, and filth recur in these texts. The streets of Naples, Serao writes, are invariably "sporche e oscure; e ognuna puzza in modo diverso" (dirty and dark, and everyone stinks in different ways), while inside a lugubrious inn visited by Valera, "regna un tanfo morboso" (a noxious stench reigns). "Volere o no, si è costretti a turarsi bocca e naso per non cadere tramortiti al suolo." (Like it or not, we are forced to close our mouths and hold our noses so as not to faint.)[130] These texts emphasize dirtiness and stink to such an extent that in *Il ventre di Milano*, a humorous and light-hearted urban novel that comprises a series of articles collected and also largely written by the *scapigliato* Cletto Arrighi in 1888, the Milanese author defends his decision to bring to light the cheerful side of the city precisely by criticizing "i libri pieni di laidumi e di cattivi odori" (the books filled with filth and bad smell) that focus exclusively on that which is rotten, corrupt, and dishonest.[131] "Il pubblico," Arrighi insists, "è stufo anche di putredine e cattivi odori ... L'effettaccio retorico della vostra letteratura verminosa e puzzolente è sfatato su tutta la linea." (The public can no longer stand stench and filth ... The rhetorical effect of your malodorous and verminous literature has been debunked.)[132]

The reduced tolerance that characterizes the nineteenth century, together with ideas about miasmas and decaying matter, sanctioned the connection between smell and disease, producing fears of contagion.[133] Peter Baldwin has observed that, in this period, offensive smells and danger to health were substantially equated, with stench generally indicating the presence of unsafe putrid material.[134] While in Great Britain the social reformer Edwin Chadwick famously stated that "all smell is disease," in France nearly all literature – fictional, political, and hygienic – on the growth of Paris in the nineteenth century was characterized by a profound and fearful disgust towards the city's filth and smells.[135] Before the emergence of germ theory in the late 1880s and early 1890s, the two principal theories of disease were contagionism and anticontagionism, or miasma theory. While contagionists posited that disease was transmitted by bodies, anticontagionists, including Chadwick, Thomas Southwood Smith, and Florence Nightingale, pointed to environmental factors, including filth, lack of ventilation, and higher concentrations of bodies, as the main sources of disease. Historians have shown that while the two theories invoke different causal factors, they are much more interrelated than was previously acknowledged. Until the mid-nineteenth century, as Christopher Hamlin maintains, the definitions of miasma and contagion remained elusive, and these terms were "variously and vaguely defined and used."[136] Many scientists even considered the terms to be synonymous.[137] This changed little in the following three decades, with medical practitioners, social commentators, and even literary authors continuing to support various conceptual blends of these theories.[138] From the 1830s to the 1880s, the two doctrines were used, often simultaneously, to explain the aetiology of various infectious diseases associated with the slums, such as cholera and tuberculosis. Charles Rosenberg asserts that most nineteenth-century Europeans believed that cholera was a product of miasma, the filthy atmosphere in the streets, but they thought "the dirty" and "the intemperate" were cholera's "intended victims."[139] These theories were compelling because they called for active, positive intervention that empowered individuals: if contagion was the product of "carelessness and ignorance," as well as the proximity of human bodies, it could be prevented through "proper sanitary precautions" taken by organized, conscientious groups of healthy people.[140] The discovery of germ theory in the 1880s – thanks to the work of European scientists such as Robert Koch, Louis Pasteur, Ignaz Semmelweis, and Joseph Lister – which proved that stinks were not in themselves particularly hazardous, did not immediately help assuage sanitary anxieties.[141] Mark Jenner has explained that changes in scientific models of sensory perception were not automatically translated into equivalent transformations in subjective understandings of sensation or perception.[142] Germ theory and bacteriology would not give rise to any practical medical cures until well into the twentieth century. As Kari Nixon observes, in this conceptual space, germ theory did very little other than highlighting "human interconnection in its most horrifying configuration."[143]

It is thus not particularly striking that the conflation of contagionism and anticontagionism theories of disease continued to exert a powerful hold over the popular imagination in Italy in the decades following unification. Serao, for instance, repeatedly employs the analogy of the fetid swamp: she graphically writes that in the middle of the Via dei Mercanti, "il ruscello è nero, fetido, non si muove, impantanato" (the stream is as black, smelly, and stagnant as a bog).[144] Filth also often slides from material to moral filth. Piccini associates indigence with moral corruption when he asserts that "la corruzione morale si accumula dove stagna la vita, come i miasmi si sviluppano da certe acque morte" (moral corruption accumulates where life is torpid, like the miasmas are sometimes generated by stagnant water).[145] In the introduction to *I vermi*, Mastriani uses what, as Forgacs points out, would later become a staple device in warnings to soldiers of the risks of venereal disease, namely the image of the infective body of the woman, hidden beneath a seductive appearance: "Colla mano sulla coscienza, solleverò il velo che copre la frine impudica, non perché il vostro corpo si arresti e si diletti su quelle forme prevaricatrici, ma perché sotto quella rosa epidermide scopriate il pus venefico che vi si asconde." (With my hand on my conscience, I will lift the veil covering the immodest harlot, not so that your eyes may linger and feast upon her deceitful shape but so that you may see the poisonous pus hidden beneath that rosy skin.)[146] The woman's breath is "pestifero e morboso" (pestiferous and noxious) and hence infective.[147] Forgacs observes, then, the striving for "truth, objectivity, and validity as knowledge ... was always indissociable from fears and anxieties of touch, infection, and corruption."[148] Although the city is prevalently depicted in dichotomic terms, the association between stench and disease makes explicit the threatening possibility of contamination between the criminal underworld and the rest of society. The places frequented by criminals and indigents, Corio writes, are also populated by "moltissimi giovani di oneste famiglie, i quali incominciano in questi turpi luoghi a mettere il piede sullo sdrucciolo del vizio, per finire poi a precipitare nel baratro del delitto" (many young people from respectable families, who begin their descent down the slippery slope of vice in these depraved places and end up slipping into the depths of crime).[149] Even in Naples, where the physical segregation of the lower classes is more visible, anxieties about boundary transgressions irrupt: Serao acknowledges that in the surroundings of Via di Santa Candida, a beautiful area that constitutes the "strada della salute e della redenzione del popolo napoletano" (street of the health and redemption of Neapolitan people), unfortunately "non si aggirano, colà, che ladruncoli, camorristi, pregiudicati e donne di mala vita" (lurk only thieves, camorristi, habitual offenders, and prostitutes).[150] Italian authors realized that in the new metropolis the separation between poor and more prosperous streets was not as sharp as had been previously thought and that, although there were pockets of severe deprivation, these were frequently located in close proximity to more-affluent areas. In cities where the wealthier, lighter, cleaner, and safer areas exist side by side with the poorer, darker, dirtier, and more dangerous ones, crossing what Corio calls the "pericoloso confine" (dangerous boundary) might turn into a nightmare.[151]

The idea of contagion, regardless of its principal causal factors, contributed to the creation of a disquieting atmosphere of collective panic that facilitated social control. However, the vagueness and elusiveness of the interpretations of the phenomenon of contagion produced spaces in which writers, activists, and investigators could criticize the failures and excesses of these technologies of social control. Italian authors failed to pursue these paths of subversion, perpetuating the ideas and views promoted by the ruling class and enacted by the government. The criminalization of any form of social and cultural transgression, particularly vagrancy, testifies to a growing preoccupation with the potentially contagious nature of a way of living seen as unhealthy and dangerous. In a literal sense, as criminologists and sociologists were claiming, vagrants were sources of contagion, as they threatened public health by causing epidemics and spreading infectious disease. In a less literal sense, they infected by setting a bad example, luring others into lives of indolence and irresponsibility.

Interaction and proximity, then, become a source of real horror. Separation between what is intrinsically criminal and what is, on the contrary, simply a consequence of extreme poverty was proving unattainable. With infection spreading and the world of the slums potentially engulfing all classes, the lives of ordinary people like the reader are threatened. Piccini denounces that "la città del delitto sorge proprio in mezzo a quella delle industrie, delle chiese e delle scuole" (the city of crime is indeed located in the middle of the city of factories, churches, and schools).[152] There are numerous neighbourhoods in Florence "in condizioni di pestilenza e di contagio" (experiencing pestilence and infection) that threaten to contaminate "tante povere e buone famiglie, che abitano le prossime strade" (several poor but good families that inhabit the neighbouring streets).[153] The danger of contagion constitutes one of the deepest and most hidden fears of criminologists, social investigators, and writers alike, and it is particularly prone to Gothicization due to its invisibility, uncontrollability, and killing force. The ideal city centre, the heart of this apparently civilized environment, was supposed to engender domesticity, provide privacy and protection from the masses, and promote respectability. Instead, it is transformed, in the words of Botting, into "a dark labyrinth ... a site of nocturnal corruption and violence, a locus of real horror."[154] What finally emerges is not simply the anxiety of the middle class about the loss of control of its space but also a growing fear that Italy is deteriorating into a nationwide slum. The vision of a world in which a contagious principle threatens to reduce all differences and distinctions to a generalized incoherence is markedly and unmistakably Gothic, a dark universe in which, as Hogle argues, all the binary oppositions of our culture "cannot maintain their separations" and inevitably collapse.[155]

Although Italian authors seek to be directly involved in the social and political processes of state-building, the ideological framework underpinning their texts remains essentially elusive, and their political stance is ultimately reactionary. Piccini and Corio appeal to Florence's and Milan's (respectively) wealthier citizens' sense of responsibility, calling for an improvement of the city's welfare services, including night shelters for the homeless and schools for disadvantaged children, while Valera limits himself to suggesting, in violent language that betrays its sterility, some sort of popular uprising. These sociological enquiries are carried out within such a moralistic dimension that any fruitful sociopolitical analysis is ultimately frustrated.[156] In the preface of his book, Piccini affirms that "io ho imparato ad amare, a compatire, a esaltare chi soffre" (I learned to love, pity, and exalt those who suffer).[157] The deserving poor, Corio insists, "non hanno sentimenti bassi, se non quando si elevano alla borghesia" (do not have lowly sentiments, unless they rise into the bourgeoisie).[158] Yet the authors' treatment of the subaltern classes is always paternalistic, with the poor being presented as savages in need of essential goods (both material and spiritual) that the upper classes/colonizers are supposed to provide: in fact, charity from the wealthy is often identified as one of the few solutions to the problem of poverty.[159] The authors' political condemnation of the worst of the lower classes' living conditions remained inseparable from expressions of horror and repulsion. The messages that these novels circulate ultimately become functional to a project of policing and medical and social control.

While the administration of the state is denounced as inefficient in these novels, no alternative is proposed. Valera admits the difficulty of establishing order in a society in which inequality is so widespread – "È possibile infrenare o estinguere la razza dei malviventi nello stato attuale? È possibile arginare la furia se essa ingrossa sempre? È possibile esigere moralità, dove il vizio è una necessità ineluttabile, imperiosa, assoluta?" (Is it possible to halt or extinguish the race of criminals in the current situation? Is it possible to stem the rage if it continues to grow? Is it possible to demand morality where vice is an unavoidable, imperious, and absolute necessity?) – and when a physician asks him what could be done given the lack of action on the part of the state, he avoids answering and simply places his hope in future generations: "Bisognerebbe prima sostituire alle vostre teste venerande e quadrangolari quelle della generazione crescente" (First we must replace your esteemed, square heads with those of the rising generation).[160] These texts convey a very pessimistic view of the prospects of the newborn state. The South, in particular, is depicted as a dark and hopeless region, devastated by injustice and corruption. Mastriani is deeply sceptical about the possibility of his homeland ever improving: "Non è quistione né di forma di governo, né di riforme politiche, né di più accomodata amministrazione. Sia questo o quel governo, sia monarchia assoluta o repubblica, le cose non muteranno giammai in bene, ove il sistema sociale resti il medesimo." (It is not a question of the type of government or political reform or more efficient administration. Under any kind of government, whether an absolute monarchy or a republic, things will never change for the better if the social system remains the same.)[161] The way in which cities are represented in these urban novels symbolizes the worrying prospects of the country, a place that was only formally unified but is, in fact, plagued by criminality, socio-economic inequality, and an unshakeable sense of ineluctability.

Although Italian authors critique the unificatory process, they fail to formulate and put forward any concrete proposals to resolve the problems of poverty and criminality, besides resorting to violence. The only exception involves repressive intervention and consists in the eradication of some of the most notorious slums – a practice that, significantly, was widely carried out by the Italian government at the end of the nineteenth century.[162] Mastriani, in *I vermi*, writes ironically that "sempre è più *pericolosa* alla società la classe de' *medici* che quella de' *mendici*" (the *medical* class is always more *dangerous* to society than that of the *beggars*), but he finally admits that "bisogna demolire que' tenebrosi nidi di bruchi" (we need to destroy those gloomy nests of worms) so that "gli abitanti di quelle contrade possano uniqua fruire de' vantaggi che la civiltà e la libertà arrecano a' popoli" (the inhabitants of those quarters can equally enjoy the benefits that civilization and freedom grant to peoples).[163] Serao holds the government responsible for the conditions of the proletariat in Naples and refuses to endorse the dismantlement of the underbelly of the city propounded by Prime Minister Depretis. Nonetheless, when it comes to suggesting some kind of political intervention, she simply replaces Depretis's idea of "sventrare" (gutting) Naples with a particularly vague "rifare" (redo), which still implies the destruction of the slums.[164] After all, this is the same expression that Piccini uses to advocate the disembowelment and subsequent renovation of the centre of Florence, an initiative actually put into practice in 1885: "Bisogna abbattere varii punti di Firenze e ricostruirli di nuovo" (it is necessary to dismantle several areas of Florence and build them anew).[165] Those subjected to these laws and initiatives tended to be the wretched of the city slums, depicted in Italian narratives as victims of poverty, injustice, and misfortune but also as a major menace to the health of the state. Supporting the political act of cleaning up slums was considered progressive and conducive to improving living conditions. In reality, it eventually reinforced classist and racist essentializing discourses that metonymically identified the poor with their insalubrious environments.

This phenomenon was certainly not new. The process of generalized, undefined medicalization of society in the eighteenth and nineteenth centuries described by Foucault is, according to Esposito, characterized by the leading role given to medicine in the fight against the risk of infection: "Connected with this prophylactic need is the importance granted to public hygiene as a prerequisite of sanitary practice, but also the function of social control that was associated with it from the outset."[166] For instance, the separation between rich neighbourhoods and poor neighbourhoods carried out in many nineteenth-century English cities was the direct consequence of the cholera epidemic of 1832. More broadly, all the urbanization that occurred in Europe from the middle of the eighteenth century, Esposito argues, took on the appearance of "a dense network of fences between places, zones, and territories protected by boundaries established according to political and administrative rules that went well beyond sanitary needs."[167] What is striking in the post-unification Italian context is that fears and anxieties concerning contagion were often disconnected from real infectious diseases and, as we have seen, were directly related to the intrinsic otherness and contagious nature of certain socially and culturally marginalized groups of people.

The promotion and validation of eugenic measures and physical confinement in the construction of the modern state seem to indicate disturbing instances of connection between post-unification Italy and Nazi Germany. Michael Berkowitz, who has written extensively on crime and disease in Nazi Germany, argues that exaggerated tendencies towards criminality and debilitating disease "were part of essentialist Nazi constructs of Jews that were a spur to, guide, and justification for actions that culminated in genocide. Suspected of a proclivity to fatal 'contagions,' Jews were treated as criminals."[168] For Berkowitz, it is possible to "conceive their treatment in ghettos and concentration camps as a sort of 'preventive' measure in light of the supposed relationship between Jews and contagious diseases – especially the dreaded typhus, as exemplified in film, poster, and press campaigns." The Nazis consistently portrayed "disease-ridden Jews as swarming in a morass of 'filth.'"[169] Jews needed to be contained and closely watched because of "their propensity for criminality," and they "had to be dealt with aggressively, because Jewish communal existence was said to be an incubator for vice, and their habits, a crucible for disease."[170] Fears of contagion resulted in deliberate attempts to physically separate the healthy and the sick. Despite the radically different contexts, both Italian theorists of the dangerous classes and Nazi theorists of criminality promoted the erection of physical barriers separating healthy areas from unhealthy areas and good subjects from bad, contagious subjects. Furthermore, both created the impression of rampant criminality in circumscribed, apparently dangerous places, that is, the poorest and most remote areas of the city and the ghettos. It is true that the promotion of secluded spaces and the call for the establishment of physical boundaries were not, in liberal Italy, intended to facilitate mass murder, but both German and Italian specialists took disturbing actions on the basis of their notions of crime and disease. Late nineteenth- and early twentieth-century Italian criminologists and legal experts advocated and encouraged the spatial and symbolic separation of lower-class bodies from the expensive and expansive living spaces of the middle and upper classes, actively promoting the elimination of these marginalized subjects, both physically and metaphorically, in order to reimagine and reconfigure the national community. Crucially, Italian urban literature, in both its high and more popular forms, failed to open sites of dissension and to challenge the ruling ideology. Instead, it replicated and perpetuated stereotypes and paradigms that, in the years to come, continued to be fed, with their inevitable and dramatic conclusion taking the form of a totalitarian regime following the First World War.

The Anthropology of the Lower Classes

In retrospect, what is striking about the novels analysed here is, on the one hand, their ability to capture the contours of a debate about the dangerous classes that was progressively mutating and, on the other, their capacity to feed and shape that very same debate. The narratives examined in this chapter came, perhaps paradoxically, to serve the interests of politics by valorizing the repressive, violent choices of the state and by naturalizing class difference. The representation of the underclasses as other and inherently dangerous offers narratives of scientific justification for many of the racial, national, and gender prejudices that formed the political justification for the creation of the state. Instead of providing answers to the problem of criminality and finding remedies to the desperate socio-economic conditions of the poor, Italian writers' portrayal of low life contributed to the further marginalization of a vast range of cultural others that made no discrimination between criminals and the various outcasts roaming the underbelly of the city, including vagrants, beggars, and prostitutes. However, the continual emphasis on the insanitary conditions of the locales frequented by criminals and indigents reveals the importance of the environment in the production of crime. The literary texts are thus the result of the mediation and re-elaboration of different theories and values in circulation at that precise historical moment. Although in a way they fundamentally reproduce the same ruling ideology they were supposed to challenge, in another way they set the ground for a new interpretation of the phenomenon of urban criminality that encompasses discordant ideas and perspectives.

From the late 1880s and early 1890s, socio-economic and environmental explanations of the lower classes' transgressive behaviour started to gain ground. An early example is that of the socialist and political economist Achille Loria. Without neglecting the importance of biology and heredity in the production of crime, Loria argues in an 1886 work that poverty, unhealthy living conditions, bad food, and possibly alcohol reduce people to a level of misery that inevitably promotes lawbreaking, thus leading to profound degradation that progressively worsens with each generation.[171] This combination of social and biological factors is likewise cited by a major exponent of Italian positivist criminology, Raffaele Garofalo, who claimed in 1885 that poverty can make the organism vulnerable to degenerative disorders and flaws, which are likely to be passed on to the next generation.[172] Connections between economy and crime were also made by the statistician Ettore Fornasari di Verce and the socialist and criminologist Napoleone Colajanni. In a survey published in 1893, Fornasari di Verce argues that, in the year 1889, of every hundred prisoners in Italy, fifty-six were indigent, thirty-two were slightly above the threshold of poverty, ten were reasonably well off, and just under two qualified as wealthy or comfortable.[173] Meanwhile, Colajanni, in his 1889 *Sociologia criminale*, emphasizes the impact of the structure and the performance of the economy on morality: "Pare impossibile ci siano ancora pensatori i quali mettano in forse la preminenza e la precedenza dell'azione del fattore economico nell'evoluzione sociale." (It seems impossible that there are still thinkers who call into question the pre-eminence and precedence of the influence of economic factors in social evolution.)[174] Although he cautions that scholars such as Loria exaggerate when they claim that "ogni avvenimento sociale – politico, religioso, estetico, morale – è il prodotto diretto ed esclusivo di un fenomeno economico" (every social occurrence – political, religious, aesthetic, moral – is the direct and exclusive product of an economic factor), he nonetheless affirms that "il delitto è soprattutto un fenomeno sociale o storico" (crime is above all a social or historical phenomenon) directly correlated to poverty levels and fluctuations in the economy: the "causa prima e vera della condizione morale, e perciò della delinquenza" (primary and true cause of the moral condition and hence of delinquency) lies in the "condizione economica" (economy) of "capitalismo moderno" (modern capitalism).[175]

The most influential theorizations in this debate were those of Alfredo Niceforo.[176] In these years, Niceforo, the last of Lombroso's pupils, founded a new scientific discipline – the anthropology of the lower classes – which integrated criminology, anthropology, physiology, and statistics to provide a comprehensive and more accurate understanding of the moral inferiority of the subaltern classes and their abnormal inclination to commit crimes. In a series of studies written in both French and Italian – *Les classes pauvres: Recherches anthropologiques et sociales* (1905), *Forza e ricchezza: Studi sulla vita fisica ed economica delle classi sociali* (1906), and *Antropologia delle classi povere* (1910) – Niceforo directs Lombroso's criminology towards environmental eugenics, inscribing socio-economic causes within an anthropological and racial scheme of interpretation.[177] A voracious reader and acute investigator of popular forms of writing, Niceforo likely came across the texts I examine here. As well as providing a precious testimony of a rapidly mutating cultural climate, and on which Niceforo was ready to capitalize, this literature may have had a direct influence on the criminologist's work. In the sociological exploration of Roman criminality *La mala vita a Roma* (1898), written by Niceforo with the help of Sighele, the label "dangerous classes" – which encompasses both petty criminals and professional delinquents, as well as prostitutes and vagrants – recurs frequently, indicating that it was ostensibly still an integral part of criminological language.[178] In the fight against crime, which sadly remained "la piaga ... più grave del nostro paese" (the most serious scourge of our country), Niceforo and Sighele argue for the need to "chiudere il rubinetto alla delinquenza incorreggibile – bisogna incanalare, d'altra parte, la delinquenza correggibile in un ambiente diverso da quello ove si tengono sotto chiave i vecchi ladri, gli omicidi nati, i recidivi continui" (cut off the flow of inveterate criminals, while at the same time moving corrigible delinquents into different places from those where the old thieves, born murderers, and habitual criminals are locked up).[179]

It is revealing that they appropriate urban novels' rhetorical strategies, Gothic imagery, and atmosphere for the socio-anthropological descriptions of such criminals. Precisely like novelists, the two scientists stage stories of murder and mystery, recreate dialogues between delinquents, and address the reader directly. The proximity of human bodies continues to represent a cause of transgression. As they put it, "l'agglomero di troppe anime in un dato spazio" (the agglomeration of too many people in a single space) is the principal reason behind the spread of criminality within the city.[180] The largest and most developed cities tend to attract "certi individui ... *suggestionabili*" (certain *suggestible* types), and, as the crowd is naturally subversive, the seed of delinquency is found in the interaction between bodies.[181] *La mala vita a Roma* constitutes a compelling example of the extent to which, at the end of the century, social investigators continued to study the crimes "nelle grandi città" (in the large cities) perpetrated "da una oscura popolazione, che ne forma il sotto-suolo immondo e pericoloso" (by an obscure population that forms their disgusting and dangerous underbelly).[182] Interestingly, the two authors realize this by taking the reader "attraverso i labirinti oscuri dei bassifondi romani" (through the dark labyrinths of Roman slums).[183] The sociopolitical situation had changed in fin de siècle Italy, but the city was still portrayed as labyrinthine and frightening, and the ghost of the dangerous classes continued to haunt Italy's modernity and to frustrate the country's entry into civilized Europe.

2 Gothic Minds

As I suggest in the introduction, despite its apparently polarized nature, the fin de siècle Italian debate on the criminogenic factors underlying criminal behaviour was, in reality, far more complex than had been acknowledged until very recently. While positivists progressively came to include social and environmental factors in their aetiology of crime, over time biology acquired increasing centrality in the explanation of transgressive behaviour, even among those who identified crime as a prevalently socio-historical phenomenon; as Ashley noted, experts fundamentally agreed that, "if not the result of atavism or of atavism alone, organic anomalies nonetheless contributed to crime."[1] For instance, Enrico Ferri, the principal and most influential pupil of Lombroso, argued in 1881 that "l'ambiente naturale e sociale, combinato colle tendenze ereditarie ed acquisite individuali e cogli impulsi occasionali, determina necessariamente un relativo contingente di reati" (the natural and social environment, combined with individual tendencies, both hereditary and acquired, and with occasional impulses, necessarily accounts for a certain number of crimes).[2] The human being is not "fatto a macchina" (made like a machine) but is rather "un meccanismo vivente, che ha una propria e speciale rispondenza alle cause esterne" (a living mechanism that has its own special way of responding to external causes).[3] On the other hand, even Colajanni, possibly the most ardent critic of the Lombrosian school, shared the idea of atavism as a determinant in inherited forms of delinquency: "Se il Lombroso rinunziando alla sua abituale instabilità si fosse fermato al concetto dell'atavismo ... avrebbe spiegato facilmente e semplicemente il delinquente nato." (If Lombroso, renouncing his habitual instability, had stopped after developing the concept of atavism ... he would have easily and convincingly explained the born criminal.)[4] Colajanni also came to accept as a fact "la trasmissione ereditaria delle cattive tendenze e dell'animo malvagio dei genitori nei figli" (the hereditary transmission of bad tendencies and mean-spiritedness from parents to their children), particularly when it came to mental diseases.[5]

Recent scholarship has revealed the permeability of the boundaries between different schools of criminology and has demonstrated the existence of a large number of specialists whose work is situated at the crossroads of competing ideologies.[6] Garfinkel's monumental *Criminal Law in Liberal and Fascist Italy* (2016), for instance, is largely concerned with a towering figure in the legal history of liberal Italy, Ugo Conti, whose work, like that of many of the specialists encountered in the previous chapter, straddles the two conflicting schools rather than adhering to one: his view of crime and punishment appeared to fit with the so-called classical school, while his concepts of social defence and criminal dangerousness seemed to embrace the penology of the rival positivist school. Gibson has also shown how the internal complexity of the Italian school of positivist criminology, whose exponents belonged to a variety of different disciplines, produced considerable methodological diversity and debate even among its own members.[7] Despite agreeing on the general differences between types of criminals, they nonetheless disagreed on specifics. Consequently, even within the same theoretical framework, research into criminality's origins remained varied, unsystematic, and inconsistent. Positivist thinking about the causes of crime was often incoherent, and scientists' explanations for criminal behaviour were occasionally self-contradictory. They never found a single, universal law of delinquency, obliging them to continuously identify variables, outline exceptions, and thus redesign the whole system of classification. The evidence of such problems can be found in the proliferation of specific types of criminals whose common matrix proved impossible to find.

Trans-medial discussions of the states of mind, psyches, and brains of criminals abounded at the intersection of literature, popular publishing, and the press. Specialists, particularly until the turn of the century, primarily focused on male criminals, and what is striking about the different ways in which male and female forms of criminality were explored is the importance accorded to the (male) criminal mind and, as we will see in the following chapter, the (female) criminal body.[8] After all, as Simona Mori points out, the scientific and technical specification of intellectual activity was, in the nineteenth century, "a quality of male distinction that enjoyed broad support in the cultured classes,"[9] with attributes such as rationality and problem-solving being culturally coded as specifically masculine. The criminal mind, as well as its feelings and thoughts, became, for the first time, the object of prodigious attention, generating a great response in the field of literature. In one often cited passage of Bram Stoker's *Dracula* (1897), Mina Harker responds to Professor Van Helsing's urgings to describe the count by stressing that Lombroso would classify him as "a criminal type" due to his "imperfectly formed mind."[10] It is unsurprising that contemporary research on the criminal mind – and more broadly on the very nature of criminality – filtered into Italian fictional narratives. This lack of homogeneous, organic, and uniform theories of crime contributed to enriching literary configurations, which in turn played a crucial role in disseminating and shaping discourses on the roots and manifestations of evil. Textual representations of delinquency responded to this complex intellectual climate in different ways, reinforcing, challenging, or manipulating dominant and subordinate views.

On this premise, this chapter analyses a variety of transgressor-centred stories in which crime is represented as an outward manifestation of the internal workings of the criminal's mind. These texts variously scrutinize types of criminals and the innermost recesses of their minds, offering powerful explorations of evil human potential. In the second half of the nineteenth century, Botting observes, Gothic tropes and motifs were no longer able to embody and externalize fears and anxieties, which were thus internalized and centred on the individual.[11] The texts that I consider present psychologically unstable protagonists involved in physically and psychologically dangerous situations, emphasize feeling and sensation, and celebrate excess, either in the extremity of the violence of the crime itself or in the way in which the narrative is told.[12] These stories anticipate future literary trends and especially the development of the psychological thriller, a hybrid, permeable, and mobile form that blurs the boundaries between Gothic and crime writing and, according to many scholars, emerged only in the second half of the twentieth century.[13] This chapter is divided into two main sections. The first investigates the crime-confession nexus, a paradigm that typifies many stories of the time, which apparently treat the criminal not as an aberration of nature but as a product of society's weaknesses and anomalies. The second section looks at the figure of the sexual monster in the context of emerging sexology and examines how the issue of homosexuality is articulated through the connection between disease and crime. In probing the boundaries and constant interaction between scientific and (Gothicized) cultural discourses, this chapter shows that, while criminology generated a varied and composite spectrum of approaches to the exploration of criminal minds, narratives of criminal transgression proved central to the modern construction of deviance in the Italian cultural imaginary.

The Guilty Mind

The exploration of guilt constitutes a peculiar characteristic of much nineteenth-century literature concerned with crime and transgression. One of the most famous examples is Fyodor Dostoevsky's *Crime and Punishment* (1866), which narrates the mental anguish and the moral dilemmas of a young student, Rodion Raskolnikov, following his murder of an old woman. Much of the novel focuses on the murderer's increasing need to confess, which he finally does under psychological pressure exerted by a judicial investigator. In an 1893 article devoted to the study of the criminal in contemporary literature and theatre, Lombroso praises Dostoevsky for his accurate portrayal of what the criminologist defines as the occasional criminal, that is, one who experiences insanity as a result of his egotism and jealousy, kills his old pawnbroker for utilitarian reasons, and is then so overwhelmed with remorse that he finally confesses.[14] In his *I delinquenti nell'arte* (1896), which explores both past and present figures of criminality against the backdrop of positivist criminology's findings, Ferri celebrates Dostoevsky's talent as a criminal anthropologist, although he disagrees with Lombroso on the nature of Raskolnikov's deviance, considering the protagonist of the novel the archetypal insane criminal.[15]

The crime-confession pattern frequently recurs in Italian literature from this period, with numerous writers investigating the mentally devastating consequences of committing a crime upon a subject who is not, apparently, a habitual offender. An excellent example is Italo Svevo's short story "L'assassinio di via Belpoggio," which appeared in nine instalments in the newspaper *L'Indipendente* under the name Enrico Samigli from 4 October to 13 October 1890.[16] Giorgio, a porter suffering financial hardship, impulsively kills a near stranger to steal his money. He is an "inept," like many of Svevo's main characters, "che col suo carattere poco energico, inerte, avrebbe sempre cercato mezzi e modi e finito col non agire che al sicuro, dunque mai" (who, because of his lack of energy and his inertia, would always look for a way out and would only take action when the outcome was certain – in other words, never).[17] Profoundly frustrated, not having been able to live up to his mother's expectations, both economically and work-wise, Giorgio kills in part because of his indigence but mostly because he seeks self-affirmation. Soon after though, when the news of the murder spreads through the city, Giorgio begins to feel increasingly haunted and then entrapped. Svevo describes in detail Giorgio's interior ontological struggles, which lead him to make a banal mistake that eventually proves fatal: after discovering that an eyewitness has given the police a profile of the killer and his hat, Giorgio goes to a shop to purchase a new one but, on his way out, inadvertently leaves the old hat in the shop, as a result of which the police are able to identify and incriminate him.

A writer who frequently used the crime-confession pattern was Gabriele D'Annunzio, whose work was heavily influenced by Dostoevsky's analyses of introspection and spiritual struggle.[18] In *Giovanni Episcopo* (1891), set in Rome, the protagonist is a meek clerk whose life is suddenly turned upside down when he meets Giulio Wanzer, a vicious and wicked manipulator to whom he eventually succumbs. After a while, however, Giulio disappears from Rome after having stolen money from the Treasury. Giovanni marries Ginevra, a mysterious and promiscuous woman who gives birth to a boy, Ciro, whose paternity remains uncertain. Years later, Giulio resurfaces and installs himself in their household, beginning an affair with Ginevra; however, only when Giovanni discovers that Giulio has beaten both Ginevra and Ciro does he angrily stab and kill the criminal. This novel, which displays perfect reproductions of Lombrosian criminals – Giulio is a born criminal; Giovanni is an occasional criminal; Ginevra is the archetypal prostitute – is also remarkable in that it is written from Giovanni's first-person point of view. Giovanni's invisible, enigmatic interlocutor is most likely a criminologist interrogating him, not with the intent of establishing his guilt – we learn early on that he was discovered over the victim's corpse with a knife in his hand – but in an attempt to obtain a complete picture of the physical and mental constitution of such a peculiar murderer. Another classic example that I examine in greater detail in the following chapter is *L'innocente* (1892), which consists of Tullio Hermil's confession of the murder of his wife's illegitimate infant son and an account of the events leading up to the killing. These novels, whose plots seem like "cases" reminiscent of psychological studies, are deeply infused with the language of positivist criminology. *L'innocente* is arguably D'Annunzio's most Lombrosian work and is extensively analysed by Ferri in *I delinquenti nell'arte*, where the criminologist describes Tullio as a "man of genius" convinced of his intellectual and moral superiority who feels that his every action finds its justification in his exceptional nature and is thus beyond reproach.[19]

The same crime-confession pattern is also explored in two major novels – Emilio De Marchi's *Il cappello del prete* (1887) and Luigi Capuana's *Il marchese di Roccaverdina* (1901) – which offer complex types of murderers who are not, apparently, congenitally evil.[20] Both De Marchi and Capuana are interested in depicting the mental struggles of people who resort to murder for various motives – money, self-affirmation, jealousy – but are then somehow forced to confess the crime. Although these novels do not employ a first-person narrator, which has an inherently confessional nature and involves direct focalization on the protagonist, they are portraits of murderers and accurate studies of their psyches, which are always centre stage. The inverted structure typical of certain detective novels – the culprit is known from the beginning of the story and the reader waits for the repercussions to be revealed – is used to generate suspense and make the readers experience the warped world view of the protagonist. As in typical examples of psychological thrillers, in which treacherous confusions regarding the role of the protagonist constitute key structural elements, in these two novels the main characters are initially depicted as hunters, but they suddenly turn into the hunted when an investigation begins and the fear of discovery builds within them.[21] Moreover, their fatally doomed relationship with society generates themes of alienation and entrapment that eventually culminate in their tragic psychic demise.[22] Ultimately, these are not, as most scholars claim, detective stories, for detection plays a very small part in the construction of the plot.[23] In *Il cappello del prete*, exponents of the judicial system appear only towards the end of the novel. In "L'assassinio di via Belpoggio," the police are pushed into the background until the final scene, when a couple of officers burst into Giorgio's house, while they are virtually absent in *Il marchese di Roccaverdina*. These stories in fact constitute embryonic forms of the psychological thriller, in which the focus on the emotional life of the transgressor moves the stories so far towards the Gothic that the typical aspects of the rational detective story are inevitably overshadowed and undermined.

Il cappello del prete, set in Naples, was originally published in 1887 in instalments both in the journal *L'Italia del popolo* in Milan and in the *Corriere di Napoli* in Naples, before being collected into a volume the following year.[24] De Marchi was influenced by the story of Count Alessandro Faella, who, in 1881, killed a priest to steal his money, was arrested, and then took his own life in prison without having confessed his crime. The case provoked a scandal and generated enormous media attention that resulted in several popular and more serious publications, including Lombroso and Ferri's scientific study of the murderer.[25] De Marchi reworked this case and used it as a starting point for examining the psychology of Baron Carlo Coriolano di Santafusca, a vicious individual, a libertine, and an atheist. He has major financial problems, having mortgaged his property and borrowed from his tenants to pay for his gambling habits. He persuades a usurer priest to buy his family property but then kills him to steal the money the priest had brought with him for the sale. Shortly afterwards, he realizes he has left a crucial piece of evidence at the crime scene: the priest's hat. He immediately tries to retrieve the hat and get rid of it, but the hat that he manages to obtain and destroy – by throwing it into the sea – turns out to be the wrong one. When the examining magistrate summons the baron to discuss the case and shows him the real hat, the criminal loses his self-control and confesses to the murder.

The genesis of *Il marchese di Roccaverdina* can be traced to the early 1880s, but the novel was serialized in the journal *L'ora* only in 1900 and published in book format the following year.[26] The protagonist of the novel, set in post-unification rural Sicily, is the marquis Antonio Schirardi, an uncultivated, feudal despot, the product of a turbulent age of transition and transformations, torn between conflicting feudal and bourgeois impulses. The marquis was raised as a noble with strict models of aristocratic behaviour, such as the baroness of Lagomorto, his father, and his grandfather. Yet the central figures in his life are peasants, including his nurse and caretaker Mamma Grazia, the faithful servant Rocco, and the young and attractive Agrippina, with whom he has a relationship. After ten years with Agrippina, however, the marquis succumbs to the pressure exerted by the family to eliminate external influences and to suppress his attraction to and affection for her. He thus decides to arrange what is supposed to be a contrived marriage between Agrippina and Rocco. After a while, however, the marquis begins to fear that Rocco has seduced Agrippina and so, devoured by jealousy, he kills him. After the murder, the marquis attempts to fully embrace the aristocratic dynamic by marrying the noble-born Zòsima. He is unable, however, to recapture the aristocratic identity of his grandfather's generation, to forget his affection for Agrippina, and to put the crime behind him. Although he initially allows another man to be charged and convicted for the murder in his place, when he finds out that the man has died in prison, his integrity and his sanity begin to unravel.

To begin with, consider that the two main characters of *Il cappello del prete* and *Il marchese di Roccaverdina* have absolutely no intention of turning themselves in, because they are not willing to compromise their reputation. They simply cannot accept their noble lineage being associated with a violent crime. It is revealing, as Sergia Adamo points out, that De Marchi and Capuana set their novels in Southern Italy in a period in which the members of the aristocracy did not intend on complying with the social and political changes that the newborn state was experiencing.[27] In a way, the representation of these criminals is a response to wider contemporary cultural and sociopolitical concerns, including the problem of class difference in Southern Italy and the abusive role of the aristocracy. Both the baron and the marquis feel legitimized in eluding the law and share feudal assumptions about the right to kill. In this respect, the authors seem to betray a fear of the possibility of an adaptable nobility's continued domination. Here, the villain, as in early Gothic texts, takes the form of the vicious nobleman, a parasite, the residual trace of a past that still permeates the country and frustrates its attempts at modernization.[28]

Moreover, the relatively minimal presence of the police allows both Capuana and De Marchi to construct a strong critique of the Italian legal system and its injustices. In *Il marchese di Roccaverdina*, an innocent man is wrongly incarcerated and dies in prison, while in *Il cappello del prete*, the examining magistrate questions the baron without knowing that he might have been involved in the case. Instead, it is the lawyer Don Ciccio Scuotto who is presented as a clever sleuth by De Marchi's narrator – "uomo fino, tenace, nemico dei giornali liberali e dei tempi scellerati" (a shrewd, tenacious man, who hated the liberal newspapers and the abandoned times we live in) – and through his words the author stigmatizes the Italian justice system, the influence of the media in the legal processes, and the superficial way in which murder investigations are generally conducted: "A don Ciccio non parea vero che tutto il gran processo ... dovesse finire come una bolla di sapone. Secondo lui le cose erano state condotte pessimamente, col solito sistema bislacco delle procedure nostre, con troppo intervento dei giornalisti, con troppo pettegolezzo." (To don Ciccio it seemed incredible that this great case ... should vanish like a burst soap bubble. According to him, the matter had been very badly managed, in the usual crooked manner of our legal procedure, with too many interventions by journalists and too much chatter.)[29] It is thus unsurprising that in both novels human justice is frustrated and the two criminals' ultimate inability to escape their fate is due to a sudden yet unavoidable breakdown that unmasks them.

The reasons behind their final loss of sanity are controversial. A considerable part of the critical discussion has focused on the protagonists' remorse, and the nature of guilt constitutes the most debated motif of these novels. Alessandra Briganti affirms that *Il cappello del prete*'s principal and most explicit model is Dostoevsky, for the primary theme of the novel is precisely "il rimorso" (the remorse), which functions, in De Marchi's view, as "prova dell'esistenza dell'anima" (evidence of the existence of the soul).[30] Fabio Pierangeli asserts that the novel pivots on the protagonist's "lotta con il rimorso e il senso di colpa" (conflict with remorse and the sense of guilt) and sees the final sequence as the result of the baron's "desiderio inconscio di confessarsi ad una autorità istituzionale" (unconscious desire to confess to an institutional authority).[31] Ettore Caccia defines *Il marchese di Roccaverdina* as "il dramma del rimorso – il rimorso che gli sconvolge l'animo ... e porta alla pazzia" (a drama of remorse – the remorse that upsets the soul ... and leads to insanity), while, for Angelo Piero Cappello, "il dramma intimo del marchese" (the intimate drama of the marquis) resides "nei due sentimenti del rimorso del delitto commesso e della paura di essere scoperto" (in both the feelings of remorse for the murder committed and the fear of getting caught).[32] For Carlo Madrignani, Capuana renounces positivist psychopathology in favour of a nebulous "dramma di coscienza" (drama of conscience) and explains the marquis's descent into madness as a consequence of the ethical remorse triggered by the crime.[33]

The centrality of guilt, remorse, and confession in the analysis of the novels is understandable considering the inextricable relation between these three paradigms in modern and contemporary culture. For Foucault, confession resides at the heart of religious, scientific, and political systems and has become "one of the main rituals we rely on for the production of truth."[34] Western society has "become a confessing society" and "Western man has become a confessing animal."[35] As Peter Brooks maintains, the notion that possible redemption depends on confession is deeply ingrained in our culture, and Raskolnikov's choice of confession and expiation in Dostoevsky's *Crime and Punishment* still holds much power.[36] However, while Raskolnikov's confession results in punishment, penance, and ultimately atonement, as Dostoevsky suggests at the end of the novel, in De Marchi's and Capuana's texts there is no space for redemption. Although the baron and the marquis occasionally express feelings of guilt in their own thoughts, they fail to actively repent and consciously expiate their crime. They never make a conscious and legitimate confession to civil authorities because they never blame themselves. Unlike the protagonist of *Crime and Punishment*, the two noblemen are not trying to understand their motives, because they seem to be perfectly aware of the reasons behind their murders. The baron needed money and believed that between him and the priest "si è combattuta la grande lotta per la vita. La vittoria, come sempre, fu del più forte, vedi Carlo Darwin" (the great fight for life has been fought. The strongest, as always happens, was victorious; see Charles Darwin).[37] The fear of being caught progressively corrodes his mental sanity, but he never regrets having taken the priest's life. The marquis cannot seriously experience pangs of remorse for having killed his most trusted servant, who had betrayed him. In his feudalistic world view, in which the power of a nobleman is absolute, there is no room for such treachery. Neither protagonist, then, takes responsibility for his actions. For the baron, like the marquis, confession is not, as Brooks suggests, "the way to contrition and to absolution, which permits a reintegration into the community of the faithful."[38] Rather, it is endless persecution of an entirely preternatural nature that causes the texts to veer towards the terrain of the Gothic.

Divine retribution constitutes an important subtext in these novels. In *Il cappello del prete*, crime is still an integral part of a Christian narrative whose inevitable conclusion is punishment. De Marchi stages a conflict between materialism (epitomized by the physician Panterre, to whom the baron refers every time his mental strength starts to vacillate) and divine power. As the baron initially says to himself, using Panterre's words, the conscience is merely "il lusso, l'eleganza dell'uomo felice" (the luxury, the elegance of the fortunate man), and God is "una capocchia di spillo puntato nel cuscino del cielo" (the head of a pin stuck into heaven's cushion).[39] Yet this tension in the baron's psyche between human reason and supernaturalism cannot result in the former prevailing: "Troppo diseguale era la lotta tra un vivo e un morto ... se uccidere un uomo significa farlo vivere più di prima; se nasconderlo in una cisterna vuol dire fare in modo che egli occupi di sé tutta una città ... è segno che la ragione non è ragione." (This struggle between a living man and a dead man was too unequal ... if to kill means to make a man live more than ever, if to hide him in a cistern means that he will make a whole city busy themselves about him ... it is a sign that reason is unreason.)[40] For a Catholic like De Marchi, who saw literature as a powerful instrument of edification, the man who challenges God must pay the highest price. The Milanese author, as testified by the figure of the avaricious priest, stood against the church, which he viewed as a wealthy, largely corrupt political powerhouse. It is thus possible to see the retributive ghost of the priest, which takes the form of his hat in order to haunt the criminal like a spectre, as an instrument of punishment. In the afterlife, he turns into a divine tool, becoming a symbol of divine justice and the implacable wrath of God: "Il cappello del prete si alzava dal mucchio, grande, nero, sozzo, peloso come un osceno pipistrello, come un fantasma accusatore." (The priest's hat stood up from the heap, large, black, filthy, hairy, like an obscene bat, like an accusing ghost.)[41] The ghostly persecution is subtle yet incessant – "era uno spavento, un castigo, un tormento insopportabile di sentire qualcuno che camminava, incalzava dietro le spalle e di non poter fermare quel fantasma" (it was a terror, a punishment, an unbearable torment, to hear someone walking, coming up behind one's back, and not to be able to stop that spectre) – and has the final effect of leading the baron to his psychic demise.[42]

The marquis's reaction following the murder in *Il marchese di Roccaverdina* is more complex and contradictory than that of the baron, but, in some ways, it is still characterized as a conflict between human reason and the supernatural. The marquis is described as voraciously reading books on scientific materialism in an attempt to exorcise his fears of the dreadful afterlife depicted by Catholicism. Yet he also contradictorily uses religious stances as a means of justifying his actions and soothing his conscience: "Se Dio intanto aveva permesso che costui fosse condannato, voleva dire probabilmente che gli pesava addosso qualche altro grave delitto rimasto occulto." (If God had allowed another person to be convicted, it probably meant that some other crime, still concealed, weighed heavily upon him.)[43] The fear of God's punishment, though, never stops haunting him. Annamaria Pagliaro suggests that, rather than concentrating on the representation of ethical remorse, Capuana focuses on the depiction of a psychological state in which "domina un senso di aver trasgredito un comandamento religioso fondamentale e, conseguentemente, la paura di una vendetta divina derivante da questa trasgressione" (there is a prevailing sense of having violated a fundamental religious commandment, and as a result there is fear of divine vengeance deriving from this violation).[44] Saved from suicide by Agrippina, the marquis experiences a moment of religious dread. In his dark and malodorous cellar, he discovers a carving of Christ on the cross: "Nel salire le scale gli sembrava che quegli occhi semispenti continuassero a guardarlo a traverso la spessezza dei muri, e che quelle livide labbra contratte dalla suprema convulsione dell'agonia si agitassero, forse, per gridargli dietro qualche terribile parola!" (Upon climbing the steps, he imagined those half-closed eyes continuing to watch him through the thick walls and those dark lips, contracted from the greatest agonizing convulsions, moving in order to scream some terrible denunciation at him!)[45] The author implies here that the marquis, in spite of his own unforgivable behaviour, does not possess the sacrilegious calm of his forebears. The image of the sacrificed Christ does not, as Paul Barnaby has suggested, remind the marquis of his blame but rather symbolizes the revenge of his repressed Catholic education and is a transparent cipher of his fear of divine punishment.[46] It is true that this symbolic resurrection drives him to confess his guilt to Don Silvio, but even though the priest refuses to absolve him, the conscience of the marquis seems entirely appeased: the very act of confession, he believes, must have placated God somewhat, and moreover, a more permissive and benevolent priest would have simply ordered private penance.

Another crucial yet often neglected element of the marquis's breakdown pertains once again to the supernatural world. His friend and lawyer, Don Aquilante, is a spiritualist who tells the marquis that he is in touch with the spirit of the dead man and is about to discover who the real perpetrator is. Although Don Aquilante is repeatedly ridiculed by the other characters, the narrator suggests that the victim, precisely like the priest in *Il cappello del prete*, is haunting the marquis like a ghost. Not only does Rocco visit the marquis in his dreams, but his presence is continually perceived at the crime scene. On one occasion, Don Aquilante says he has sensed the presence of Rocco, who "si è fermato presso il ponticello ed è rimasto un istante in ascolto" (stopped near the little bridge and remained listening).[47] One of the peasants goes as far as to say that he saw, in the same place in which Rocco was killed, an apparition of a man and his mule, both of which vanished almost immediately into thin air.[48] The fear of unknown, vengeful ghosts condemns the marquis to a state of social alienation and existential disorientation. Persecution metamorphoses into possession when, as he is talking to himself one night in a voice that seems like that of "un altro" (another) – an entity "senza forma" (without form) and "senza nome" (without a name) that speaks like "un terribile misterioso fantasma" (a terrible, mysterious ghost) – the marquis cries out:[49]

Eh? Ti sarebbe piaciuto che Dio non esistesse! Ti sarebbe piaciuto che l'anima non fosse immortale! Hai tolto la vita a una creatura umana, hai fatto morire in carcere un innocente, e volevi goderti in pace la vita quasi non avessi operato niente di male! Ma lo hai visto: c'è stato sempre qualcuno che ha tenuto sveglio in fondo al tuo cuore il rimorso ... E questo qualcuno non si arresterà, non si stancherà, finché tu non abbia pagato il tuo debito, finché tu non abbia espiato anche quaggiù!

(Eh! Would it please you if God did not exist? Would it please you if the soul were not immortal? You have ruined the life of a human creature, you have allowed an innocent man to die in prison, and you wanted to enjoy your life in peace as if you had done nothing wrong! But you have seen him: there has always been someone who has kept remorse awake at the bottom of your heart ... And this someone will never stop, will never tire, until you have paid your debt, until you have expiated your sin in this world too.)[50]

The marquis has now lost his rationality and begins to live in a completely hallucinatory state. One night, he takes his rifle and goes to where the homicide was committed, shooting and screaming at the ghost of the victim and confessing his crime.

There is a complex interplay between different factors that eventually results in these criminals' madness. Insanity itself, which constitutes a key component of the psychological thriller, plays such a major role throughout both texts that it should be discussed in greater depth. There are strong grounds for considering the possibility that moral insanity could be a pathological phenomenon that motivates, to a certain extent, the crimes. Moral insanity, a term originally coined by the early nineteenth-century British physician James Cowles Prichard, designated individuals who seemed normal in physique and intelligence but were unable to distinguish between good and evil behaviour.[51] In a famous 1885 article, Lombroso defines moral insanity as a constitutional anomaly and "una delle forme più gravi di alienazioni mentali" (one of the most serious forms of mental alienation), arguing that epilepsy, moral insanity, and congenital criminality frequently overlap, with one often being a manifestation of the others.[52] Here Lombroso explores the connections between these different yet interrelated types of mental disorders by looking at various physical and especially psychological factors that frequently recur among these subjects. He concludes that, notwithstanding their apparent lucid behaviour and mental stability, they tend to commit impulsive, excessive, and unreasonable acts of violence: in their compulsion to harm others and in their lack of remorse, morally insane individuals are, in Lombroso's view, akin to atavistic, born criminals.[53]

In *Il cappello del prete*, the baron is described from the very beginning of the novel as a vicious man who regularly commits antisocial acts. He is an atheist, a gambler, a libertine, perhaps even an alcoholic, and, above all, a cold-blooded murderer. Although the narrator never touches upon the possibility of an innate predisposition to criminality, it is undeniable that the baron is, in many ways, a serious and habitual offender. It would thus be superficial to classify him merely as, in Lombrosian terms, an occasional delinquent. This type of criminal does not exhibit any sort of degenerative anomaly and usually commits his or her initial offence later in life and always for some adequate reason: occasional delinquents, for Lombroso, possess a hidden predisposition to crime that certain conditions, particularly external circumstances, abruptly activate.[54] However, Lombroso remarks that occasional delinquents tend to openly and consciously confess their misdeeds: this is precisely what distinguishes them from born criminals.[55] The baron, in contrast, keeps his murder concealed for as long as his mental strength allows him to, and he tends to justify his act as necessary in the context of the struggle for life that, in Darwinian terms, constitutes the essence of our world.

Lombroso, when it comes to the type of criminal he defines as "pazzo morale" (morally insane), claims that such delinquents believe they have the right to kill: this "delirio di grandezza" (delusion of grandeur) results in them believing themselves to be "superiori ad ogni altro, li fa sorpassare su ogni riguardo e non veder gli ostacoli" (superior to everyone else; it causes them to disregard all considerations and overlook all obstacles).[56] Similarly, in his analysis of the "delinquente pazzo" (mad criminal), Lombroso stresses that "in molti omicidi pazzi, si ha quella mancanza di rimorso, che è pure negli omicidi nati" (in many insane murderers, there is that lack of remorse that likewise characterizes the born criminals).[57] As has been noted, Lombroso's criminology is not systematic, and these definitions are loose, volatile, poorly articulated, and often self-contradictory. Suzanne Stewart-Steinberg aptly affirmed that "Lombrosian categories are an amorphous flux of divisions and subdivisions that ultimately undermine the very possibility of all categorization."[58] What I intend to draw attention to, however, is the notion of moral insanity underlying all these different categories of criminals. The word *pazzia* recurs several times in *Il cappello del prete* and seems to indicate the presence of psychosis that gradually progresses, culminates in the act of murder, and continues after the crime has occurred. After having committed the murder, the baron hoped "Napoli lo vedesse sano" (Naples could see him sane), implying that the homicide might have accentuated a process of deterioration of the mind that had already been in action.[59] Before speaking to the magistrate, devoured by the seed of doubt, he asks himself whether "non era da uomo pazzo il soffrir tanto per una sì meschina contingenza" (it was not madness to suffer so much for such a trifling contingency).[60] The conversation with the magistrate possibly intensifies and eventually brings to light a latent form of mental illness. The baron's body is ultimately betrayed by his own destabilized psyche, and only when he realizes that he is entrapped does he start revealing the truth, in what the author describes as a "furioso delirio, mentre legato come un toro che si trae al macello, dibattevasi nelle convulsioni di una pazzia spaventosa" (furious delirium, while, bound like a bull led to the slaughter, he struggled in the convulsions of raving madness).[61]

Remaining within the complicated Lombrosian framework, the baron might also be categorized as a "delinquente pazzo" due to the premeditation of the crime. Lombroso affirms, "La premeditazione non è molte volte ... che l'effetto di quella coesistenza e sovrapposizione di più delirii nello stesso individuo ... e per la quale avviene che la premeditazione di un omicidio sia l'effetto di un delirio cronico e l'esecuzione invece lo sia di un impulso più o meno vertiginoso." (Premeditation is often only ... the effect of the coexistence and overlapping of several delusions in the same individual ... it thus happens that the planning of a murder is the effect of chronic delirium, while its execution is that of a more or less frenetic impulse.)[62] At the same time, we could consider the baron a "reo-latente" (latent criminal), a complex combination of the occasional delinquent and the born criminal. It is illuminating that Lombroso inserts into the section devoted to mad criminals examples of wealthy aristocrats with a natural predisposition to criminal behaviour who are able to avoid prison thanks to their social status: "Così come vi è il reo d'occasione, così vi è quello che nato delinquente non si manifesta tale perché gli manca l'occasione, o perché la ricchezza o la potenza gli diedero modo di soddisfare i pravi istinti senza urtare nel codice." (In the same way that there exists the occasional criminal, there is also the born delinquent who does not manifest himself as such because wealth or power gave him the means of satisfying his depraved instincts without coming up against the law.)[63] The baron could coherently be described, in this respect, as a habitual offender affected by some kind of psychosis who deliberately uses his social status to act as if he were above the law. There is, ultimately, no unambiguous classification of the baron's criminal profile, the composite character of which mirrors the varied and conflicting nature of contemporary assumptions regarding criminality. In any case, the possibility of a latent form of madness as a factor in the crime should not be ruled out.

The classification of the marquis is perhaps more intricate, but we can follow the same path. On the surface, he seems to constitute an example of the criminal of passion. For Lombroso, like occasional criminals, criminals of passion respond to circumstances rather than to organic conditions. Their principal motive resides in "l'adulterio o la fiducia tradita" (adultery or betrayed trust).[64] They act on impulse, driven by overwhelming rage, love, or offended honour, and ultimately regret their acts and spontaneously confess.[65] The marquis's final confession, though, is far from spontaneous. In addition, Lombroso distinguishes between criminals of passion and various other types of insane criminals on the basis of their lifestyle and moral integrity: "L'onestà della vita anteriore, il rapido pentimento, la causa gravissima, tracciano una differenza nettissima coi delitti ispirati dalle passioni, anche non ignobili, ai delinquenti abituali, che ne portano nella faccia e nel cranio e nella trista loro storia anteriore tutta l'impronta." (The righteousness of one's past life, the promptness of repentance, the seriousness of the motive – all of these factors indicate a clear difference between crimes of passion, even when the passion is not ignoble, and habitual delinquents, whose character is inscribed on their faces and skulls and in their sorrowful pasts.)[66] The marquis's behaviour during his life was far from irreproachable. Finally, Capuana's admiration for Lombroso and his criminological work may suggest a more advanced and sophisticated use of the criminologist's theories of crime.[67] Mario Zangara, who considers the protagonist's actions to be typical of family traditions in a feudal society and regards his remorse as a reaction to the endangerment of his noble name, perceptively suggests in the final line of his analysis that the confession of the marquis is also determined by "cause oscure di carattere prevalentemente cerebrale e fisiologico" (obscure causes of a prevalently cerebral and physiological nature).[68] Annamaria Cavalli Pasini cites Lombroso's influence on Capuana but claims that madness is only "oscuramente" (obscurely) at the origins of the murder, "essendo l'abbandono agli istinti deteriori che conduce l'uomo alla morte psichica" (as surrendering to the inferior instincts is what leads the man to psychic death).[69] The possibility that some kind of psychosis might be behind the marquis's deviant behaviour is not unfounded.

To begin with, the writer provides at least two clues that imply the presence of madness in the marquis's family. The baroness states, "Noi Roccaverdina siamo, chi più chi meno, col cervello bacato" (we Roccaverdinas are a bit crazy, some more than others), and Don Pietro acknowledges that "i Roccaverdina sono stati sempre uno più matto dell'altro; e il marchese non dirazza" (as for the Roccaverdinas, each has been more insane than the last, and the marquis is no exception).[70] The marquis does not undergo a significant evolution in the book. In fact, Judith Davies correctly underlines how he is "in essence psychologically static."[71] His mental instability, therefore, predates the beginning of the novel and distinctly emerges long before its conclusion, when the marquis definitively loses his sanity and reveals the truth. As he tells the priest during his confession, the homicide was committed impulsively and out of a ferocious jealousy that temporarily made him lose his reason: "Ero pazzo" (I was mad), he fearfully acknowledges, "in quella terribile notte!" (on that terrible night!).[72] This temporary moment of insanity must be seen as a crucial symptom of the man's unstable mind, which has been repeatedly eroded over the years by his enduring and unbearable jealousy in relation to Agrippina, a selfish thought that gradually turns into a pathological form of monomania: the marquis admits, the woman should be "o tutta mia, o né mia né di altri!" (either mine or no one's!). For him, it is a "pensiero fisso che mi ribolliva nel cervello, e mi offuscava la ragione" (fixed idea that boiled up in my head and clouded my judgment).[73] At the end of the novel, the Cavalier Pergola (a relative of the marquis) recognizes that the marquis "da più giorni si lagnava di una trafittura al cervello, di un chiodo, diceva, conficcato nella fronte. Il male ha lavorato, lavorato sottomano" (has, for several days, been complaining of a piercing sensation in his brain, as if, he said, a nail were stuck in his forehead. The evil has worked, has worked insidiously).[74] He validates the diagnosis of the physician La Greca, asserting that the marquis's downward spiral into madness constitutes a direct consequence of "esquilibri di nervi, sconvolgimento di cervello prodotto dal pensiero fisso, fisso sempre su la stessa idea" (an imbalance of nerves, a devastation of the brain produced by a fixation, a fixation always on the same idea).[75] The criminal mind of the marquis is thus represented in a complex manner, and it is difficult to discern whether crime leads to madness or the other way round. It is unfortunate that Lombroso never had the chance to review the novel. He could have probably classified the protagonist of *Il marchese di Roccaverdina* as a morally insane individual affected by what the criminologist calls "tendenze istintive infrenabili" (uncontrollable impulsive tendencies), whose "pervertita affettività" (perverted affectivity) becomes a "forza irresistibile" (irresistible force) that compels him to commit a murder.[76]

This categorization, however, is inevitably incomplete. The criminals in the novels analysed here resist scientific systematization, and their portrayal is more the result of a complex and heterogeneous blending of diverse formulations than the product of a single, straightforward view of criminal behaviour. This is partly the obvious consequence of their fictionality, but it also mirrors the manifold nature of late nineteenth-century criminology and its inability to provide coherent formulations. On the one hand, the two characters' trajectories of crime and punishment can be traced, to a certain extent, to a conflict between an elusive and ultimately unreplicable feudal ideology and repressed Christian values, which resurface in the form of retributive ghosts. The two writers seem to locate responsibility in acts and consequences, establishing a close relationship between free will, responsibility, and punishment, thus apparently contesting deterministic views of criminal behaviour. On the other hand, both authors place great emphasis on madness, the consideration of which helps us obtain a broader and more detailed picture of the criminals' psyches. In fact, a close look at the texts reveals the centrality of the concept of moral insanity, which ultimately remains deeply problematic, as it undermines the role of external factors and weakens the idea of remorse, opening up a variety of different interpretations.[77]

Sexual Monsters

Although the underlying moral insight of the texts I have examined is that murderous potential can be found in everyone, by giving their murderers a motive to kill, De Marchi and Capuana seem to suggest a dividing line between being an evil human being and being a wicked and ruthless monster. This latter, Foucault explains, was a central element of responses to the problematic question of abnormality in the early nineteenth century, particularly with regard to those crimes that seemed completely irrational and motiveless.[78] The figure of the monster progressively linked up with the figure of the sexual deviant towards the fin de siècle. In these years, when sexuality represented, as Foucault puts it, "the precise point where the disciplinary and the regulatory, the body and the population, are articulated," growing importance was attributed to the universality of sexual deviance, which "emerges as the root, foundation, and general etiological principle of most other forms of abnormality."[79] Moreover, the most excessive form of crime, serial killing, often sexually motivated, entered the Gothic repertoire towards the end of the century: in Italy, two murders were committed by Vincenzo Verzeni between 1869 and 1873; in Germany – in Bochum, to be precise – Wilhelm Schiff raped, killed, and then mutilated three women between 1878 and 1882; and in Great Britain, the unidentified Jack the Ripper committed six gruesome murders of women in Whitechapel in 1888.[80]

Sexual murders resonated strongly throughout Europe, and, inevitably, the figure of the sexual monster emerged in extraordinarily different kinds of discourse and practice, including literature.[81] Abigail Lee Six and Hannah Thompson have shown that increasing interest in sexology was one factor that changed the way in which monstrosity was depicted in late nineteenth-century literature: rather than focusing on the story of the monster's suffering and the impact that monstrosity has on the afflicted character, fin de siècle texts "are interested in the causes of physical or moral monstrosity and their ramifications for society more generally."[82]

Late nineteenth- and early twentieth-century Italian narratives present the figure of the sexual monster in interesting ways. A noteworthy example is the protagonist of the forgotten novel *La moralità del male* (1906) by Ugo De Amicis.[83] De Amicis vicariously takes the reader through a variety of antisocial activities, including rape and murder, which are committed to satisfy the character's innermost sexual desires, without any remorse: "Confesso le mie follie, le malvagie opere, gl'incendi, gli stupri, gli omicidi, l'immenso amore che trema in ogni mia fibra, e l'impulso generoso del mio essere, che mi spinge alla confessione." (I confess my acts of madness and wickedness, the fires, rapes and murders, the immense love which vibrates in all of my fibres, and the generous impulse of my being, which urges me to confession.)[84] In this section, I provide a close reading of another little-known text, the short story "L'ossessione rossa," written by the journalist and politician Giuseppe Bevione and originally published in the leading journal *La Lettura* in 1906.[85] Narrated in the first person, this is a powerfully Gothic psychological thriller in which there is nothing to mediate the warped perceptions of the narrator and the horror of his crime. The focus is exclusively on the criminal, who engages in a violent struggle with the destructive impulses of his own mind, a struggle that eventually leads to the murder. According to the preface, the text is the manuscript of confessions written in prison by the criminal Michele Songina, who was sentenced to death for murder and then executed. These confessions are said to have been collected and published by a friend of the prison director who is particularly interested in the profiling of murderers, "perché imparassimo a temere l'oscura combinazione organica ch'è il nostro cervello" (so as to learn to fear the dark organic combination that is our brain).[86] Unlike the novels analysed in the first section, then, in which the authors do not explicitly intend to provide answers about the origins of evil, Bevione speculates about the problem of aberrant behaviour in an in-depth manner, drawing attention, albeit never explicitly, as we will see, to the relationship between homosexuality and crime.

This story appeared in the context of emerging sexology and research on monstrous sexual conduct. At the beginning of the twentieth century, Italy had apparently entered a more tolerant phase of its short history – legally, culturally, and medically. Articles 420 to 425 of the Sardinian-Piedmontese criminal code of 1859, which was subsequently extended to most of the peninsula in 1865, punished homosexual acts between men (but not between women). In Southern Italy, however, the laws against homosexual acts were not enforced due to the peculiar characteristics of those who lived in this geographical area.[87] The government acknowledged that in Mediterranean culture it was considered normal for young boys to engage in same-sex practices, thereby acknowledging a cultural difference between the country's northern and southern regions. With the promulgation of the 1889 criminal code, private homosexual behaviour between consenting adults stopped being a punishable offence, except in cases that involved violence or "public scandal."[88] Homosexuality was thus effectively decriminalized in the entire country and tolerated as long as it remained private and discreet. In the 1887 parliamentary discussion that led to the decriminalization of male same-sex practices, as Lorenzo Benadusi has revealed, the then minister for justice and future prime minister Giuseppe Zanardelli followed the precepts of the legal professor Giovanni Carmignani, in whose view the best way of confronting the "vice" of same-sex practices was to deny their existence; Zanardelli explained that, in dealing with "acts against nature," ignorance of the "vice" was more useful than its advertisement through the law.[89] The lack of specific criminal laws targeting homosexual men and the emergence of a more indulgent cultural approach to homosexuality meant that, as Yuri Guaiana and Mark Seymour note, before the rise of Fascism in 1922, and particularly for foreigners, "Italy developed a reputation for tolerance of same-sex sexuality. In the second half of the nineteenth century, certain alluring sites such as Venice, Capri, and Taormina became legendary precursors of modern gay tourism. Such places attracted well-to-do, homosexually-inclined foreigners from the harsher legal climates of Northern Europe, particularly Britain and Germany."[90]

In the medical sphere, too, the early twentieth century was characterized by a somewhat more indulgent attitude towards homosexuality. This was a time when, as Derek Duncan puts it, "modern homosexuals were coming to the fore," and in which medicine also had ultimately replaced the church as the arbiter of sexual mores, framing and feeding the discussion on what were regarded as sexual pathologies.[91] Alongside renowned personalities such as the German psychiatrist Richard von Krafft-Ebing and the English physician Havelock Ellis,[92] Italian positivist criminologists played a major role in the transnational production and circulation of knowledge on sexual deviance. In the 1870s and 1880s, the basic assumption underlying much sexological research was that individuals were not responsible for their sexual drives. The predominant determinant of most sexual abnormalities was believed to be heredity and degeneration, with sexual deviants inheriting anatomical or functional defects or at least the predisposition to develop them.[93] The association between aberrant sexual behaviour and antisocial activity was seen as a matter of fact. According to Krafft-Ebing, homosexuality constitutes a "functional sign of degeneration," one that is "a partial manifestation of a neuro- (psycho-) pathic state" and, in most cases, "hereditary."[94] Nearly always, he maintains, "neuroses, psychoses, degenerative signs have been found in the families."[95] The physician Arrigo Tamassia, appointed professor of legal medicine at the University of Pavia in 1876 after Lombroso, was the one who, in 1878, introduced in Italy the concept of "inversione dell'istinto sessuale" (sexual inversion), coined by the German psychiatrist Carl Westphal in 1870.[96] Starting from the premise that "l'istinto sessuale" (sexual instinct) represents "uno dei fattori, dei modificatori più potenti della vita dell'individuo" (one of the most potent factors and modifiers of the individual's psychic life),[97] Tamassia challenges the suggestion made by his German colleague, according to whom "sexual inversion" constitutes a partial form of insanity, a "nevropatico" (neuropathic) state rather than a "psicopatico" (psychopathic) one.[98] For Tamassia, homosexuality is not a nervous disorder but rather a fully fledged, mostly hereditary mental disorder because it affects the individual's whole personality and sense of self: following Krafft-Ebing, he defines it as a "profondo stato psicopatico" (deep psychopathic state) and "una grave degenerazione funzionale" (a serious functional degeneration).[99] Tamassia concludes that homosexual behaviour can lead to criminal deeds, including murder, but specifies that "sexual inverts" suffer from mental pathologies and thus cannot be considered legally responsible for their actions.[100]

Sexual abnormality was one of the many forms of deviance that Lombroso investigated throughout his career. By the 1890s, he was recognized by the international medical community as a pioneer of the emerging medical field of sexology, which was increasingly drawn to the study of sexual perversion, particularly homosexuality. In her landmark history of sexology, Chiara Beccalossi shows that, over the course of his career, Lombroso articulated different explanations of same-sex desires, with the result that his work on the topic remains clouded and complicated by contradictions and shifting positions – not unlike his study of criminality.[101] Lombroso began to publish in the field of sexual inversion in 1881, with a pioneering and widely influential article entitled "L'amore nei pazzi," which explores the variety of sexual aberrations committed by mentally abnormal individuals, such as sadism, zoophilia, and nymphomania.[102] In the second part of this article, Lombroso examines various case studies of what he calls, following Tamassia, "tendenza sessuale invertita" (sexual inversion), a pathological condition and a form of degeneration that is the result of arrested development.[103] This approach was widely accepted at the time, as shown by Morselli's *Manuale di semejotica delle malattie mentali* (1885–9), in which it is stated that sexual perversion could be caused either by morbid heredity or by a corrupt environment, but the latter was only possible in those individuals who were already tainted by degeneration.[104] In 1889, Lombroso directly related deviant sexual inclinations with criminal behaviour when he affirmed that "la precocità del pervertimento sessuale" (the precocity of sexual perverts) has been identified "dal Krafft-Ebing nei pazzi morali come da me nei rei" (by Krafft-Ebing in morally insane individuals and by me in criminals).[105]

Throughout the 1890s, research on sexual abnormality took different directions and the idea of degeneration as the central explanation of aberrant sexual behaviour was progressively replaced. This is testified to by the larger variety of approaches adopted by Italian specialists, who contributed to making Italy one of the most important laboratories for the study of sexual deviance and its relationship with crime. A major figure was the physician and criminologist Pasquale Penta, professor of psychiatry and then criminal anthropology at the University of Naples, who founded, in 1896, the first scientific journal in Europe to be entirely devoted to sexual problems, *L'archivio delle psicopatie sessuali*.[106] Turning away from the strictly biological explanations for deviance typical of Lombrosian criminology, Penta advocated for more psychological explanations of crime and deviant sexuality. Other important figures include the psychiatrists Eugenio Tanzi and Leonardo Bianchi, who called into question the conflation of same-sex desires and mental pathology.[107] By the beginning of the twentieth century, the idea that homosexuality was a serious mental disorder had been partially challenged and the theory of degeneration was no longer considered sufficient as the sole explanation of deviant sexualities; purely congenital explanations were gradually abandoned in favour of a more comprehensive approach to homosexuality that included the study of the individual's environment and early life. Lombroso himself, in the fourth edition of *L'uomo delinquente* (1889), proposed the thesis that same-sex desire was generally first experienced during childhood: "L'inversione del senso genitale fu notata quasi sempre precocemente" (inverted sexual instinct was almost always noted in precocious subjects).[108] At this time, Italian psychiatrists turned more and more towards the childhood of homosexuals for answers, exhibiting a growing interest in the mechanisms of mental association and memory and the influence of the environment upon mental development.[109] Tanzi, in the chapter of the fundamental *Trattato delle malattie mentali* (1905) devoted to "i pervertimenti sessuali" (sexual perversions), offers a view that is symptomatic of a more nuanced medical approach to homosexuality. He does premise that in those cases in which the "inversione" (inversion) is most "profonda" (profound) and "completa" (complete), namely those in which men are attracted by other masculine, virile, brave, and strong men, the reason is "manifestamente congenita" (manifestly congenital).[110] However, he nonetheless places great emphasis on the critical role of the memory in determining sexual inversion, which gave erotic impressions from childhood an irresistible charm: "Le tendenze psichiche che fissano l'ideale erotico ... rappresentano l'ultimo prodotto del differenziamento sessuale, l'ultima tappa dell'istinto erotico" (the psychical tendencies that fix the erotic ideal ... represent the final product of sexual differentiation, the last stage of the erotic instinct).[111]

Thus, when Bevione's short story "L'ossessione rossa" was published in 1906, legal culture seemed to be characterized by a more tolerant approach to homosexuality, while medical research increasingly questioned the inseparable links between homosexual and criminal behaviour. This text, however, tells a different story. "L'ossessione rossa" represents an excellent example of the complex ways in which literature incorporates, rearticulates, and reframes diverse, often conflicting theories and ideas of homosexuality. The story captures and promotes a homophobic, anti-homosexual sentiment while also disseminating dangerous views that both influence readers and contribute to shaping the direction of future medical research; it is not coincidental that, within a few years, with Fascism rising to power, homosexuality came to be persecuted for the first time in Italian history. The character of Michele in "L'ossessione rossa" represents a nuanced mixture of different, intertwining ideas about homosexuality, abnormal sexual conduct, and criminal behaviour. It is significant that the confession starts with Michele's difficult and violent childhood, in keeping with the emphasis placed on early life in contemporary sexual deviance research. He mentions the death of his mother, which happened when he was very young, and his fraught relationship with his stepmother: "Mio padre mi voleva bene e tuttavia mi diede una matrigna" (my father loved me yet he gave me a stepmother).[112] At the age of thirteen, when his father and mother were already dead, Michele began to be subjected to abuse and violence by his stepmother: in his memoir, he particularly and painfully recalls the "ire e le percosse della matrigna, la mancanza di libri e spesso del pane" (anger and blows of his stepmother, the absence of books and often of food).[113] He spent most of his time alone, lacking food and education, which inevitably contributed to the deterioration of an already imbalanced psyche. Indeed, Michele immediately suggests that his mother was mentally disturbed and that this hereditary defect might have been transferred to him:

Molte volte però, durante la mia infanzia e la mia adolescenza, sentii dire, non dal papà, ma dagli zii, dalla matrigna e da altri del vicinato: – "Come Michele rassomiglia a sua mamma, negli occhi, nella bocca, nella fronte! Purché ..." Qui abbassavano la voce, dicevano fra loro parole ch'io non comprendevo e mi guardavano con infinita pietà.

(Even so, during my childhood and adolescence I often heard it said, not by my father but by my uncles, my stepmother, and others in the neighbourhood, "See how Michele resembles his mother – his eyes, his mouth, his forehead! But then again ..." At this point they would lower their voices and exchange words that I couldn't understand, while they looked at me with deep pity.)[114]

80 Gothic Italy

At the time, it was commonly accepted by specialists that women, who were more prone to insanity than men, transmitted habits and traits to their offspring more easily.[115] As Jean-Étienne-Dominique Esquirol famously argued, "insanity is rather transmissible by mothers, than fathers."[116]

In the 1890s and 1900s, Beccalossi explains, Alfred Binet's research on sexual arousal in relation to non-living objects gave rise to a theory that greatly affected Italian psychiatrists working on same-sex desires, including Penta.[117] Basing his observations on the phenomenon of "fetishism" (a term he personally coined), Binet suggests that sexual psychopathologies such as fetishism and "sexual inversion," which are experienced by subjects tainted by hereditary defects, are psychologically acquired by accidental exposure to events in early childhood.[118] The "sexual inversion," then, commonly takes place when there is an early and enduring association between fixed ideas and pleasurable feelings: quoting Binet, Krafft-Ebing writes, "In the life of every fetishist there may be assumed to have been some event which determined the association of lustful feeling with the single impression," an event, the author specifies, that must have happened "in the early youth."[119] It is significant that Michele shows strong erotic attachment to the colour red and, in particular, to blood. In this passage, in which the word "penetrated" has strong homosexual connotations, Michele explains his obsession with red and blood. He describes in great detail the pleasure he experienced at the sight of blood flowing from a dead calf in a butcher's shop during his childhood:

> Quando l'animale fu levato sulle carrucole, e nel collo gli fu piantata la larga lama arrossata, e il grosso flutto di sangue precipitò gorgogliando, io bevetti quella vista con le pupille dilatate, e provai come se un'onda di tiepida soavità mi avesse coperto e penetrato.

> (When the animal was lifted onto the pulleys and a wide reddened blade planted in its neck, when the copious flow of blood came gurgling down, I drank in that scene with dilated pupils, feeling as if a wave of tepid tenderness had engulfed and penetrated me.)[120]

When Michele starts practising as a barber in his stepfather's barber shop, his sexual fantasies concerning blood become stronger. Initially, he limits himself to inflicting superficial wounds on some of his clients, giving rise to indescribable pleasure: "Negli inizii del mio mestiere avveniva sovente che io per imperizia facessi qualche piccola ferita ai miei avventori, e il sangue naturalmente ne spicciava, portandomi la sua solita ineffabile felicità." (During my first years in the trade it often happened that out of inexperience I would cause small injuries to my clients, and blood naturally dripped out, bringing me its usual ineffable joy.)[121] Although at first he is able to "controbilanciare gli istinti anormali della mia creatura interna" (counterbalance the abnormal instincts coming from my inner creature) with his talent in the art of barbering, as time passes, his violent impulses prevail:

> Cedetti al demone, e cominciai a procurarmi *col mio mestiere, col mio rasoio* il perfido godimento ... mi misi a regalare uno, due, tre piccoli tagli ai miei avventori ... Mai nessuno se ne accorgeva ... e nessuno, fuorché Dio, se mi vedeva, si accorgeva del mio dolce uragano interno.

> (I gave in to the demon: as I became more proficient in *my trade*, I would use *my razor* to give myself that malicious pleasure ... by giving my clients one, two, or three small nicks ... But no one noticed ... and no one but God, if He was watching, noticed the sweet storm inside me.)[122]

For Michele, the sadistic satisfaction seems initially to derive from the process of killing and not from the death. In inflicting small and subtle wounds on his clients, he is highly sexually stimulated: "Ebbi trasporti, ebbrezze, deliri, voli d'anima, gridi interiori tali, che nessun amante, nessun santo nella contemplazione di Dio ebbe mai." (I experienced rapture, exhilaration, and delirium; my soul took flight and my inner self screamed for a joy that had never been felt by any lover or any saint contemplating God.)[123] However, the serious fantasies of seeing and drinking blood that Michele expresses eventually drive him to commit a murder. The description of the victim, a duke, has strong sexual connotations – "possedeva due mandibole enormi che avrebbero sgretolato la coscia di un montone ... due labbra umide, carnose" (he had two enormous jaws that would have crushed the thigh of a ram ... two moist, fleshy lips) – with the duke defined as the ideal man: "Era l'esaltazione del tipo che da anni cercavo, e che non avevo mai trovato, l'uomo ideale, il sangue perfetto, che doveva darmi tutta la gioia di cui sentivo capace la mia infermità." (It was the sort of excitement that for years I'd been looking for and that I'd never found: the ideal man, the perfect blood, which should have been able to give me all the joy that, in my infirm condition, I was capable of taking in.)[124] Unlike in previously considered stories, in which corpses are essentially sacrificial and possess a reassuring corporeal integrity, the body of this victim is constantly violated, abjected, and repulsive. The victim is objectified and repeatedly called "l'oggetto del mio amore" (the object of my love), and the act of killing is described as an intense and lengthy sexual experience: "L'emozione ... si faceva più viva e più bramosa in ogni attimo, e mi rendeva, come gli amanti, cupido ad ogni secondo di una più completa voluttà" (the emotion ... became livelier and keener each moment; like lovers, I lusted for more complete satisfaction with every passing second).[125] When the duke has a fit of apoplexy and becomes paralytic, Michele is driven into the arms of evil. The realization that he can exercise absolute power over the body of a man who is incapable of moving causes him to give in to his destructive impulses. The scene of the murder is disturbingly Gothic in its extreme violence and its richness of gruesome details, with the killer describing how he ripped off his victim's skin and then removed his eyes:

> Cominciai a raderlo, ma nella pelle e non più nei peli. Gli affondai il rasoio di due millimetri nel volto e gli trassi via, a grandi pezze, l'epidermide. Compii la difficile operazione con la squisita precisione d'un chirurgo ... L'anima ubbriaca di felicità. Gli rasi così le guance, poi il mento, poi la fronte fino alla chioma, poi il naso: e recisi anche le palpebre, che restavano stranamente bianche in quell'immensa piaga.
>
> (I began to shave him, but to shave his skin and not his hair. I pressed the razor two millimetres into his face and scraped away his skin in large pieces. I completed this difficult operation with the delicate perfection of a surgeon ... My soul was drunk with happiness. In this way I shaved his cheeks, then his chin, then his forehead up to the hairline, then his nose. I also cut off his eyelids, which were strangely white in that immense wound.)[126]

This passage is illuminating because it reveals Michele's heightened aesthetic sense, which, according to most specialists, is a typical characteristic of homosexuals. For Krafft-Ebing, homosexuals frequently display "psychical anomalies" such as "brilliant endowment in art, especially music and poetry."[127] In an essay on the artistic skills of male "sexual inverts" published in the *Archivio delle psicopatie sessuali*, Ellis builds on the observations of the German psychiatrist Albert Moll, according to whom many homosexuals had to constantly act to disguise their sexual preferences, in order to argue that these subjects had mental characteristics that promoted artistic genius.[128] Lombroso, in a paper that was, significantly, presented at the Sixth International Congress of Criminal Anthropology in Turin the same year the short story "L'ossessione rossa" was published, argues that homosexuals tend to be aesthetes, which is why artists, musicians, and actors often engage in same-sex practices.[129] Michele is thus not only a degenerate with a troubled family history but also a sort of mad artist who darkly and humorously aestheticizes the murder, refashioning the body of his victim in the image of his own psychic wounds.

The representation of the moment when Michele completely loses control of his body seems to replicate the symptoms of a seizure. As well as degeneration theory, specialists stressed that external circumstances could activate an inborn and unhealthy predisposition to transgressive sexual behaviour. Disease, often degenerative in nature or origin, could produce sexual abnormalities; epilepsy, in particular, was thought to affect sexual impulses in striking ways.[130] In his major 1886 work, Krafft-Ebing claimed that epileptoid states are common among homosexuals: their sexual desire "is accompanied by an abnormally powerful feeling of lustful pleasure, which may be so intense as to suggest a feeling of 'magnetic' currents passing through the body."[131] In "L'amore nei pazzi," Lombroso asserted that in most cases involving "sexual inversion," specialists have found "anomalie che indicavano arresto di sviluppo ... e spesso epilessia" (anomalies that indicate arrested development ... and often epilepsy);[132] eight years later, he would extend the range of biological factors that produced habitual criminals, identifying epilepsy as the key to linking moral insanity and born criminality.[133] In his 1893 study on sexual deviancy, the French criminologist Julien Chevalier, who studied medicine in Lyon under Alexandre Lacassagne and became one of the most important French sexologists of the time, presents the case of a twenty-six-year-old patient – an ordinary man from a good, wealthy family, with a normal sex life – who periodically fell into a sort of pederastic rage of unbelievable violence. Chevalier notes that on one occasion, when seized by an epileptic attack, the patient chased a young boy with indescribable fury and abused him.[134] In "L'ossessione rossa," Bevione also links epilepsy to sexual deviancy. Michele is said to suffer from a seizure, and his perturbed mental state is attested by his abnormal sensitivity to sounds: "Non ero più padrone di me; sentivo la mia povera testa naufragare in un mare di folgori, udivo voci misteriose e irresistibili che mi chiamavano, mi consigliavano cose orrende." (I was no longer master of myself. I felt my poor head drowning in a sea of lightning flashes and heard mysterious, irresistible voices calling me and urging me to carry out horrific deeds.)[135] During the seizure, aberrant sexual behaviour erupts suddenly in the form of an uncontrollable impulse that leads to the murder. For Lombroso, "spesso gli accessi epilettici [sono] accompagnati da propensione al coito" (seizures are frequently accompanied by a propensity to engage in coitus).[136] Coherently, the moment of the duke's death, when Michele cuts his throat, is distinctly represented as an orgasm; this impression is enhanced by Michele's drinking of the blood emerging from the victim's neck:

> Con un colpo vibrato gli tagliai l'arteria carotide. Ne scoppiò fuori un getto caldo, violentissimo ... Piegai la faccia in quell'amorosa onda e la ricevetti a mezzo il viso, nel centro della fronte, nelle pupille spalancate. Me ne abbeverai, me ne saziai, me ne accecai. Varcai le invalicabili frontiere della delizia terrena e partecipai per un lampo alle felicità eterne.
>
> (With a decisive blow I cut the carotid artery. Out came a warm jet, gushing violently ... I bent over that loving wave and let it strike the middle of my face, the centre of my forehead, and my open eyes. I drank it till I was full; I let it blind me. I stepped over the insuperable limits of earthly pleasure and for an instant experienced eternal happiness.)[137]

Immediately after having killed the duke, Michele passes out, again in keeping with Lombroso's hypotheses, according to whom a seizure accompanied by coitus might eventually provoke a "perdita della conoscenza" (loss of conscience).[138]

Bevione's short story, then, situates itself at the crossroads of different medical paradigms, combining old yet deep-rooted explanations of sexual deviance, particularly heredity and degeneration, with modern takes on the subject, including allusions to early life and environment and a focus on fetishism and epilepsy. What is striking is that although this story is imbued with homosexual references, homosexuality as a disease is never explicitly mentioned. This may be explained by the general uneasiness Italians exhibited towards what was perceived as sexual deviance. Penta's *Archivio delle psicopatie sessuali*, despite its great popularity in the scientific community, was terminated after only one year; as he remarked later in his career, what probably forced him to stop publishing the journal was the great difficulty he experienced in dealing with the prudery of Italian society, which saw certain subjects as shameful and disrespectful.[139] Read in this context, it is less surprising that Bevione, writing for a leading and widely read literary journal, chose not to address homosexuality directly. What the story clearly symptomizes, however, is the author's fear of same-sex desire. When Michele admits "io invece per la donna non ebbi mai un palpito ... non amo che il rosso, la fiamma, il sangue, il rosso senza sesso" (I never felt any attraction for women ... I only love what's red – flames, blood, redness without sex), he excludes women – but not men – and subtly implies that killing is a substitute for socially and morally forbidden sex.[140] In this story, criminal behaviour serves to police the boundaries between "normal" and deviant sexuality, with the narrative voice of the prologue's author firmly positioned on the side of the normal. "L'ossessione rossa" seems thus to intercept a complex and mutating cultural climate that saw, on the one hand, medical research debating the boundaries between normality and abnormality in the context of sexual conduct and, on the other hand, a growing intolerance and spreading anxieties in relation to homosexuality, the terrible outcome of which was the repression experienced by homosexual men during the Fascist regime.[141] The fact that the Fascist government enacted such repressive measures with a certain ease suggests that the tolerance for which Italy had become known prior the First World War was fundamentally superficial and that the 1889 criminal code's silence on homosexual acts had done nothing to substantially change public attitudes that, deeply rooted and widely promoted by the Catholic Church, continued to be displayed in the years to come.

Michele, as we saw, exhibits a disturbing obsession with blood. This is one of the characteristics that most obviously relates him to the literary vampire, a familiar Gothic figure that re-emerged in new shapes in the late nineteenth century in famous novels such as Stoker's *Dracula*, in which Lombroso's theories are directly referenced. I return to this in the following chapter; suffice to say, the nature of the vampire was somewhat distorted by Italian writers at the turn of the century, with the Italian vampire owing very little to the classics of British fiction. Blood is almost entirely absent, and the sexual connotations take on different meanings.[142] Unlike many other Italian texts centred on vampiric figures, blood is everywhere in "L'ossessione rossa," and from the beginning, Michele's vampiric traits are associated with blood and sexuality. In the fin de siècle Italian cultural imaginary, the vampire was still very much associated with the sexual murderer Vincenzo Verzeni – the association between the vampire and the serial killer continues to be seen in both the popular imagination and criminological thinking in the contemporary period, as Jörg Waltje explains when he claims that the serial killer "has become the vampire's modern successor."[143] Between 1868 and 1873, in his early twenties, Verzeni assaulted numerous women, resulting in the death of two of them: a girl of fourteen and a woman of twenty-eight. He rose to fame as the Italian vampire because of the postmortem mutilations found on his victims' bodies. The victims' bodies were mutilated, their genitals removed, their limbs smashed to pieces, and their abdomens cut open lengthwise. It is particularly striking that, as the ensuing legal hearing revealed, Verzeni had bitten his victims and sucked their blood.[144] This is what led newspapers to call him the "Vampire of Bottanuco." The image of the vampire was not, then, that of the seducer aristocrat, like Lord Ruthven, Carmilla, or Dracula, but rather that of the monstrous, aggressive, sexual serial killer.

Italian newspapers exhibited a morbid curiosity about the case, and psychiatrists from different countries drew great attention to Verzeni as a clinical subject. Krafft-Ebing, for instance, devoted a number of pages to Verzeni, who was described as the "prototype" of the lust murderer, for whom "the sadistic crime becomes the equivalent of coitus."[145] Lombroso, who participated in the trial as a member of the defence, wrote extensively about this case in subsequent years.[146] Verzeni's singular mental characteristics were the subject of great debate; a total of eleven psychiatrists examined him in the course of the trial. One of the critical points of the debate was whether Verzeni could be diagnosed with moral insanity: some psychiatrists thought that Verzeni retained his rational capabilities and hence emphasized the murderer's depravity, while the defence psychiatrists tried to show that he was insane and unable to distinguish right from wrong.[147] Lombroso, Krafft-Ebing reports, found numerous "signs of degeneration" in Verzeni, including an "asymmetrical cranium," "defective ears in the inferior half of the helix," and "enormous development of the *zygomæ* and inferior *maxilla*," which led him to conclude that "there is a congenital arrest of development of the right frontal lobe."[148] Moreover, Verzeni, who had "bad ancestry" and came from a "low-minded family," exhibited "no trace of moral sense, remorse and the like."[149] However, in the end, Lombroso failed to persuade the Court of Justice in Bergamo and, in 1873, Verzeni was sentenced to life imprisonment with hard labour.

At the beginning of the twentieth century, the Verzeni case was still very popular. Indeed, it was Verzeni who first piqued Penta's interest in human sexuality. In 1887, while working as a psychiatrist in the Santo Stefano prison in Naples, Penta came across Verzeni, who became his patient. His notes on his psychiatric examination of Verzeni were first published in 1890 in the leading journal *La Tribuna Giudiziaria* and then expanded for his first monograph, *I pervertimenti sessuali*, which came out in 1893. It is thus unsurprising that there are remarkable similarities between Verzeni and the character of Michele in "L'ossessione rossa." From a medical perspective, they share similar psychological characteristics. First, both psyches are altered by genetic defects. Michele, as we saw, suffered from congenital anomalies. For Penta, who starts from the premise that "in tutti i casi [di perversione sessuale] vi è una eredità morbosa grave" (in all cases of sexual perversion there is a form of serious pathological heredity),[150] Verzeni's family is marred by several cases of mental illness, including a criminal cousin and a degenerate uncle.[151] Second, Michele, who obtains sexual gratification from the act of violating the body of a person who appears to be in a vegetative state, can be labelled as a necrophiliac, a condition from which, according to Lombroso, Verzeni suffered.[152] Third, both are defined as epileptic. In the second volume of the 1889 edition of *L'uomo delinquente*, which was largely devoted to epileptic criminals, Lombroso described Verzeni as an individual who occasionally suffered from seizures and exhibited a morbid perversion of his feelings, which led him to act in a confused and uncontrollable manner: during his crimes, "si sentiva una forza enorme e non vedeva più niente; ebbe amnesia, e non ricordò come avesse tagliato quelle donne e come vi avesse immersi gli spilli. Ebbe vertigini." (He felt exceptionally strong and could not see anything; he suffered from amnesia and could not remember how he mutilated those women and how he wounded them with pins. He suffered from vertigo.)[153] Fifth, it is important to mention Binet's theory of fetishism. Lombroso, Krafft-Ebing, and subsequently Penta all drew attention to the fact that Verzeni experienced great pleasure when, at age twelve, he strangled chickens for the first time: "Verzeni arrived at his perverse acts quite independently, after having noticed, when he was twelve years old, that he experienced a peculiar feeling of pleasure while wringing the necks of chickens. After this he had often killed great numbers of them and then said that a weasel had been in the hen-coop."[154] Compare this to Michele's sexual gratification in witnessing the brutal killing of a calf. Both, then, associate sexual pleasure with an erotic image that had been a source of pleasure in early childhood. From a very early age, sexual craving and violence had been experienced simultaneously, so that sexual gratification must always be accompanied by a violent component.

Finally, both experience sexual pleasure in the act of killing, rather than in the death of their victims, and in drinking blood. As Verzeni later admitted, he had experienced orgasms while pressing his victims' throats without killing them and, particularly, he felt spasms of sensual pleasure when mutilating bodies or biting his victims and sucking their blood: "I had an unspeakable delight in strangling women, experiencing during the act erections and real sexual pleasure ... It never occurred to me to touch or look at the genitals or such things. It satisfied me to seize the women by their neck and suck their blood."[155] Therefore, their crimes are principally sexually motivated and a substitute for normal sex.[156] Ultimately, the two men were considered degenerate beings, whose propensity for committing crimes is explained by a combination of biological predisposition and sociocultural influences. Both are thus sexual serial murderers, whose principal motive to kill is, as Maurice Cusson and Jean Proulx remark, "the quest for sexual satisfaction," obtained through the acts of killing and drinking the blood of their victims.[157]

It is most likely that Verzeni represented a major influence on Bevione. If this is the case, we can argue that the author transforms a horror story of heterosexual murder into one in which same-sex desire is stigmatized, pathologized, and ultimately criminalized, thus reinforcing deep-seated views regarding the connection between homosexuality, insanity, and crime. Again, both Michele and Verzeni experienced the same fate. Both suffered from mental illness – at least according to Michele's biographer and criminologists such as Lombroso, Krafft-Ebing, and Penta – and yet both were considered fully rational beings by the jury charged with evaluating their sanity. Positivists were united in arguing for the reduced responsibility of sexual offenders – Tamassia, as mentioned above, was the first to argue that homosexuals who commit criminal acts do not act freely and that their legal responsibility must be mitigated.[158] Lombroso sought in vain to prove the mental instability of Verzeni and thus the necessity to reduce his sentence. The failure to convince the jury is typical of nineteenth-century clashes between legal and psychiatric interpretations of deviant behaviour; psychiatric theories were often regarded with suspicion in the courtrooms. However, this also signals the progressive shift in the location of the monstrous in modern culture. In his anthropological and biological study of Verzeni, Penta claims that Verzeni displays "parecchie e gravi anomalie antropologiche" (several serious anthropological anomalies) that would have been otherwise imperceptible to non-experts, but he finally admits that "non portava sul volto lo stampo dell'animale o dell'uomo selvaggio" (his face did not bear the features of the beast or the savage).[159] Lombroso also concluded that Verzeni did not possess the physical deformities characteristic of insanity, conceding that the man "offre alle indagini antropologiche tutti i caratteri dell'uomo sano" (offers to anthropological analyses all the characteristics of the sane person).[160] Likewise, there is nothing unusual in the physical appearance and everyday behaviour of Michele, at least as long as he is able to repress his destructive impulses. Both are not, then, evolutionary throwbacks whose propensity for committing crime is discernible through an obvious physical malformation.

Monstrosity, as these examples show, no longer constitutes an aberration of nature that is entirely and easily discernible but is rather something alien harboured within the obscure, unknowable mind of apparently civilized, normal, and respectable individuals. These stories, whether real or fictional, bring to light the power but also the ambiguities of claims by criminologists, who were never able to find reassuring, unequivocal answers to the question of delinquency and were forced to constantly revise their theories. Bevione's original aim to understand the criminal's mind is thus ultimately frustrated. The conclusion of the story, in which the jury rules out insanity and condemns Michele to death, confirms the impossibility of capturing and understanding the elusive roots of evil. This is precisely why these narratives retain their disturbing power. It is unsurprising, in my view, that Verzeni's case, shrouded in mystery and imbued with Gothicism, continues to haunt contemporary literary and criminological discourses.[161] The criminal's mind was, and still is, a Gothic object of horror, an obscure repertoire of monstrosities that never ceases to fascinate because its inner workings remain fundamentally incomprehensible.

3 Gothic Bodies

The last two decades of the nineteenth century and the early years of the twentieth century saw criminologists, jurists, and sexologists drawing increasing attention to what was specifically seen as female deviance.[1] In her work on the origins of biological criminology in modern Italy, Gibson has situated this process within the larger nineteenth-century woman question; in these years, women's gradual entrance into the workforce and their intensifying demands for legal and political changes, economic and sexual independence, access to education, equality within the family, and the right to vote spawned growing anxieties in male-dominated, deeply Catholic Italian society. Moreover, statistics in this period highlighted a surprisingly sharp rise in violent crimes committed by women and, as a result of the expanding urban population, an increase in activities related to prostitution.[2] Although not all specialists were against changes to women's status, most were profoundly troubled by the potential destabilization of established hierarchies of power and the prospect of a fundamental restructuring of gender roles and relations. It is thus unsurprising that scientists and commentators from different schools of thought united in an attempt to scientifically validate and recirculate received cultural stereotypes of women as a way of neutralizing the threat of female emancipationists. They placed major emphasis on women's physical and intellectual inferiority and essential psychological instability, especially during the pathological states of puberty, menstruation, pregnancy, and menopause. This reinforced the widespread belief in women's latent deviance,[3] which could be counterbalanced only by the experience of maternity and needed to be controlled by the techniques and technologies of the state.

Childbearing, as Cristina Mazzoni points out, "is too central to the reproduction both of the species and of culture to be left out of that process of medical colonization of the body" that reached its climax in the late nineteenth century.[4] Thus, normative female behaviour became increasingly associated, from a medical perspective, with maternity, monogamy, chastity, modesty, sexual passivity, and even frigidity, as proven by the research of specialists such as the anthropologist Giuseppe Sergi.[5] While these characteristics were natural in normal, healthy women, the mere presence of sexual desire outside of the context of procreation represented a deviant nature because it made women dangerously more similar to men. In *La donna delinquente: La prostituta e la donna normale* (1893), arguably the most influential criminological study on women in Western history,[6] Lombroso and his collaborator Guglielmo Ferrero, a sociologist as well as Lombroso's son-in-law, note in criminal women "una tendenza fortissima a confondersi col tipo maschile" (a very strong resemblance to the masculine type), which translates into "l'erotismo eccessivo, la debole maternità, il piacere della vita dissipata, l'intelligenza, l'audacia, il predominio sugli esseri deboli e suggestionabili, talora anche per la forza muscolare, il gusto degli esercizi violenti, dei vizi" (excessive eroticism, a weak maternal instinct, pleasure in a dissipated life, intelligence, audacity, subordination of weaker and more impressionable persons sometimes using muscular strength, a taste for violent exercise [and] vices).[7] At the same time, female criminals, despite their different categorizations – which, as always with Lombroso, are permeable and volatile – share both physical and psychological characteristics traditionally assigned to deviant women, including a tendency to have long, thick, dark hair and dark eyes and an "esageratissima inclinazione alla vendetta, l'astuzia, la crudeltà, la passione per il vestiario, la menzogna" (extreme predilection for revenge, cunningness, cruelty, a passion for clothes, dishonesty).[8] For Lombroso and Ferrero, the criminal woman is "una eccezione a doppio titolo" (a double exception) – both as a criminal, representing a deviation from normative behaviour, and as a woman, being a relatively rare anomaly among female subjects – and thus even "più mostruosa" (more monstrous) than her male counterpart.[9]

This conceptualization of female deviance encountered very little resistance in cultural, medical, and legal circles. Italian feminists and emancipationists saw femininity and motherhood as inextricably connected and, as Alba Amoia has argued, there was a lack of "dissentient voices" even among the most courageous contemporary women writers.[10] In the widely read *Dizionario d'igiene per le famiglie* (1881), written by the writer Neera (the pseudonym of Anna Maria Radius Zuccari) with the aid of the physician Paolo Mantegazza, the authors promote the return to traditional values, emphasizing that maternity is the "missione primissima della donna" (first and foremost mission of woman), that chastity "non è solamente una virtù, è un precetto santo di igiene" (is not merely a virtue but a sacred precept of hygiene), and that marriage, for a woman, represents "il suo stato di perfezione" (her perfect status).[11] Traditional critics of positivist criminology, including Napoleone Colajanni, Francesco Carrara, and Pietro Ellero, did little to discredit Lombroso's theses.[12] Indeed, they all substantially adhered to the ideology of the organic inferiority of women, validating and reinforcing the belief that all female behaviour, including its deviant manifestations, is governed by women's sexual organs. Candida Carrino reminds us that the document physicians were asked to complete in order to support the request for a woman's institutionalization contained specific questions about menstruation, pregnancies, number of births, and breastfeeding, which reveals how elements associated with female sexuality were crucial in determining a diagnosis of insanity.[13]

What emerged from these studies, Horn comments, "was less the (hoped for) transparent pathology of the female offender than the barely legible *potential* dangerousness of the normal woman."[14] The medicalization of female behaviour and the scientific validation of the idea of woman's innate predisposition to instability brought about significant changes in criminal law, including greater participation of medical experts in courtrooms during criminal cases. This process is situated within Foucault's genealogy of "dangerousness," a historical and cultural process through which some of positivist criminology's "most fundamental theses, often those most foreign to traditional law," gradually took root "in penal thought and practice."[15] Drawing on Foucault, Horn comments that this process did not occur because of the truth value or persuasive power of positivist theories of criminality. Rather, he suggests, changes in civil law – relating to notions of accidents, risk, and responsibility – made "the articulation of the legal code and of science in penal law" possible.[16] This allowed the instantiation of a new regime of norms that served to control the female body and transform it into an object for the practices of surveillance, prevention, and punishment.[17] Tony Ward has aptly suggested how "courts are more likely to accept portrayals of women offenders as 'sad' or 'mad' rather than 'bad,' and less inclined to treat them as rational, autonomous subjects."[18] Many jurists, such as Tancredi Canonico and Francesco Scarlata, and psychiatrists, such as Tito Vignoli, saw the organic constitution of women – their emotionality, irritability, sensitivity, and fragility – as a mitigating factor and thus a reason for the diminution of criminal responsibility.[19]

The process of the derationalization of women is particularly evident, in the literary sphere, in the novella *Il processo di Frine* (1884), written by the Neapolitan author and journalist Edoardo Scarfoglio.[20] It tells the story of Mariantonia Desideri, a twenty-six-year-old woman who poisons and kills her husband's mother to punish her for her tyrannical behaviour in their house. Mariantonia spontaneously confesses to the crime and, when the trial begins, the outcome seems like a formality, with the death sentence being a given. However, the defence lawyer manages to convince the jury that a woman of such "bellezza perfetta" (perfect beauty) could not rationally kill a person: "Mancherebbe la ragione fisiologica del delitto, che procede assai spesso dalla coscienza ... della propria inferiorità" (there is no physiological reason for the murder, which often arises from the awareness ... of one's own inferiority).[21] It does not matter, he argues, that the murder was meticulously calculated because Mariantonia suffers from insanity and hence cannot be convicted: "La colpa di questa donna non è nel cuore, è nel cervello. Gli appetiti suoi son quelli appunto dei cretini e degl'idioti: questa donna, e la sciocca ingenuità del delitto ve lo prova, è ammalata di mente." (The guilt of this woman resides not in her heart but in her brain. Her appetites are the same as those of idiots and cretins; this woman – and the silly naivety of her murder proves it – is mentally ill.)[22] At the end of a farcical trial, all the extenuating circumstances are taken into account, and Mariantonia ends up being sentenced to only three years in prison. What is striking in the courtroom debate is that the woman's ability to premeditate a murder and carry out a plan with cold-heartedness and precision – thereby challenging the idea of female emotionality, fragility, and irrationality – is removed from the legal discourse. That which a woman might state in court is, in fact, fundamentally irrelevant, because she has neither knowledge of nor control over her actions. Although she manifests autonomy and self-control and takes responsibility for her actions, her pathologization calls into question and ultimately countermands her agency and her accountability. The medicalization of Mariantonia's act reduces her nature to the biological and deprives her of all legal responsibility, thus transforming the female transgressor from a reasoning individual into an irrational being uncapable of distinguishing right from wrong, a mere object of social and scientific investigation that needs to be placed within a systematic network of surveillance and discipline.

Scholarship on transgressive women in Italian literature has traditionally emphasized the conservative and un-subversive nature of such narratives. Edwige Comoy Fusaro, for instance, argues that literature conveys the same ideology as contemporary medical discourse; scientists and writers "si uniscono nella repressione della sessualità femminile, vista come un agente sovversivo dell'ordine" (unite in the repression of female sexuality, seen as an agent of subversion of order).[23] In this chapter, however, I contend that literary and criminological representations operate in dialogue, though not invariably in harmony, with one another and that Gothic narratives concerned with female transgression occupy a privileged position in the exploration of such interactions. They provide an excellent space for examining how ideas of female criminality were culturally negotiated and rearticulated, creating potential areas of subversion and giving rise to possibilities for reimagining women's roles both in fiction and in reality. The first two sections, devoted to femmes fatales and infanticidal mothers respectively, illustrate the intersections between the different discourses that contributed to the construction of images of the criminal woman, rethinking the issue of female criminality more broadly, beyond the limits of traditional disciplinary divisions. Fictional uses of female criminals were, in fact, neither subversive nor reactionary per se but had the potential to be both, and occasionally actually were. The third section is concerned with the fears and anxieties engendered by the emergence of new, confrontational models of womanhood and the increasing demands for status, independence, and rights for women. As I show, the figure of the male vampire, which irrupts from the shadows to punish women who have engaged in deviant behaviour, perfectly captures a post-unification cultural climate in which questions of male performativity, female sexuality, and the body politic intertwine in complex and significant ways.

Femmes Fatales

Post-unification Italian writers find themselves in the difficult position of having to negotiate between the new freedoms offered to women by modernity and the constraining circumscriptions that a male-dominated society imposes upon them. This is mirrored in a variety of strong and powerful women characters whose desire to satisfy their carnal pleasures is socially and culturally framed as deviant and must be physically repressed. A paradigmatic example is Giovanni Verga's short story "La lupa," contained in the volume *Vita dei campi* (1880).[24] The protagonist, Pina, is a sexually independent woman who roams the streets of a Sicilian village like a dangerous, insatiable she-wolf looking for male prey.[25] Pina seduces her daughter's husband, Nanni, who, incapable of resisting the temptation of incest, decides to mete out what he believes to be justice. Pina is a fascinating character that challenges the culturally enforced expectations of passive, demure femininity. She is an estate owner and a harvester who enjoys routinely performing heavy lifting, exhibiting the muscular strength and the taste for violent exercise that, as we saw, Lombroso and Ferrero catalogue as symptoms of virility and therefore signs of female deviance.[26] She leads an independent, unconventional life that defies gender expectations and proves to be unbearable and unacceptable for the men of the village. Although the story's conclusion is open and ambiguous – Nanni walks towards Pina with an axe in his hand, determined to finish her off – the assumption underlying it is that physical punishment constitutes the only way of reclaiming control of a female body that seems uncontrollable.

Pina is an example of a character that figured prominently in Italian literature of the 1880s and 1890s.[27] This character would later be labelled as the femme fatale, a disruptive and troublesome figure that problematizes received notions of women's passivity, nurturing nature, and social conformity.[28] It is, as Virginia Allen indicates, "the dark half of the dualistic concept of the eternal feminine, the Mary/Eve dichotomy."[29] Recent scholarship, particularly in the fields of gender and film studies, has challenged the long-standing, deep-rooted idea of the femme fatale as a marionette manipulated to feed the lusts of the audience and finally invariably punished for her anti-normative behaviour. Although femmes fatales are physical signifiers of sexual excess and danger, they do not function merely as archetypes of female seduction and destructive sexuality. Representations of the femme fatale can expose how women rupture traditional notions of female transgression and containment, creating a space for reimagining female agency in the fictional world.

A fascinating case in point is Ippolita Sanzio in Gabriele D'Annunzio's *Trionfo della morte* (1894).[30] The novel relates the turbulent, draining relationship between Giorgio Aurispa, a cultivated young man of noble origins, and Ippolita Sanzio, a woman trapped inside a complicated and often violent marriage from which she chooses to escape. As the novel progresses, Giorgio loses control over Ippolita: initially perceived as the "ideal figura ... buona, tenera, sommessa" (ideal woman ... fond, docile, quiet), she becomes progressively stronger, more physically resilient, and more emotionally independent, metamorphosing, in Giorgio's eyes, into a "semplice strumento di piacere e di lascivia, strumento di ruina e di morte" (mere instrument of pleasure and lust, an instrument of ruin and death).[31] This progressive loss of masculine power eventually leads Giorgio to murder Ippolita and simultaneously kill himself.

In her famous feminist and psychoanalytic reading of the femme fatale, Ann Doane argues that this figure has an agency independent of her consciousness – she "has power *despite herself*." For Doane, the femme fatale encounters an "evacuation of intention," rendering her no more than an "articulation of fears surrounding the loss of stability and centrality of the [male's] self."[32] Ippolita, however, is not merely a "symptom of male fears about feminism"[33] but is rather an active and potent character who escapes the hands of both her creator and her partner; she is the subject of her own will and desire, and she uses her sexual appeal to gain power. Ippolita's unrestrained sexuality, in the words of Rebecca Stott in her analysis of the late-Victorian femme fatale, gives rise to Giorgio's fear of "losing his self" and "being absorbed into" that of the woman.[34] Ippolita's passions have a debilitating effect upon Giorgio, with sexual intercourse taking on a corrosive nature and serving as an obstacle to the full realization of his intellectual and artistic aspirations: "Che cosa mi manca? Qual è il difetto del mio organismo morale? Qual è la causa della mia impotenza?" (What do I lack? What is this defect in my moral nature? What is the cause of my impotence?), he keeps asking himself throughout the novel.[35]

The invisible, irresistible source of energy that attracts Giorgio to Ippolita progressively assumes monstrous guises. Ippolita is not only an adulteress, a temptress endowed with a serpentine body, but also a woman who suffers from sterility: "Il suo ventre è colpito di maledizione" (her womb is accursed), as the narrator puts it.[36] The impossibility of procreating makes her sexual exuberance a monstrosity: "L'inutilità del suo amore gli apparve come una trasgressione mostruosa alla suprema legge" (the uselessness of her love seemed to him a monstrous transgression against the supreme law).[37] Beyond the alluring facade, Giorgio gradually comes to discover her hidden, deviant nature. In an emblematic passage, Ippolita is caught torturing a butterfly with a pin, an act of gratuitous cruelty to which Giorgio reacts with horror and disgust: "Che crudeltà!" (How cruel of you!), he screams. "Come sei crudele!" (How dreadfully cruel!)[38] Giorgio here seems to share Lombroso's coeval position on the latent deviance of all women – "la crudeltà è latente in fondo al suo amore" (cruelty is latent even in her love), he observes – but he also acknowledges Ippolita's ability to act freely, without social restraints, and to fulfil her own desires, even when this has destructive repercussions: "Qualche cosa di distruttivo è in lei, più palese quanto più forte è il suo orgasmo nelle carezze" (there is something destructive in her that manifests itself more clearly the more ardent her caresses become).[39] Sexually, indeed, Ippolita becomes increasingly confident, authoritative, and powerful: "Ella era divenuta così esperta, così certa de' suoi effetti" (she had become so confident, so certain of her powers), laments Giorgio, exhibiting a certain unease.[40]

Right before the tragic end of the novel, there is a significant sex scene that sheds more light on Giorgio's warped world view and the active role that Ippolita plays in the text's dénouement. This scene troubles the misogynistic stereotyping of the femme fatale as an archetype of seduction and manipulation, exposing Ippolita's powerful agency and her capability to destabilize male mastery using her body. Here, we witness Ippolita thoroughly enjoying sex on her own, to which Giorgio reacts with alarm and repulsion: he is described as "soffocato dal disgusto, vedendola spasimare, udendo lo strano rumore che le mettevano nel ventre i sussulti del viscere sterile e infermo" (disgusted while he saw her gasping and while he heard the strange sounds that came out of her sterile and ill womb).[41] At the apex of sexual gratification, Ippolita bursts suddenly into laughter: "Fu presa da un riso nervoso, frenetico, incoercibile, – lugubre come il riso d'una demente" (she was seized by hysterical laughter, frenzied, uncontrollable, – ghastly like the laughter of madness).[42] Here, as Michela Barisonzi aptly suggests, Ippolita's progressive loss of bodily control eventually undermines Giorgio's attempt to sexually instrumentalize the female body for his own pleasure.[43] She knows the power of her body, even when she cannot completely control it, and consciously uses it to fulfil her desires. In blurring the demarcation between activity and passivity, self and other, Ippolita brings Giorgio beyond what is, for him, understandable, normal, and safe. Being simultaneously, as Julia Kristeva writes, "desirable and terrifying, nourishing and murderous," the (non)maternal body of the femme fatale becomes abjected.[44] Caught up between excitement and repulsion, Giorgio, in the words of Noëlle McAfee, "spits out, rejects, almost violently excludes [the abject] from" himself.[45] Horrified and frightened, he distances himself from Ippolita and keeps wondering, dismayed, "È la follia?" (Has she gone mad?)[46]

What Giorgio has realized here is Ippolita's concealed deviance. Sexual gratification was, for women, aberrant and symptomatic of unfeminine monstrosity. One of the principal ways in which the hidden savagery of criminals was thought to be revealed was in the sexual act. The criminologist Giovan Battista Moraglia, for instance, notes in an 1895 article that female criminals tend to unmask their false exterior beauty by exhibiting "un'espressione feroce" (a ferocious expression) at the climax of orgasm during sexual intercourse; this, for Moraglia, constitutes "un carattere atavico" (an atavistic character) that is historically and evolutionarily rooted in those ancient times when men forcefully subjugated women against their will.[47] The realization of Ippolita's criminal nature, concealed behind a pleasing exterior, eventually prompts Giorgio's decision to inflict a final form of punishment on the woman who has subjugated him. Until that moment, Giorgio had been almost exclusively obsessed with his own death. After that realization, however, a horrific thought infiltrates his deranged mind: "Debbo io morire solo?" (Ought I die alone?), he starts asking himself.[48] The threat posed by excessive female sexuality to the fragile male self thus leads to the final crime, an act of violence that radically changes the reader's perceptions of Ippolita.

In another important reading of the femme fatale, Elisabeth Bronfen contends that the femme fatale "chooses to accept the tragic consequences of her actions and manipulates the outcome of their fatal meeting." She knows all along that she is doomed and can, therefore, "turn what is inevitable into a source of power."[49] This interpretation is, however, hardly applicable to this novel, as Ippolita seems to be totally unaware of her tragic destiny. She never stops making life plans with Giorgio, and she has no idea of the man's murderous obsessions. In the final scene, she is caught completely off guard and when Giorgio carries her over the cliff, she screams "murderer!" at him several times. At the same time, their simultaneous demise complicates straightforward readings that see the textual eradication of the femme fatale as the reassertion of control by the threatened male subject. Unlike Giovanni Episcopo, who, in the eponymous novel, ultimately kills his wicked magnetizer, Giulio Wanzer, to regain control of his mental sanity, or Tullio Hermil in *L'innocente*, who murders the intruder to recover his masculine power, Giorgio is forced to kill himself while simultaneously eliminating his magnetizer and object of desire. Ippolita's sexual power over Giorgio is so strong that it transforms the man into a succubus subject, unable to devote himself to any intellectual pursuits, with murder being the only solution he can imagine.

The final repression of sexually transgressive women, be it through murder, suicide, or imprisonment, is what typifies femme fatale novels. Exceptions are scarce, and it is interesting – and perhaps surprising, given the author – that a novel that deviates from this path is *Peccatrice moderna*, one of Carolina Invernizio's last novels, published in 1915. Invernizio's stories are characterized by a strong ambiguity in relation to women's role in society; they address the gradual emergence of the model of the twentieth-century woman, simultaneously accepting and destabilizing apparently coded and innate gendered constructions. As a consequence of her ambivalent and sometimes even conservative view of womanhood, the work of Invernizio has been systematically overlooked in books on Italian women writers published over the last forty years that have reintroduced into the canon forgotten but certainly more progressive female authors, such as Neera, Marchesa Colombi, and Matilde Serao.[50] Although it is indisputable, as Katharine Mitchell argues, that these writers engage far more than Invernizio with "the issues with which the moderate emancipationists were concerned, such as better access to education and the professions," it is equally true that Invernizio's enormous popularity and appeal inevitably and greatly influenced her female readers, teaching them how to deal with their possibilities and limitations as women, wives, and mothers.[51] Significantly, she was asked in 1890 to address the Società operaia di Napoli on the subject *Le operaie italiane* (Italian female workers): while admitting that the situation had improved and that women must now be respected for their work, she expressed worry about the condition of women workers and denounced their subjection and exploitation but also recognized their need for escapist literature.[52]

Invernizio's narratives are potentially very subversive, entirely written "for women, about women," as Anna Laura Lepschy puts it, and always concerned with crime and deviance.[53] In her long career, spanning over a hundred novels, she repeatedly chose to investigate women's stories and explored the various roles available to women of her time, whether within the boundaries of the heterosexual love relationship or in the mother-daughter dyad. In many of her novels, we find courageous and intelligent female characters taking on the role of unofficial investigators in an attempt to recover their loved ones (as in *I ladri dell'onore*, 1894) or to defend the honour and protect the stability of the family (as in *La felicità nel delitto*, 1907). At the same time, female villains are nearly invariably punished for their actions, ultimately reinstating the indissoluble, however artificial, nature of family ties and relations. Invernizio's heteronormative narratives conventionally pit different, often opposite women – blonde/brunette, angelic/demonic – against each other, warning of the dangers of female deviance and emancipation and emphasizing the importance of motherhood and the family. This binary model, which usually serves to legitimize the text's conclusion and the punishment of the villain, undergoes a radical shift in *Peccatrice moderna*, whose title points to a new and more modern type of criminal. Sultana Sigrano, whose exotic name immediately reveals her duplicitous nature, is an example of the femme fatale, a beautiful, extremely intelligent yet wicked, vicious, and ambitious twenty-two-year-old countess, married to a loving husband, a rich lawyer, with whom she has two children. Her angelic exterior and her "modi austeri" (austere manners) conceal a nature that is "falsa" (false) and "corrotta" (corrupt).[54] As the narrator describes her, she is the "peccatrice moderna" (modern sinner) who "seguiva la via del vizio senza provarne rimorsi" (followed the path of vice without feeling any remorse).[55] The plot begins with Sultana murdering one of her lovers, the chauffeur Alceste, who, after being told that the relationship was over, attempted to blackmail her to force her to continue the affair. She manages to frame the murder as legitimate defence and avoids punishment. The convoluted and melodramatic story that follows sees Sultana seeking to cover up the murder, and a variety of other misdeeds, while also trying to preserve her affair with a young count, Mario Herbert, who starts to have doubts about the relationship.

Sultana possesses both those features typically considered feminine, including beauty, weakness, and a general languor, as well as those typically considered masculine, such as sexual desire, strength, and mental power over others. Her radical behaviour is described as lustful and predatory, and the narrator emphasizes her exploitation of appearances, blurring any distinctions between sexuality and danger: "I suoi occhi azzurri si fissarono in quelli di Alceste come se avesse voluto magnetizzarlo" (her blue eyes were fixed upon those of Alceste as if they wanted to magnetize him).[56] Alceste, in a letter sent before his death to what was supposed to be his future bride, describes Sultana as the typical femme fatale, a serpentine figure capable of injecting some kind of "veleno" (poison) into men's veins in order to corrode their "povera anima" (poor soul).[57] Lombroso and Ferrero would probably identify her as the "adultera incorreggibile" (incorrigible adulteress), a subcategory of the born prostitute, who exhibits a "precoce tendenza al vizio" (precocious tendency to vice), little in the way of maternal instincts, and abnormal sexuality;[58] she is generally "impudente" (impudent), "impulsiva" (impulsive), and "menzognera" (deceitful).[59] Not even the childbearing function acts as a moral antidote to criminality; the more Sultana pursues her sexual desire, the more she loses her motherly role. She is, in fact, an absent mother: the narrator comments at one point, "Dove era andata in quel pomeriggio, trascurando i figli, come se non esistessero per essa?" (Where did she go that afternoon, neglecting her children, as if they did not exist for her?)[60] She immediately remarries when her husband dies and, after having obtained an inheritance from a distant uncle, decides to send her children to boarding school so she can fully enjoy the rest of her life.

Sultana represents a new, threatening, and specifically public form of femininity for a culture that was redefining public and private in the context of modern social change. A male friend of Sultana's husband tells him, without concealing a certain pleasure, that "abbiamo due perle rare in mezzo alle donne moderne" (we have two rare pearls among modern women), hinting at the difficulty of dealing with the emerging models of womanhood and women's increasing demands for emancipation.[61] Sultana is a unique character who successfully mobilizes her skills in a male-dominated milieu, defying normative conceptions and expectations of gender roles by challenging the pattern of female submission, domesticity, and dependence. She uses her wiles and her power as a femme fatale to achieve her ambitions of success and social and economic mobility. In the conclusion, unlike what usually happens in these cautionary tales, Sultana manages to overcome all difficulties and continues to commit acts of transgression and misdeeds. The narrator comments at the end, "La peccatrice aveva vinto ancora. Ed essa proseguirà nella sua vita d'inganni, di corruzione, fino a che giungerà anche per lei l'ora del castigo. Se così non fosse, dove sarebbe la giustizia?" (The sinner had won once again. And she will continue her life of deceit and corruption, until one day the time for punishment arrives for her too. Otherwise, where would justice be?)[62] Seeking to negotiate between her conservative world view and her fascination with women's power, Invernizio concludes the novel on an ambiguous note, suggesting that punishment, whether human or divine, might never be meted out to Sultana. At the dawn of a new world, Invernizio seems to foresee the emergence of a new type of woman that – despite her deviant behaviour, or perhaps because of it – would be more successful and less prone to containment and punishment than her male counterparts.

Infanticidal Mothers

What connects many of the deviant women in literature of the time, from Pina to Ippolita through Sultana, is their problematic relationship with maternity. Given that, in normal women, "la sessualità è subordinata alla maternità" (sexuality is subordinated to maternity), as Lombroso and Ferrero posit, the absence of maternal instincts was seen as "una stigmata grave di degenerazione" (a grave stigma of degeneration) and a major sign of a criminal nature.[63] In a cultural climate that considered the essence of normal womanhood to be motherliness, the most subversive criminal act was killing your own offspring. Gibson has noted that "illegitimacy rates peaked in the late nineteenth century. The two decades between 1871 and 1891 saw the highest rates of illegitimacy, with over 7 per cent of all babies being born outside of marriage."[64] In tandem with this, a major debate about the crime of infanticide, or more precisely about the infanticidal mother, developed during the last two decades of the nineteenth century.[65] During this period, infanticide constituted a major problem, largely the result of the significant lack of any legal or practical safeguards for unmarried mothers and illegitimate children: Silvia Chiletti writes in her recent analysis of this phenomenon, "Along with the practice of abortion and the abandonment of infants outside foundling hospitals, infanticide in fact represents one of the most common strategies used by women to circumvent the codes imposed by society and by the law, and, very often, to preserve their own reputations as 'honest women.'"[66]

As we saw, from 1861 to 1889, the code in force was the Sardinian-Piedmontese Code of 1859. Infanticide was legally considered murder and was punishable by death, except for those cases in which, as stated by the modified article 532, the offspring was illegitimate.[67] The introduction of this clause foregrounded woman's honour, an element that would progressively become central to the debate.[68] Stewart-Steinberg observes that theorists of infanticide rearticulated this traditional Catholic element "for their own secularizing and modernizing purposes," upholding it and celebrating it.[69] One of the first to draw attention to the central importance of honour in defining infanticide as a crime was the jurist and politician Francesco Carrara.[70] For him, if a crime is motivated by the necessity to defend and protect the woman's honour, criminal responsibility is diminished because – and here Carrara seems to promote principles of social defence that positivists would later embrace – "codesta causa non presenta il delinquente come pericoloso alla società quanto il comune omicida" (this cause does not imply the presence of a delinquent who is as dangerous to society as the common murderer). "Volere o non volere" (Whether one wishes it or not), Carrara contends, "è un fatto che lo spettacolo di una infanticida eccita ribrezzo, indignazione, pietà per la vittima, ma non genera spavento e timore di sé nell'universale dei cittadini" (it is a fact that the spectacle of an infanticide arouses horror, indignation, pity for the victim, but does not in itself engender dread and fear in the general public).[71] However, the legal definition of honour remained elusive, making its application in criminal law particularly complicated. For Carrara, the line of clear separation was represented by the character of the woman to be judged, namely her conformation to the image of the "honest woman." When the crime is committed by an "infanticida recidiva" (infanticide recidivist) or a prostitute, indeed, "obbligare il giudice ad usarle benignità … è cosa meno ingiusta che risibile" (forcing the judge to be indulgent with her … is ludicrous as well as unjust).[72]

Carrara's theorizations about infanticide would have lasting implications. Preceding and following the promulgation of the 1889 criminal code, both medical doctors and jurists from different schools of thought came to agree that honour was the only motive relevant to a definition of infanticide. For Lino Ferriani, a lawyer and theorist of infanticide, "poiché il sentimento che spinge la giovane già onesta è l'*onore*" (given that the sentiment that drives the honest woman is her *honour*), infanticidal mothers "non possono dividersi che in due grandi categorie: *donne oneste* e *donne perdute*" (can only be divided into two main categories: *honest women* and *fallen women*).[73] Honour thus constitutes the clear line of separation between the former and the latter; to the honest women, the author explains, we extend "tutta la nostra simpatia, la nostra pietà, la nostra clemenza" (all our sympathy, pity, and clemency), while to lost women we extend "solo quel tanto di compassione che il principio umanitario esige" (only so much compassion as the humanitarian principle demands).[74] These widely shared positions on infanticide led to its progressive depenalization in criminal law. For instance, Sighele, who produced a famous article on infanticide in 1889, argued that killing an infant cannot be considered "una perdita grave per la società" (a serious loss for society) and the mother, in light of her relatively negligible social dangerousness, should be punished accordingly.[75] The invocation of honour as the motivation for a crime, which consequently became the principal and most reliable argument lawyers used in court to defend women accused of infanticide, moved juries to acquit or apply lesser sentences in most criminal cases. The infanticidal mother thus became an exceptional criminal figure, in Italy as well as in other parts of Europe. Referring to the French context, Ann-Louise Shapiro asserts that "the poor and desperate murdering mother did not inhabit the same imaginative space" as other criminal women.[76] Crime and the criminal were discursively separated, reducing the accountability of the mother. As the inevitable conclusion of the vibrant debate in the preceding years, the 1889 code removed all references to illegitimacy and emphasized the woman's honour as central to the definition of the crime – technically, infanticide remained a form of homicide, only becoming a separate type of crime upon the introduction of the 1930 code. Given the widespread assumption of women's innate instability, the association between the infanticidal mother and irrational behaviour remained strong.[77] However, legal scholars have shown that insanity as a defence strategy was only very rarely invoked in the late nineteenth century,[78] whereas it became much more prominent from the early 1900s, when infanticide was increasingly pathologized as a result of the popularization of puerperal mania and honour as a motive was demoted to second place.[79]

As well as being progressively decriminalized, in the 1880s and 1890s infanticide paradoxically came to acquire positive connotations. Chiletti writes that the woman who committed infanticide "almost came to be seen in a 'positive' light, as if she were a sort of heroine who sacrificed her own nature as a mother in order to preserve intact the 'patrimony,' at once individual and collective, of honour."[80] The corollary of this process of both depenalization of and desensitization to infanticide was the progressive erosion of the rigid dichotomy between honest and fallen women. Chiletti notes that from the late 1880s some legal commentators, including the criminal lawyer Alessandro Stoppato and the jurist Pasquale Arena, began to call into question the strict division between the two types of women, thus toning down the distinction imposed by the doctrine of honour.[81] Lombroso and Ferrero's views on infanticide represent a major example of this: they regard the infanticidal mother as a minor threat to society and include the crime among those committed "per passione" (for pure love).[82] The act of infanticide, they argue, is determined by a variety of factors, including the "passione imprudente" (powerful amorous passion) of the woman, which leads to engagement in irregular love affairs condemned by social customs, the fear of dishonour, the desire to exact revenge against the unfaithful father of the child, and the anxieties generated by the prejudices and severity of both public opinion and the families involved.[83] The infanticidal mother, according to Lombroso and Ferrero, exhibits very few, if any, atavistic traits, which leads the authors to conclude that such criminals could hardly be distinguished from normal women; indeed, they assert that psychological examinations reveal that infanticidal mothers are generally not deficient in the particular sentiment characteristic of the normal woman, namely the maternal instinct, which is conversely absent in prostitutes and female criminals.[84] The distinction between honest and fallen women seems less rigid and dichotomic here: these criminals, the two criminologists conclude, are "in genere donne oneste e anche onestissime" (generally honest and even very honest).[85] Such a perspective gradually was widely embraced by other specialists. The jurist Giovanni Battista Impallomeni, writing in 1900, contends that infanticide is not a symptom of a mother's perversive nature but rather the result of the naivety of honest women led astray by vicious seducers.[86] This attenuation of the boundaries between honest and fallen women, Chiletti points out, was not the result of "a transformation of the moral canons and sexual norms of Italian society"; rather, it was due to "a masking" of the dimension of female sexuality "consigned on the one hand to the implicit codes that regulated sexual ties within society and on the other to scientific observation in the first studies of sexual psychology."[87]

This view on infanticide apparently met with very little resistance even outside medical and legal circles. Despite the obsession that journalists, lawyers, and the wider public showed for sensational criminal trials, cases of infanticide remained peripheral on the pages of contemporary judicial journals and reviews, volumes collecting criminal trials, and newspapers.[88] The book *I processi celebri di tutti i popoli*, edited by Italian and French legal experts and published originally in 1868, features only one infanticidal case that occurred in France in 1858, while the volume *Processi celebri contemporanei italiani e stranieri* (1889), edited by the lawyers Oscar Pio and Nicola Argenti, and the popular judicial magazine *I Grandi Processi Illustrati* (1896) do not contain references to infanticide. It may also be surprising that newspaper articles focusing on suspected cases of infanticide published in the 1880s and 1890s very rarely sensationalized such crimes. Most consisted of brief summaries of the events surrounding the murder, generally devoid of emotion, personal opinion, and allusions to theatre-like courtroom scenes, which instead frequently appeared in articles devoted to other murder trials.[89] Journalists of leading newspapers such as *Il Corriere della Sera* and the *Gazzetta Piemontese* (which would become *La stampa* in 1894) offered mostly sympathetic portrayals of infanticidal mothers, particularly when the crime was committed to protect the woman's honour and reputation. Negative representations were particularly scarce in this period and largely concerned women who either premeditated their crimes or caused the deaths of their children through physical abuse: most were also older women (age was linked with knowledge, experience, and hence agency), as shown by the case of an old Sicilian widower who in 1884 committed an "atroce infanticidio" (atrocious infanticide) as a result of an illicit relationship with a man.[90] The majority of newspaper articles on infanticidal crimes provided compassionate portrayals of women, with journalists emphasizing their youth, attractiveness, and femininity, but also their paleness and emaciated physical aspect: for instance, a woman tried in the Court of Assizes of Milan in 1892 for strangling her newborn child to protect her honour – she would eventually be sentenced to one year and fifteen days in prison due to major extenuating circumstances – appeared before the jury "come una donnetta pallida, magra, dall'aspetto sofferente" (as a pale, frail, and suffering woman).[91]

These reports contributed to constructing the image of a "desperate" woman from a poor background who had been forced by circumstances outside of her control to murder her infant. A twenty-one-year-old peasant who killed her son because her lover did not agree to marry her is depicted as "sventurata" (unfortunate),[92] while a "bellissima" (beautiful) twenty-six-year-old maid who became pregnant from an affair with a member of the family for which she was working is described as a suffering woman who "pianse per tutta l'udienza e non disse una parola d'allusione su colui che l'aveva resa madre" (cried during the entire judicial hearing and did not say a word regarding the person who impregnated her).[93] Again, a washerwoman who murdered her son because he was the fruit of a relationship with a married man is depicted as "pallida, magra, affetta da malattia che la rende degna di pietà" (pale, thin, affected by a disease that makes her worthy of compassion) – significantly, she was later acquitted.[94] These women were thus mostly represented as victims and described as weak and repentant in court, showing remorse and regret for the loss of both their child and their virtue. What emerges from these reports, crucially, is the perpetrator's fundamental lack of agency.

It can be argued here, then, that the creation of the good, honest, yet corrupted infanticidal mother, an unfortunate figure who killed reluctantly and without cruelty, served to reaffirm rather than challenge contemporary ideals of motherhood, neutralizing threats to gender norms and roles that might otherwise disrupt the process of nation-building. The specialists' willingness to diminish the culpability of the infanticidal mother was not, in fact, the result of a recognition of the dramatic social conditions in which most lower-class women were forced to live; actually, this apparent act of compassion silenced and further derationalized women, reinforcing the assumption of their irrationality, instability, and lack of agency – manipulated by their seducers, women did not deliberately choose to fall but were led astray. This is mirrored in one of the most famous cases of infanticide in late nineteenth-century Italian literature, D'Annunzio's *L'innocente*. The novel features Tullio Hermil, a libertine and unfaithful man who discovers that his wife Giuliana, who had remained with him despite his repeated extramarital affairs, is pregnant by another man, the famous writer Filippo Arborio. He cannot condemn her on moral grounds, but he is horrified and repulsed by the fact that she has been irremediably tainted. After the birth, with Giuliana's tacit consent, Tullio kills the child by inducing pneumonia. In D'Annunzio's narrative world, in which blood plays a major role in society, infanticide represents a particularly forceful act of resistance to patriarchal hegemony and threatens the very foundations of society. Here, however, its transgressive component is undermined and ultimately neutralized. Giuliana, semantically depicted mostly in terms of sickness and fragility, is deprived of agency and legal responsibility, transformed into the helpless mother corrupted by a cunning seducer. Physically confined to bed for most of the story, she is coerced by Tullio and convinced to accept a criminal act that is purely reactionary, perpetrated to protect the name and lineage of the family.

The conservative dimension of this novel should not lead us to presume substantial congruence between literary and medico-legal narratives. Italian writers' responses to the changing perspectives on infanticide were varied and conflictual, testifying to the complexity of the debate, which transcended disciplinary boundaries and escaped the medical and legal spheres. Here, I focus on two novels published in the early 1880s and 1890s, respectively, that mingle Gothic elements, melodrama, and sensationalism. A comparative reading of the way in which infanticide was negotiated, discussed, and re-elaborated in the literary domain surrounding the promulgation of the 1889 code sheds further light on the larger battlefield on which this debate took place and the contradictions inherent in it, thus revealing the more complex and elusive nature of the infanticidal mother. The first text I consider is Francesco Mastriani's *La Medea di Porta Medina*, serialized in the journal *Roma* between 12 October and 29 December 1881 and published in a single volume in 1882.[95] Set in late eighteenth-century Naples, it tells the story of Coletta Esposito, a young, sexually independent woman from the lower class who kills her daughter, Cesarina, and her partner's mistress, Teresina, when she realizes that her partner and his lover have planned to escape together, bringing the child with them. Coletta is convicted and sentenced to decapitation, in accordance with the law at the time,[96] and her head is displayed as a macabre trophy at Castel Capuano. The second novel is Carolina Invernizio's *Storia d'una sartina* (1892).[97] Set in late nineteenth-century Florence, it relates the tragic story of the seamstress Giselda, who strangles her own child immediately after the birth to take revenge on the man who had seduced and abandoned her, Count Gerardo. To dispose of the body, she leaves the house in the middle of the night and throws the bundle into the river, where she is seen by a witness who denounces her. At the end of a dramatic trial, all the extenuating circumstances are taken into account, and she is sentenced to three years in prison. She serves her time and, as soon as she is out, she visits and kills her former lover before taking her own life.

Both Giselda and Coletta are, on one level, positioned as victims of an unjust legal system that denies women full juridical agency and uses honour as a weapon to silence and subordinate them. During the trial, Giselda is unwilling to reveal the name of the man with whom she had a sexual relationship. This greatly disconcerts the audience, the judge, the members of the jury, and the defence lawyer, who strongly encourages Giselda to name the person who seduced and dishonoured her. This is not to punish the man; rather, according to the lawyer, it is the easiest way to prove Giselda's honour and thus reduce the gravity of her crime: as he exclaims, "Se l'accusata si decidesse a parlare ... la sua colpa ci apparirebbe meno grave, il suo delitto meno abominevole" (If the accused decided to talk ... her fault would appear less serious to us and her murder less abhorrent).[98] This echoes the words of Patrizia

Guarnieri, one of the leading Italian historians on infanticide, who suggests that the indulgence shown towards late nineteenth-century infanticidal women assumed the form of a self-indulgence for the benefit and protection of the male world only: women are punished less because men are not punished at all.[99] Coletta is not given the same opportunity. She is a victim of a patriarchal society that puts honour and respectability over natural and family relationships, forcing young women to carry the burden of what was seen as sexual impropriety by their parents. Indeed, Coletta is an orphan, given by her mother, a countess, to the Ruota dell'Annunziata, a charitable institution for the care of abandoned infants, because she was the result of an adulterous relationship. She is irremediably doomed, not because of biological factors but due to the monstrous operations of patriarchal authority. Her surname, Esposito, is the one given to "children of guilt."[100] These unfortunate women, Mastriani writes, are scarred forever and destined to a life of crime and prostitution they do not deserve: "Il destino" (Fate), Mastriani remarks, "non ci entr[a] per nulla in questa faccenda" (has nothing to do with this matter).[101] By addressing the social mechanisms underlying women's oppression, both stories expose how infanticidal mothers were sentenced based on their social class or level of "social respectability" rather than on evidence. While an unmarried girl of a poor but essentially respectable family such as Giselda, who killed her child to hide her dishonour after having been seduced and abandoned, was punished in a clement way, a dishonoured, sexually unrestrained woman like Coletta, who had no economic or social imperative to commit infanticide, was harshly judged and most likely convicted.

Although victims of an unjust legal system, both women actively try to fight their miserable fate. In this respect, they appear to be capable and rational subjects. Despite their physical differences – Coletta with her dark skin, thick black hair, and voluptuous lips, Giselda as the embodiment of traditional femininity, virtuous, angelic, and blond – both possess psychological features conventionally coded as virile and masculine, including intelligence, strength, courage, and determination. In particular, the premeditation of both crimes complicates those familiar discourses that attributed physicality to the female and cerebrality to the male: "Pochi esempi d'una feroce vendetta sì freddamente meditata ed eseguita offre la storia dei delitti celebri" (The history of notorious trials has seen very few examples that can match a revenge like this, so ferocious and so coldly premeditated and executed), the narrator of Mastriani's novel notes.[102] In Invernizio's story, what disturbs other women, particularly during the trial, is that the crime was clearly carefully planned: "Si capiva che l'aveva a lungo meditata"

(It was clear that the murder was long premeditated).[103] What is most horrifying about the female murderer, then, is not her excess, for excess is always constructed as feminine, but her paradoxical cerebrality, her agency, and even her creativity – the plan orchestrated by Coletta, who kills her daughter and throws her corpse at the two lovers during the wedding ceremony, is a masterful, spectacular act of theatre of the macabre.

However, the portrayal of these women is ultimately contradictory, for they are also ostensibly described as victims of their own instability as female subjects. Mastriani, for instance, links Coletta's violence with the possibilities of hysteria. When Coletta publicly declares her love to her future husband Cipriano, the people around her – all men, significantly – label her as mentally ill: "Questa giovane è pazza" (this young woman is crazy), one of the characters shouts, while the narrator notes that "il suo aspetto accusava davvero uno stato di demenza" (her physical appearance truly signalled a state of dementia).[104] Plus, Coletta's lawyer does try, however unsuccessfully, to use temporary insanity as a defence strategy, invoking the "condizioni anormali della giovane nel momento di compiere l'atroce vendetta" (abnormal conditions of the woman while carrying out the atrocious revenge).[105] What is more, Coletta is framed as deviant because of her lack of maternal instincts. Contrary to "good women," who "feel a primary and primal connection to their children,"[106] as Loralee MacPike remarks, Coletta has a fraught relationship with her daughter: "Me non ama questa creatura" (She does not love me), Coletta laments. "Se non fossi certa di averla partorita io, direi che non è mia figlia" (If I were not sure I had given birth to her, I would say she is not my daughter).[107] In the absence of the father, Cesarina feels uncomfortable – "la piccola Cesarina mandava acutissime grida quasi avesse avuto paura di star sola con la mamma" (the little Cesarina screamed loudly as if she were scared to be alone with her mother) – a feeling that gives rise to furious and often violent reactions, culminating in the final murder.[108]

Giselda is likewise frequently associated with insanity. The defence lawyer, to add a layer to his argument, suggests the possibility of temporary insanity: "Ella deve essere stata colta da un momento di pazzia, che la rese irresponsabile dei suoi atti" (She must have been seized by a moment of insanity, which absolves her from responsibility for her acts).[109] It is impossible, he insists, that "scientemente, con freddezza d'animo" (deliberately, with cold-heartedness), she could have committed such a crime; "La sciagurata agisce sotto un impulso più potente della sua volontà" (The poor woman acts under an impulse that is more powerful than her own will), he concludes.[110] Significantly, this claim reflects the words used by the narrator at the beginning of the book to describe Giselda strangling the infant: "Bisognava credere che Giselda fosse stata colta da un momento di pazzia!" (It was necessary to believe that Giselda had been seized by a moment of insanity!), the narrator states, hinting at the unnaturalness of infanticide: "È forse possibile che scientemente, freddamente, potesse commettere un così mostruoso delitto!?" (Is it perhaps possible that knowingly, coldly, she could have committed such a monstrous crime!?)[111] After the murder, Giselda seems scared, desperate, and even regretful. However, she deliberately decides not to confess the crime and instead gets rid of the corpse: "Aveva conservato il suo sangue freddo o agiva sotto l'impeto di una ispirazione esaltata, folle?" (Had she had remained composed or was she acting under the influence of a mad, impetuous drive?), the narrator rhetorically asks, instilling once again doubt regarding her sanity.[112]

Women's underlying instability serves here as a lens through which their monstrous nature is revealed. Monstrosity, Marie Mulvey-Roberts argues, "is invariably a perception relating to bodily confusion and the blurring of boundaries out of which liminality manifests as an object of fear."[113] In both novels, as the idea of killing their children takes shape, the women's pleasing exteriors mutate, they become increasingly less feminine, growing bigger, darker, and more masculine. On the night of the murder, Coletta's entire body seems to change for apparently natural reasons: "Si trasformarono le sue sembianze ... Era la maledizione della natura." (Her lineaments changed ... It was nature's curse.)[114] Invernizio also emphasizes Giselda's mutating physical appearance as she commits the crime; she progressively assumes deformed, even evil features: "I lineamenti di Giselda si contrassero con un'espressione infernale ... Con una mano afferrò attraverso il corpo la sua creaturina, coll'altra la cinse per il collo ... La sua creatura aveva mandato un altro lievissimo gemito, un lamento indefinibile, ed ella continuava a stringerla per il collo." (Giselda's features contracted with an infernal expression ... With one hand she grasped her child around its body, with the other she clutched its neck ... Her child had managed another fragile whimper, an indefinable lament, and she continued to squeeze its neck.)[115] During the act of murder, both women are transformed into androgynous, monstrous beings that, in their violation of the norms of both femininity and the law, dismantle the gendered boundaries between reason and unreason, mind and body, agency and passivity.

The monsterization of the mother reveals that the apparently discarded (or, better, rearticulated) Catholic view of infanticide as a crime against nature, rooted in and reinforced by the idea that the purpose of women's existence was essentially procreation and motherhood, did not disappear but rather continued to circulate widely, particularly in the realm of popular literature. For Mastriani, infanticide is always inexcusable, and no extenuating circumstances could ever mitigate the crime: "Una madre che strangola una sua innocente creatura di pochi mesi non può trovare difesa neanche ove fosse comprovata la sua demenza" (A woman who strangles her own innocent creature cannot be defended even in those circumstances in which her demented state is established beyond reasonable doubt).[116] Infanticide is, for him, rationally incomprehensible, monstrous, and unnatural: "Non comprendiamo la madre che uccide il frutto innocente delle visceri sue. Questa singolarità esce eziandio dall'ordine dei mostri." (We cannot understand a mother who kills the innocent fruit of her own womb. This singularity is not even found in the realm of monsters.)[117] Coletta's supposed innate criminal nature is confirmed in many passages in which the author intrudes upon the narration and highlights biological and anthropological determinants to account for the woman's transgressive behaviour: "Coletta Esposito offre agli studi antropologici un tipo straordinario" (Coletta Esposito represents an extraordinary subject for anthropological studies), Mastriani remarks.[118] He even points out that "un amatore di studii antropologici, di nazione inglese, comperò dal governo napolitano il teschio di Coletta Esposito" (an amateur of anthropological studies, of British nationality, purchased the skull of Coletta Esposito from the Neapolitan government)[119] and confirms that this acquisition was well worth what had been paid for it: "Il teschio di quella nuova Medea valeva la spesa" (The skull of that new Medea was worth the price).[120]

Likewise, Invernizio does not refrain from sharing her horrified reaction to the act of infanticide. She writes, "La sciagurata stava dunque per compiere uno dei delitti più orribili, che abbiano spaventato l'umanità. Uccideva la sua creatura, il sangue suo!" (The wicked woman was, then, about to commit one of the most horrible crimes ever to have shocked humanity. She was killing her child, blood of her blood!)[121] Other women, all mothers, react with horror and disgust upon the discovery of the crime. They would have killed Giselda if they had the chance: "Si sarebbero scagliate su Giselda, ne avrebbero fatta giustizia sommaria" (They would have jumped on Giselda and they would have done perfunctory justice).[122] Though Giselda was seen as a beautiful, loving person before the murder, her crime renders her a despicable woman and a social outcast: "Nessuno la compiangeva, nessuna era sorta a difenderla" (No one felt sorry for her, no one was willing to defend her).[123] Infanticide is a crime so monstrous that it eventually has devastating consequences for everyone; by the end of the story, all the characters involved – Giselda, Gerardo, Gerardo's fiancée, and Giselda's parents – have died as a result of murder, suicide, or grief. It is thus perhaps paradoxical that, in critiquing the dominant view of the good, innocent infanticidal mother, both novels reinstate the widespread assumption of women as fundamentally irrational beings through their emphasis on insanity. Despite presenting two diametrically opposite views on infanticide – women as fundamentally virtuous beings who kill to protect their honour on the one hand, and women as unstable and abnormal subjects on the other – both authors end up circulating the same problematic stereotype.

The ambiguous nature of these two female characters ultimately mirrors the ambivalence of the novels themselves, which exhibit a contradiction deeply ingrained in Gothic narratives, both policing and transgressing the borders between conservatism and resistance. While they allow the idea that female biology is linked to insane violence to remain unchallenged, the texts also question the extent to which those links are inseparable from problems of class, gender, and the patriarchy. Although these women deliberately reject the role of procreators and refuse to be controlled, posing a danger to male sexual self-management, heredity, and social containment, the literary expression of their abnormal sexual behaviour is used to re-enforce control over women, ultimately reinstating the ideological message that all forms of female deviance must be repressed and punished. While, in Invernizio's novel, Giselda decides to inflict the final punishment on herself, in Mastriani's this is more explicit. The author converts a tragic story of female violence into a narrative that sanctions and strengthens controls enforced by a bourgeois- and male-driven culture, with Coletta's final decapitation representing a further stage in the process of the desexualization of the woman and the final act of repression.

As we have seen, literary depictions of deviant women work their way through a large and complex web of ideas – medical, legal, and cultural – connected to what was perceived and classified as female transgression. This results in a pluralization of approaches that problematize a straightforward, linear reading of science and literature as operating within the same deeply moralizing and paternalistic cultural framework that suppresses female emancipation and reinforces patriarchal ideologies. The texts analysed here occupy a conflictual space, exposing the tension between the conventional order and the demonized, othered woman, ultimately revealing the permeability and fictionality of these two poles. The stories are deeply nuanced and often ambivalent; they either reinforce the cultural, social, and legal marginalization of women in Italian society or challenge problematic stereotypes and constricting practices – and sometimes they do both. On the one hand, most female criminals do little to resist their fate, with death ending their deviance and contributing to the final re-establishment of the status quo. Writers, confined within the dominant ideology, produced stereotypical constructions, often merely confirming the disadvantages suffered by women, especially the denial of their right to control their own sexuality. On the other hand, these texts exhibit spaces of potential subversion and lend themselves to counter-readings with a potentially liberating effect. In its various guises and manifestations, the female criminal emerges in post-unification Italy as a Gothic figure that blurs the boundaries between activity and passivity, normality and abnormality, public and private, forcing readers to confront a reality that, however gradually, was finally mutating.

Vampires

The cultural phase that spans the late nineteenth and the early twentieth centuries was seen for a long time as the triumph of the empiricist method and a materialist approach to reality, with science gradually but inexorably supplanting religion and the occult as the ultimate authority on the natural world. However, recent scholarship has redefined this period as ambivalent and problematic, characterized by a pervasive tension between the rational and irrational, in which apparently contradictory fields such as science, technology, and magical and supernatural thinking interacted and intertwined.[124] The rise of occultism in the nineteenth century was not merely a reaction against the increasingly dogmatic materialism of science. Shane McCorristine suggests, "Instead of reading spiritualism and the occult as *responses* to things, we can take the alternative perspective of seeing the engagement with supernatural other worlds as *discoveries* which ran alongside secularization and scientific naturalism."[125] The very idea of the "supernatural" poses a problem at the fin de siècle. Nicola Bown, Carolyn Burdett, and Pamela Thurschwell, who have edited a fundamental volume on the Victorian supernatural, argue that the complexity of the concept of the supernatural and its "slipper[y]" nature, which make it "resistant to definition," increased its appeal: the supernatural, they say, had a "protean quality of being a cause, a place, a kind of being, a realm, a possibility, a new form of nature, [and] a hope for the future."[126] Ultimately, the supernatural was often predicated on the idea that apparently occult manifestations were, in reality, phenomena governed by laws that had not yet been fully grasped by humans. Timothy Jarvis sees the collapse of the occult/science binary at the fin de siècle as the result of this new dialectical relationship between scientism and occultism:

114   Gothic Italy

"If spiritualism and other occult movements had endeavoured to become more scientific, science was also becoming more occult."[127] Positivist science aimed to deprive the world of its mysterious and supernatural aura, exploring phenomena, from mesmerism to spiritualism, that had been previously ascribed to superstition and religion, thus engendering a new form of syncretism. It was the development of science and technology, then, that helped foster the resurgence of discarded popular beliefs and traditions, which were re-evaluated in the light of recent discoveries and reassessed within a new, apparently more scientific system of knowledge.

It is unsurprising that a time marked by an increasing number of both amateur and professional incursions into the occult saw the re-emergence of a powerfully Gothic figure that had appeared only sporadically in the Italian literary sphere throughout the nineteenth century.[128] The literary vampire featured in an assortment of stories, including Francesco Morando's "Vampiro innocente" (1885), Giuseppe Tonsi's "Il vampiro" (1902), Daniele Oberto Marrama's "Il dottor Nero" (1904), Luigi Capuana's "Un vampiro" (1904), Enrico Boni's "Un vampiro" (1908), and Vittorio Martella's "Il vampiro" (1917). The very limited circulation of classic British Gothic texts in nineteenth-century Italy, Camilletti also notes, is one reason why Italian writers developed the theme of vampirism differently and autonomously.[129] These texts are, in fact, an echo more of European folklore than of the literary vampires created by Anglophone writers. Common motifs associated with folkloric vampires that are central in these stories include the appearance of vampire fantasies in circumstances of acute object loss and intense grief on the part of survivors; the marginalization of blood, with vampires mainly being recognized on account of their consumption of the life force of victims; and the idea that recurring visitations to family members by the recently deceased man-turned-vampire bring malevolence, bad luck, or death.[130]

The vampire, a figure that transgresses the categories that make the world intelligible, escaping attempts at identification and engendering unease and panic in those who confront it, mutated and adapted to the fin de siècle Italian environment to challenge not simply its rationality but also accepted assumptions about family, gender, and sexuality. In this section, I first refer to Marrama's "Il dottor Nero" and then consider, in greater depth, Capuana's "Un vampiro," two short stories that exhibit similar patterns in that they both depict the vampire as a dead man who comes back from the grave and attacks his widow because of her recent new marriage.[131] In "Il dottor Nero," a mysterious Spanish doctor "dalla barba nerissima, dagli occhi penetranti" (with a black beard and penetrating eyes) keeps a beautiful, suggestible young woman bound to him through a sort of diabolical "influsso magnetico" (magnetic influence).[132] When he leaves for a long expedition to South America, he warns her that "uomini come me non si debbono dimenticare" (men like me cannot be forgotten) because "essi si vendicano del tradimento come dell'abbandono, *con armi che nessun uomo al mondo conosce!*" (they avenge betrayal as well as abandonment *with weapons that no one knows*).[133] After a while, the man is found dead, killed, according to local sources, by a mysterious vampire bat. The woman, suddenly relieved and free, embarks on a new relationship, but the promised revenge of the doctor, who has now taken the form of a vampire bat, is inescapable.

In "Un vampiro," the unfortunate Lelio Giorgi asks his physician friend Mongeri for help as his new wife, Luisa, seems to be possessed by the spirit-vampire of her dead former husband, who torments the couple with his violent jealousy at her perceived betrayal and attempts to kill their child by sucking the life out of him. In some ways, the story constitutes a parody of the motif of the man coming back from the dead to denounce his own murder. The spirit openly accuses his former wife of having disposed of him, but the physician refuses to take this possibility into consideration. He rules out the culpability of the woman, and his intervention eventually saves the lives of the couple and their newborn son. Whereas "Il dottor Nero" has been neglected by critics, Capuana's "Un vampiro" has received more attention, though scholars have only superficially considered the relationship between science and the occult. Giuseppe Tardiola, in his study of the fantastic in Italian literature, argues that "si tratta di una novella di forte impronta positivistica e che pertanto riconduce il tema fantastico all'interno di un dibattito critico fra scienza e irrazionalità" (it is a positivism-inflected novella that traces the theme of the fantastic back to a critical debate between science and irrationalism), while for Annamaria Loria, the story should be read as a "polemica nei confronti della scienza ufficiale" (polemic against mainstream science).[134]

I contend that, in these texts, the invariably male vampire represents an extraordinarily potent catalyst that attracts and refracts some of the most pressing fears and anxieties of fin de siècle Italian society. Vampirism constitutes a disruptive factor through which male writers seek to conceal, contain, and exorcise objects of anxiety associated with the emergence of feminism and the so-called New Woman. In her demand for economic, political, and notably sexual independence, the late nineteenth-century woman destabilized the very concepts of femininity and womanhood and exposed her culturally constructed role in both the domestic and social spheres. Positivism, as the expression of the nation's ruling classes, was committed to constructing and organizing Italian society. A crucial part of this mission was controlling sexuality and maintaining gender hierarchies, which were fundamental to stability in social organization. As we saw earlier in this chapter, criminologists' interest in studying female offenders – a population that had hitherto seldom been mentioned in the history of criminology – must be understood as a response to the immediacy of the woman question in Italy in the 1890s and the fears aroused by women's demands for sexual independence. Aggressive sexuality, considered an inherently virile or male characteristic, called into question the scientific assumption that normal women are feminine, necessarily monogamous, and sexually passive. Sexual instinct, Lombroso suggested, is less intense in women than men and tends to atrophy over time.[135] This led to sexual pleasure outside of marriage being viewed as an outer sign of deviance.[136] Strong female sexuality also challenged the position of the church, which saw women as exclusively dedicated to motherhood and reproduction.

It is remarkable that these stories of violence in, and towards, the family were published at a time when the institution of marriage was receiving considerable public attention. The question of marriage dominated the political scene between 1878 and 1902, when eight attempts to introduce divorce into Italian legislation were frustrated by the interventions of the church, which sought to protect the sanctity of marriage from the depredations of advancing liberalism and feminism.[137] For the Catholic hierarchy, the idea of a woman wanting to get a divorce constituted a great offence to the divine order of things but also to the patriarchal structure of society. The article "La donna degradata," published in the Catholic journal *L'Osservatore Romano*, underlined how Christian marriage protected women from becoming vile instruments of animal passion.[138] As Mark Seymour observes, many late nineteenth-century Italian men felt intimidated by the emergence of feminism, and the determination to reject divorce was linked to the attempt to protect masculinity itself, along with its attendant privileges.[139] By showing that female sexual impulses led women to commit adultery or remarry, the women protagonists of these texts, however subtly, represent a powerful menace to male power and to the very concept of masculinity. Female sexuality has dangerous connotations in many of Capuana's works, from *Giacinta* (1879), in which adultery leads to degradation, decay, and eventually suicide, to *Profumo* (1892), in which only the aid of a doctor allows the male protagonist to prevent his wife from committing adultery, helping him find a way to fulfil his marital obligations and to deal with, control, and contain the woman's sexuality within accepted boundaries.

In "Un vampiro," the physician constantly repeats that he would not marry a widow "per tutto l'oro del mondo" (for all the gold in the world) because "qualcosa permane sempre del marito morto, a dispetto di tutto, nella vedova" (some part of the dead husband always remains, despite everything, inside the widow), a reference to the contemporary idea of telegony.[140] A woman who has formerly been in a sexual relationship with another man bears the mark of her first possessor and is thus fundamentally contaminated and permanently tarnished. She threatens any man's control and is in a position to compare one man's sexual prowess with that of another. This view is reinforced by the protagonist's description of his own feelings of jealousy towards his wife and her former spouse: "Certe volte, il pensiero che il corpo della mia adorata era stato in pieno possesso, quantunque legittimo, di un altro mi dava tale stretta al cuore, che mi faceva fremere da capo a piedi" (At certain times, the thought that the body of my darling had been in the full possession, however legitimate, of another wrung my heart so that I shuddered from head to toe).[141] When the apparitions of the spirit-vampire begin, the monster again possesses the woman, using her body to speak while she is in a trance state. In this instance, it is the vampire that tries to purify the woman's body by eliminating the child she has produced with a subsequent partner. He penetrates her body, transforming it into a repulsive, corrupt, and unwanted sexual presence: "La signora Luisa si era rizzata sul busto con tal viso rabbuiato, con tale espressione di durezza nei lineamenti, da sembrare un'altra persona" (Luisa had risen from the grave, with such a darkened face, with such hardness in her features, that she seemed another person).[142]

This concern regarding the female body and the menace it presupposes conceals a strong preoccupation with male vulnerability that permeated post-unification Italian society at different levels. Drawing on Angus McLaren's study of impotence, which shows how male sexual potency has long been intertwined with ideas of the vigour of the body politic, historians such as Patriarca and Seymour have argued that the preoccupation with the nature of masculinity and its increasing vulnerability in Italy at both official and popular levels was intimately bound up with anxieties about the strength and legitimacy of the new state.[143] More specifically, Stewart-Steinberg observes that the project of making Italians relied on, but also produced, discourses of gender and sexuality whereby the problem of making an Italian subject "came to be lived as a crisis of the paternal function and hence as a crisis of male performativity."[144] Duncan argues that Lombroso's work on homosexuality in the early twentieth century was fuelled "by a perception of a crisis in reproductive sexuality. Atavistic or degenerate traits were the unpredictable symptoms of a heterosexuality gone wrong."[145] It is not a coincidence that, in "Un vampiro," the ghostly manifestations start when the woman finds out she is pregnant: as soon as she confesses to her husband "come sono felice ... che questo sia avvenuto soltanto ora" (I'm so happy ... that this has happened only now), they both distinctly hear "un gran colpo all'uscio" (a loud knock at the door).[146] Shortly thereafter we are told that "tutto l'odio di *colui* era rivolto contro il bambino" (all of *his* hatred was directed towards the baby).[147] The vampire's furious reaction to the infant, who is almost completely deprived of his life force, can be read as a refusal to accept that he himself was unable to fulfil his marital obligations and provide his wife and family with a child. Only upon the cremation of the first husband's body does the lingering, malignant influence of the vampire dissolve and moral order is restored. Anxiety surrounding virility is also present in "Il dottor Nero." In this short story, written by the Neapolitan writer Marrama, the vampire is portrayed as a foreign, specifically Spanish, entity. For centuries, Spain was a colonial power in Southern Italy, particularly the Neapolitan regions. The unificatory process was supposed to bring an end to such oppression, but it may have aggravated it. The imperial, oppressive powers of the North replaced Spain as the intruding force coming from abroad, exercising hegemony, and contaminating the Southern regions and their inhabitants. For Marrama, Spain seems to represent the metaphorical substitute for the hegemonic North and the threat from within that it posed to Southern identity, which was increasingly under attack and forced to conform to foreign powers and ideologies.[148]

These popular, critically marginalized stories powerfully reflect the generalized sense of anxiety that both pervaded and characterized post-unification Italy, an anxiety that, for Stewart-Steinberg, was crucial to Italian modernity: the formulation of an Italian national self, she notes, was "predicated on a language that posited marginalization and powerlessness as fundamental aspects of what it meant to be modern Italians."[149] Significantly, as Patriarca has shown, Italian nationalists sought to fight "the historical degeneration of the Italian" by invoking a process of "national regeneration" that was conceived as one of "almost literal re-virilization of the people."[150] In this respect, a figure who played a major role in fostering debates aimed at revitalizing Italians was D'Annunzio. Thus, it is extremely interesting to read his *L'innocente* as a vampiric text.

The novel, obsessed as it is with degeneration and regeneration, sterility and fecundity, conceals anxieties regarding masculine power, virility, and the future of the body politic. The story, as already mentioned, concerns a father, Tullio, who is preoccupied with both the biological and genealogical intrusion of an adulterine fetus who threatens to infiltrate and destroy his entire world and that of his wife, Giuliana. He has been able to give her only two daughters and now her male child seems poised to usurp him. He is obsessed with the idea of "l'intruso che avrebbe portato il mio nome, che sarebbe stato il mio erede" (the intruder who bore my name, who would be my heir).[151] According to Rhiannon Noel Welch's brilliant reading of this novel, the theme of "adulterous reproduction" is "staged as a racial intrusion."[152] Although Tullio is inserted, like Giorgio in *Trionfo della morte* after him, into a declining family line, "his primary preoccupation is not with his genetic make-up, however deficient. Instead, he positions himself with regard to flawed prospective heredity."[153] Tullio's rejection of the child even before the birth is framed in terms of blood: "Il mio avvenire era legato a un essere vivente d'una vita tenace e malefica; era legato a un estraneo, a un intruso, a una creatura abominevole contro di cui non soltanto la mia anima ma la mia carne, tutto il mio sangue e tutte le mie fibre votavano un'avversione bruta, feroce, implacabile fino alla morte, oltre la morte." (My future was fettered to a being whose life was tenacious and harmful; it was shackled to a stranger, to an intruder, to an abominable creature, against whom not only my mind but also my flesh, all my blood and every fibre, rose with a brutal, ferocious, implacable aversion, until death, beyond death.)[154] For Welch, the threat that the child poses to Tullio's heredity is "inextricable from the novel's poetics of blood."[155] As we will see, blood is omnipresent in the text. This blood, spilled during labour, is now contained within the body of the newborn infant, which progressively sucks the life out of his mother (literally) and his stepfather (metaphorically).

As figures of contamination and pollution, vampires have historically been associated with race and demonized as all-consuming monsters. In vampire narratives, Aspasia Stephanou writes, blood and race are inextricably connected: blood's "dangerous circulation underneath the skin is ... hidden but threatening. With its capacity to spill outside the body and pollute white society's categories, blood remains associated with race."[156] John Allen Stevenson famously argues that Dracula, the epitome of the vampire, threatens to "deracinate" his victims by "injecting them with a new racial identity."[157] The body of Giuliana in *L'innocente* embodies the idea of disease and threatening sexuality. We know from early on that Giuliana had suffered from unspecified "malattie complicate della matrice e dell'ovaia, quelle terribili malattie nascoste che turbano in una donna tutte le funzioni della vita" (complicated internal troubles, those terrible occult maladies that in a woman disturb all her vital functions), because of which she needed to undergo a delicate surgical intervention that would probably cause permanent sterility.[158] The institution of the clinic is one of the principal ways of disciplining the female body within the modern regime of biopower. However, during what seems to be a single instance of sexual intercourse outside of marriage, Giuliana becomes pregnant. Medicine's inability to regulate Giuliana's sexuality is a first, major symptom of the impossibility of controlling the female body, which resists legibility and rational, scientific understanding. Giuliana's body thus gradually becomes a site where anxieties proliferate about uncontrolled, weakening bodies, devouring appetites, and consumption of blood. These fears are linked to the degenerate or unhealthy status of women and their impure blood. As Elizabeth Grosz explains in *Volatile Bodies* (1994),

> the representation of female sexuality as an uncontainable flow, as seepage associated with what is unclean, coupled with the idea of female sexuality as a vessel, a container, a home empty or lacking in itself but fillable from the outside, has enabled men to associate women with infection, with disease, with the idea of festering putrefaction, no longer contained simply in female genitals but at any or all the points of the female body.[159]

In this novel, Giuliana's genitals are constantly described through references to a wound and to blood; one of the first and most emblematic depictions – "la piaga originale, la turpe ferita sempre aperta 'che sanguina e che pute'" (the original, repugnant wound, always open, which bleeds and smells)[160] – suggests the idea of the female genitals as a threat that cannot be neutralized but also uncovers them as a site that is both attractive and repulsive, an uncanny place, in Freud's words, that is for men simultaneously familiar, signifying the return home, and unfamiliar. It is precisely from this monstrous site that a creature with vampiric traits emerges.

Raimondo, Tullio's illicit son, is described as having vampiric attributes from the very beginning. Even during Giuliana's pregnancy, the vampire seems to signal its spiritual presence:

> Era di sera, era il crepuscolo, e la finestra era spalancata, e le tende si gonfiavano sbattendo, e una candela ardeva su un tavolo, contro uno specchio; e, non so perché, lo sbattito delle tende, l'agitazione disperata di quella fiammella, che lo specchio pallido rifletteva, presero nel mio spirito un significato sinistro, aumentarono il mio terrore.

(It was evening, twilight, and the window was open, and the swollen curtains shook at the breath of the wind, and a candle was burning on a table, before a mirror. And, I do know not why, the shaking of the curtains, the hopeless flickering of the tiny flame which reflected its paleness in the glass, assumed in my mind a sinister significance, and increased my terror.)[161]

Even though Tullio is unaware of Giuliana's pregnancy, he nonetheless senses that "un elemento estraneo, qualche cosa di oscuro, di convulso, di eccessivo, aveva modificata, difformata la sua personalità" (a strange element, something dark, violent, and excessive, had modified and deformed her personality).[162] Tullio uses the verb "deformare" again later, when Giuliana's apparently "deformed personality" assumes, in his mind, the physical shape of a "deformed body": he imagines her "difformata da un ventre enorme, gravida d'un feto adulterino" (deformed by an enormous stomach, pregnant with an adulterine fetus).[163] Tullio is unable to dispel the impression that something abnormal and disturbing is growing inside Giuliana's body:

Mi volsi ancora verso l'alcova, con un moto repentino, come se avessi sentito uno sguardo sopra di me. Mi parve che le cortine ondeggiassero... Qualche cosa come un'onda magnetica a traverso le cortine veniva a penetrarmi; qualche cosa a cui non resistevo. Entrai nell'alcova una seconda volta, rabbrividendo.

(I turned towards the alcove again with an abrupt movement, as if I had felt a gaze fixed on me. It seemed to me that the curtains were waving ... Something like a magnetic wave came through the curtains and penetrated me, something I could not resist. I re-entered the alcove with a shudder.)[164]

Superficially, "non v'appariva segno di contaminazione" (there was no sign of contamination),[165] Tullio acknowledges, but the vampiric presence is made increasingly evident through the deterioration of Giuliana's physical and psychological conditions. From the very beginning, Giuliana experiences a troubling pregnancy. Her pregnancy is characterized by discomfort with how her body is being shaped from the inside out by forces that now, more than ever before, elude her control. She is disgusted and "umiliata" (humiliated), suffering from "un'infermità vergognosa" (a shameful infirmity).[166] She progressively loses her beauty and her essence. The fetus is a burden that scars and disfigures Giuliana's body, which is afflicted by a "deturpante e disonorante gravezza" (disfiguring and dishonouring heaviness).[167] The sense of disempowerment and dislocation that Giuliana feels is an evocation of the unendingly uncanny state of gestation, when the body is occupied by that which is both of itself and not of itself, what Naomi Wolf calls a "benign possession"[168] – in this case, the possession is, instead, completely evil. Tullio is both horrified by and preoccupied with Giuliana's suffering: "Lo spettacolo della sua sofferenza mi dilaniava" (Seeing her suffering tormented me), he laments.[169] He sees Giuliana's body as weakened by an evil creature that grows by feeding off of her. He drains her and makes her bleed. The child, who for Tullio signifies adultery and aberrant sexual behaviour, is crucial in revealing the protagonist's dramatic loss of virility and his progressive marginalization, especially in what was supposed to be his realm, the house: "Il figliuolo non mio cresceva protetto da lei, per le cure assidue di lei; si faceva robusto e bello; diveniva capriccioso come un piccolo despota; s'impadroniva della mia casa." (The son who was not mine would grow up under her protection, benefiting from her assiduous cares; he would become robust and handsome; he would become capricious like a little despot; he would reign in my house.)[170]

Before the birth, Tullio ruminates obsessively about the child and constantly visualizes him as a monster whose destiny is to attack and destroy the whole family. Raimondo is depicted in Gothic terms as a "piccolo fantasma" (little ghost) with "occhi grigi e malvagi" (grey and evil eyes); he is imagined as "tutto nervi, bilioso, un po' felino, pieno d'intelligenza e d'istinti malvagi, duro con le sorelle, crudele verso gli animali, incapace di tenerezze, indisciplinabile" (a bundle of nerves, bilious, rather catlike, full of intelligence and evil instincts, rough with his sisters, cruel to animals, incapable of tenderness, undisciplinable).[171] After Giuliana finally gives birth to Raimondo, Tullio's fears materialize. Giuliana becomes increasingly associated with her bodily fluids, particularly blood, as she experiences a major loss of blood that puts her life in danger: "Vidi il lago rosso e, in mezzo, Giuliana boccheggiante" (I saw a pool of blood and, in the middle of it, Giuliana gasping); again, "Giuliana pareva morta, più pallida del suo guanciale, immobile ... Grandi macchie di sangue rosseggiavano sul letto, macchie di sangue tingevano il pavimento" (Giuliana seemed lifeless, paler than her own pillows, motionless ... Big bloodstains had reddened the bed and the floor).[172] Tullio is obsessed with "quelle macchie di sangue, tutto quel povero sangue sparso che aveva inzuppato i lenzuoli" (those bloodstains, all that spilled blood that had soaked the bedsheets).[173] While the constant proliferation of Giuliana's bodily fluids transforms her into an abject body, Raimondo, on the contrary, seems extraordinarily vigorous, potent, and vital – the obstetrician repeatedly exclaims, "Guardi che maschio!" (What a boy!) – as if he had fully consumed his mother's life force: "L'estrema debolezza le toglieva ogni moto, ogni segno di vita; la faceva sembrare esanime" (Extreme weakness prevented all movement, removed all expression of life, made her seem lifeless).[174]

The encounter between Tullio and Raimondo is framed as a Gothic story. The child appears physically deformed, almost inhuman: "La piccola faccia turgida, ancora un po' livida, con i globi oculati sporgenti, con la bocca gonfia, col mento obliquo, difforme, quasi non aveva aspetto umano" (The little puffed-up face, still somewhat livid, with protruding eyeballs, swollen mouth, slanting chin – that deformed visage had almost nothing human about it).[175] Tullio sees him as a "cosa ributtante" (repulsive thing) that elicits "ribrezzo" (disgust).[176] He is repulsed by the idea of physical touch: "Io sentivo che mi sarebbe stato impossibile toccare quella carne estranea" (It would be impossible for me to touch that strange flesh), and "provavo per tutta la pelle lo stesso raccapriccio che m'avrebbe dato il contatto d'un animale immondo" (I felt all over my skin the same thrill of horror that contact with an unclean animal would have caused me).[177] In spite of Tullio's hatred, Raimondo grows bigger and stronger: "Vidi il piccolo essere malefico che si gonfiava di latte, che prosperava in pace, senza alcun pericolo, circondato d'infinite cure" (I saw the little evil being who was growing fat on milk, who prospered in peace, without any danger, lavished with infinite attentions).[178] He earns his place in the family, becoming the real man while Tullio is marginalized and deprived of his masculine power. The only way of securing the health of both the mother and the family is to physically eliminate the vampire and dispose of his polluted body.

As Foucault argues, biopower establishes its domination over life and not over death, making it right to kill those who pose "a kind of biological danger to others."[179] According to him, the bourgeoisie's concern with its body is related to its hegemony. The "indefinite extension of strength, vigor, health, and life" of its body was significant because it represented "politically, economically, historically," but also biologically, the bourgeoisie's present and future.[180] Read through this lens, the corrupted blood of the racial other threatens to endanger the mother's body, contaminate Tullio's legacy, and, by extension, destroy the (feminized, weakened) body of the entire nation. This is why Tullio fantasizes about purifying Giuliana, decontaminating her organism, and revitalizing both her spirit and her body. This would entail a transfusion of blood. The question "chi le renderà tutto quel sangue?" (who will restore all that blood to her?) is answered with a fantasy of transfusion: "Come sarei felice se potessi trasfondere la metà del mio sangue nelle sue vene!" (how happy would I be if I could transfer half of my blood to those veins!), Tullio exclaims.[181] As Welch notes, after the evacuation of the other man's blood during labour, Giuliana would require a rush of Tullio's vital fluid: "Ella risorgerebbe a poco a poco, rigenerata, con un sangue nuovo. Parrebbe una creatura nuova, scevra d'ogni impurità." (She would resuscitate gradually, be regenerated with new blood. She would be like a new creature, freed from all impurity.)[182] If, in the unconscious mind, blood, as Ernest Jones writes in his *On the Nightmare* (1931), is commonly an equivalent for semen,[183] Tullio's desired transfusion is a way of sanitizing, de-vampirizing, and ultimately reclaiming Giuliana's tarnished body. The transfusion, however, is physiologically impossible, making the elimination of the vampire the only way, however partial, for Tullio to recover his masculinity and nourish a family legacy to change its direction. As in another contemporary short story involving vampirism, Morando's "Vampiro innocente" (1885) – in which a widowed father murders his son as soon as he realizes that the boy is assuming the form of a vampire, absorbing the vital essences of his sister and killing her – in *L'innocente*, Tullio must kill the monstrous intruder to protect himself and save the mother's body and the body of the state.[184]

Ultimately, in *L'innocente*, as in "Il dottor Nero" and "Un vampiro," the focus on male vampires deflects attention from the real menace subtly underlying the stories. Even when pushed into the background, female sexuality re-emerges by the back door, like a spectre that powerfully threatens the very essence of what it means to be masculine and, as a corollary, calling into question the credibility and stability of the new body politic. Questioning the virility of these men and their ability to provide for their families or defend their women from the attacks of foreign forces can thus be interpreted as a reflection of Italy's own intrinsic weakness and its lack of power, authority, and diplomatic weight.[185] In the context of the highly masculine-gendered Italian public sphere, then, vampire narratives intercept and engage with, rather than merely reflecting, cultural anxieties, opening spaces of horror that seem ultimately inescapable. The project of "making Italians" – which promised the normalization and harmonization of the social body, the reinforcement of accepted hierarchies of power and rigidly defined gender roles and relations, and the transition from dark to light, from a hostile world ruled by supernatural forces to an explainable, legible, and safer world that relied on the superior faculties and training of the physician or the criminologist – was ultimately frustrated. It is significant that, in the aftermath of his crime, Tullio is described as terrified by the possibility that the monster could escape and take his revenge:

"L'intruso non doveva uscire dalla sua stanza" (The intruder should not escape from his room), Tullio whispers while seeking to reassure himself. "Non poteva venire a perseguitarmi fin là dentro" (It could not come here and persecute me).[186] The natural world no longer seems like a safe place. The spectre of the contaminated, the monstrous, and the unknown would continue to loom large over Gothic Italy.

Conclusion

A Gothic presence lurks in the shadows of Italy's troubled path to modernity. Searching for, and trying to capture, what is inherently resistant, multiform, and unstable is inevitably a difficult, sometimes confusing, and even disorienting endeavour. With this book, however, I cast the familiar portrait of post-unification Italy in a new light, unveiling a truly Gothic place, a fragmented nation tentatively founded on ordering principles (normalization and hierarchization, policing of deviant behaviour, rationality) that are invariably contaminated by their disordering, Gothicized other (fluidity and transgression, violation of gender and power relations, supernaturalism). Gothic-inflected literature, especially that concerned with crime and deviance, represents an ideal territory for exploring how such intersections and collisions created the wider framework scaffolding the binary distinctions on which the modern state was built – the healthy and the diseased, the normal and the abnormal, the acceptable and the unacceptable – and where they found their form, sedimented, and eventually crystallized. Literary manifestations, from the most canonical to the most popular, are never neutral but always engage with the dominant discourses of the society producing them. The deep-seated idea that popular forms of fiction have the power only to placate cultural anxieties and displace them into the realm of fantasy has, for many years, prevented historians of modern Italy from examining narratives that, if read through different lenses and in dialogue with a diverse body of texts, can acquire new meanings and unleash their cultural potential, as I hope I have shown here.

The discussion in this book has illuminated the largely overlooked formal and thematic diversity of Italian Gothic narratives between approximately 1861 and 1914, bringing to light a literary landscape that was, and still is, a contested terrain, a field of cultural conflict marked by lingering ideological and aesthetical tensions. Far from being merely escapist and detached from reality, the vast corpus of Gothic stories that appeared in these years articulates a wide range of moral positions and speaks to many of the issues and anxieties that specifically troubled Italian society, ranging from class fluidity and cultural contagion to inborn criminal tendencies, aberrant sexual behaviour, female transgression, the crisis of masculinity and sexual potency, the lack of authority and state control, and positivist science's inability to develop a semiotics of the criminal body that would make deviance legible and understandable. The many stories that I have analysed were fully involved in the negotiation of power at the heart of the newborn nation. Gothic narratives reflect the contemporary scientific world, but they also contribute to the construction of science in the popular imagination. As a scientific discipline, positivist criminology is not a separate entity that operates on its own terms; rather, it is a form of knowledge production whose fresh understandings both affect and are affected by the wider society and culture. There is, then, a continuous cyclical process of influence and self-reflection within scientific and cultural disciplines that constitutes a complex channel of intercommunication.

In this conclusion, I do not wish to offer a final word on the Gothic in Italy or Gothic Italy, as attempting to do so would be presumptuous as well as counterproductive. I wish, instead, to look forward, provoke further discussion, and encourage other lines of research. The texts I consider in this book reveal the complex, and ambiguous, role of the Gothic in representing and exploring sites of dissension and spaces of subversion, as well as both policing and transgressing its own prescribed boundaries. Chapter 1 examined a series of texts, published between 1863 and 1884, that had radical and reformist intentions in that they aimed to spur the government to address the acute problems of crime, slum housing, and ill health. On the one hand, Italian authors denounced how the insanitary environments in which the underclasses were forced to live contributed to further physical and moral degeneration. On the other hand, despite their sympathetic attitude towards the poor and their supposedly denunciatory and challenging intentions, these authors ended up elaborating their versions of cultural and racial evolution and degeneration through semi-fictional formulations and theoretical discussions of the slums. The rhetoric of the Gothic was exploited to discuss various sociopolitical concerns, particularly those relating to class fluidity and infectiousness, but the final effect of this was the demonization of a vast range of racial and cultural others. Whether the prostitute or the vagrant, these others' deviant nature makes them socially dangerous, necessitating strict forms of surveillance, discipline, and control involving the techniques and technologies of the state. The attempt to document or catalogue the locales and inhabitants of the new nation was permeated by fears of contamination and infection sparked by proximity to those categories of contagion. The depiction of the poor themselves as an illness, a parasite that inevitably falls into the hands of evil and infects the rest of society, crystallized the image of the lower class as a foreign entity alien to the more progressive bourgeoisie; this depiction thus further popularizes the problematic concept of the dangerous classes, which would continue to figure in the rhetoric of novelists, criminologists, and sociologists in the following years. The body of primary literary sources considered in this chapter was, however, limited. Many more nineteenth-century texts and writers, from the most famous to the virtually unknown, would benefit from systematic investigation from more flexible perspectives, particularly transnational approaches, and much more needs to be discovered in terms of production and consumption, publishers and readerships. Considering the ambiguous interaction between science and popular fiction – with certain texts, as I have argued, having possibly influenced the direction of future anthropological research – an intriguing line of enquiry might be the role of the Gothic in the debates that took place leading up to the outbreak of the Second World War, with a particular focus on race and eugenics.[1]

Chapter 2 focused more explicitly on the fin de siècle, a period distinctly pervaded by fears of degeneration, devitalization, and feminization, to demonstrate how Gothic-infused literature engaged with dominant medical discourses regarding the mind of the criminal. The second section, which was devoted to a close reading of Giuseppe Bevione's "L'ossessione rossa" (1906), showed how literature was able to capture the fast-changing cultural climate in relation to what was increasingly perceived as aberrant sexual conduct, specifically homosexuality. It is my contention that this kind of text, subtly but deeply imbued with a rhetoric that pathologizes and criminalizes same-sex desire, helped fuel popular anxieties regarding homosexuality. These culminated in the intense politics of repression, during the Fascist regime, of those masculinities that fell outside the prescriptive boundaries of hegemonic masculinity, founded on the idea of virility. In the 1920s and 1930s, virility (or the lack of it) became central to what it meant to be good (or bad) Italians. As Barbara Spackman has famously written, "the cults of youth, of duty, of sacrifice and heroic virtues, of strength and stamina, of obedience and authority, and of physical strength and sexual potency that characterize Fascism are all inflections of that mater term, virility."[2] In the years following the First World War, when an enormous number of physically and mentally traumatized men returned home from the battlefields, the Fascist celebration of masculine virility also translated into the marginalization of war trauma in public discourse and the ensuing glorification of war's regenerative qualities and the heroization of the veteran. The peculiar sociocultural and political milieu of interwar Italy makes an exploration of the Gothic in this period especially worthwhile, perhaps homing in on the soldiers' and civilians' traumatic experiences of the war.[3]

Finally, chapter 3 considered the terrain of female deviance, showing how the Gothic operates in an ambiguous and contradictory way, both reasserting and troubling constructions of the deviant, monstrous woman. The narratives examined in the first two sections, concerned with femmes fatales and infanticidal mothers respectively, constitute a nuanced dialogue between an unquestioning representation of women and their bodies as threatening and an awareness of how such images serve to reinforce and strengthen a misogynistic and patriarchal view of the world. The Gothic female body in these narratives can ambivalently function, in the words of Marie Mulvey-Roberts, "as an ongoing critique of gender inequalities, though it can still reinforce the monstrosity of these figurations."[4] The third section focused on the male vampire, a figure that began to appear with unusual but significant consistency in Italian literature of the fin de siècle. This time frame was characterized by fears regarding the vigour and performativity of both the male body and the body politic, and in it the institution of marriage was receiving considerable public attention, with eight attempts – all frustrated – to introduce divorce into Italian legislation between 1878 and 1902. In these vampire narratives, as I argue, even when it is relegated to the margins of the story, female sexuality emerges from the shadows to destabilize ideas of male power and performativity and, by extension, to call into question the credibility and stability of a new body politic precariously founded on the rigid hierarchization of gender roles and relations. This chapter highlighted several potential areas of research that have remained largely untouched by scholars. Criminal women in Italian literature and science of the nineteenth and twentieth centuries have received little critical attention, and research on this topic would benefit from interdisciplinary and transnational approaches.[5] The study of the vampire in Italian culture has also been overlooked, except for a few notable contributions, in keeping with a tendency among scholars to neglect that which pertains to the realm of the occult in modern and contemporary Italy.[6]

It is worth noting at the end of this journey that many of the ideas, values, and practices that ripened and crystallized within the period covered by this book have continued to resonate widely in Italian culture and have never ceased to influence our attitudes towards transgression.

Significantly, a growing body of scholarship argues for the existence of strong continuities between the liberal and Fascist periods in terms of social policies, the development of the police forces, and the evolution of medical science and legal theory and practice. The studies of great scholars such as Mary Gibson, David Horn, and Jonathan Dunnage are well known.[7] However, even the work of historians who deviate somewhat from more established paths, such as that of the legal scholar Paul Garfinkel, eventually ends up reinforcing a familiar narrative, namely the nineteenth-century preoccupation with identification and social prevention, with the criminal rather than the crime, and with the dangerousness of criminals rather than their accountability, and such a narrative would have lasting implications.[8]

As part of the procedures for the criminal code reform that were set in motion in 1919, the Italian government created a commission charged with proposing a series of penal reforms that would serve to build "un più efficace e sicuro presidio contro la delinquenza abituale" (a more effective and sure defence against habitual delinquency), one that was "in armonia ai principi e ai metodi razionali della difesa della società contro il delitto in genere" (in harmony with the rational principles and methods for the defence of society against crime in general).[9] Significantly, it was Enrico Ferri, the most important of Lombroso's disciples, who drafted a revision of the criminal code in 1921. Although Ferri's draft never came into effect due to Fascism's rise to power the following year, the code authored by the jurist and politician Alfredo Rocco in 1930, as Horn has explained, takes as its principal object the defence of the body of society against the risks posed by its constituent parts.[10] The continuities between positivist and Fascist attitudes towards social prevention are also exemplified by the promulgation, in 1926, of the Testo unico delle leggi di pubblica sicurezza, which included numerous measures for maintaining social order and gave the police considerable powers to repress, control, and punish.[11] Prevention measures targeted "persone pericolose o sospette" (dangerous or suspicious persons), including vagrants, mentally unstable people, prostitutes, and many others, against whom "è autorizzato l'impiego diretto della forza pubblica" (the use of public force is authorized). The infamous policy of *confino di polizia*, an internal exile of between one and five years that could be imposed on anyone deemed to be "pericoloso alla sicurezza pubblica" (a danger to public security), was derived directly from the nineteenth-century policy of *domicilio coatto*, which allowed police to exile suspected offenders to island penal colonies with very limited judicial intervention.

The reality is that political events did not suddenly and radically change the contours of Italian medical and legal circles and that their most central figures remained influential after the Fascist seizure of power in 1922. After Lombroso's death in 1909, new generations of specialists, such as Benigno Di Tullio, Nicola Pende, and Giuseppe Vidoni, continued to apply and update his theories, while also expanding their journals and publications, obtaining university chairs, and gaining positions of power in parliament, the medical circuit, and the criminal justice system. All of this assured the popularity of positivist criminology throughout the Fascist period, which reached its "theoretical culmination," as Gibson suggests, in 1943 with the publication of the *Dizionario di criminologia*, edited by Eugenio Florian, Alfredo Niceforo, and Nicola Pende.[12]

These ideological affinities, connections, and points of convergence between positivism and Fascism have led scholars to identify clear and direct links between the criminological theories that matured within the context of liberal Italy, the rise of eugenics, and Fascist and Nazi politics of exclusion and extermination. Henry Friedlander, for example, observes, "The Nazi killers used the language of Lombroso to target the same victim groups."[13] Richard Weikart claims that positivist theories fed dictatorial regimes such as Nazism in Germany after the end of the First World War, which spread the idea that only through racial extermination could humanity improve biologically and advance to higher cultural levels, since the lower races were not mentally capable of producing culture.[14] Likewise, Joseph Crawford argues that, within the Gothicized world lying behind Lombroso's rhetoric, the otherness of marginalized groups appeared not as relative and situational "but as innate and essential, the result of a basic, ineffable monstrousness that could be erased only by extermination."[15] Correlation, however, does not imply causation, and the question of whether the trajectory that led from positivism to Fascist politics of extermination was an unavoidable one is still debatable. For one thing, Lombroso was neither a totalitarian (he was a liberal and a socialist) nor an antisemite (being Jewish himself). When the Fascists took over in 1922, Lombroso's daughters Gina and Paola, along with their husbands Guglielmo Ferrero and Mario Carrara, went into exile abroad or lost their university positions. On the other hand, it is undeniable, as Angelo Caglioti has shown,[16] that continuities between the two historical periods did exist and that the Fascist regime used the expertise of positivist criminologists as long as doing so served Mussolini's goals – namely, until the late-1930s Aryanist turn.[17]

The point I make here is the importance of Gothic narratives in the articulation, popularization, and recirculation of certain discourses on deviance. The enduring presence of such discourses was not simply a consequence of the long legacy of specific disciplines or branches –

Lombrosian criminology, for instance – but was, rather, due to their cross-disciplinary, trans-medial, and often transnational dissemination, which enabled them to penetrate more deeply into the realm of popular culture and to shape the perceptions and beliefs of the wider public. By escaping from their ostensibly scientific origins, medical and legal discourses on crime reappeared, in rearticulated and popularized guises, in literature, the popular press, both specialized and generalist journals, magazines, and reviews, facilitating the survival and proliferation of ideas, theories, practices, and values that were supposed to have dissolved or been surpassed. Although this book has neither delved into the interwar period nor offered any concrete comparisons between these different historical moments, it hopefully constitutes a valuable resource for understanding how a cultural climate that produced specific attitudes towards deviance, and was ultimately conducive to Fascism, developed and matured in the fifty years after Italy's unification.

Late nineteenth-century Gothic discourses involving innate evil, biological monsters, and ghosts that team up with diabolical human beings found their way into the ideology of eugenics and scientific racism, which continue to resonate widely and disturbingly in our world. It is remarkable that the spectral presence of the biology of crime, which lay dormant for a small portion of the twentieth century due to its association with Nazi politics, has never ceased to both fascinate and repulse and has recently resurfaced to haunt contemporary discourses on crime. Since the early 1980s, indeed, there has been a significant increase in scientific studies that again purport to trace the aetiology of crime to physical factors, without neglecting social components.

Neurocriminology, for instance, has provided evidence of how brain structures and functions are implicated in subjects with psychopathic traits, while molecular genetics has identified specific genes that apparently increase the risk of criminal behaviour.[18] The blossoming of studies on the interaction between genes and the environment has also led to an increasing number of attempts to read sexual orientation from the body by looking at, among other things, fingerprints, the size of the hypothalamus, or genetic markers on the X chromosome.[19] In 2016 and 2018, the news that DNA profiles from ancestry websites had been used in the United States to solve long-unsolved criminal investigations all over the world (these websites allow individuals to look up information about their genetic background by matching their DNA against publicly available DNA profiles).[20] In August 2019, Italian scientist Andrea Gamma at Harvard Medical School produced a large study that was extremely controversial, both in its scope and execution, on the genetic basis of sexuality. The Italian popular press rapidly capitalized on this by spreading the news that there is no "gay gene," spawning long and intense debates, particularly on social media.

Although the rise of the application of genetics to the study of deviant behaviour has been facilitated by moral discourses concerning addiction, as well as techniques in the fields of genetic engineering, neuroanatomical imaging, and virology, this complicated and alarming trend has its deepest roots in the historical period I analyse in this book. It does not come as a surprise, then, that historians of crime have increasingly turned their attention to the ways in which Lombroso's work anticipated the current genetic and neurological theorizations of crime.[21] These new studies have affected legal proceedings and court decisions across Western societies, especially in Italy, and their growing popularization by the media has changed the nature of the debate on the origin of transgression.[22] Contemporary criminology is once again tinged with the Gothic, and much Italian literature relating to crime today seems ready to intervene in these debates.

The narratives of authors and filmmakers such as Laura Grimaldi, Carlo Lucarelli, Sacha Naspini, Gianfranco Nerozzi, Barbara Baraldi, Dario Correnti, and Donato Carrisi, to name just a few, are all deeply concerned with both the roots of evil and the Gothic dimension of criminological research. The case of Lucarelli, who also co-authored several non-fiction books on infamous criminals with the criminologist Massimo Picozzi, is emblematic, but it is worth mentioning that the first novel by Dario Correnti, the pseudonym of two different authors, was *Nostalgia del sangue* (2018), which reprises the story of Vincenzo Verzeni, in which Gothic and criminological discourses intertwine. These popular narratives, with their obsessive focus on monstrous criminals whose behaviour often has unproblematic origins, border on the liminal territories of subversion and conservatism. However well they might lend themselves to collapsing rigid boundaries and breaking down societal taboos, they also have the potential to facilitate the propagation of conservative stereotypes, stigmatizing the other as embodying monstrosity and signifying dangerousness. While some of these narratives imagine and denounce the potential impact of controversial criminological research on present and future societies (the erasure of human agency, the loss of diversity, the disorienting and disempowering effects of racial discourses), they also often depict and problematically dramatize transgressive, non-normative acts, characters, and sexualities, thereby producing pathology and perversion that ultimately condemn and punish these potentials and possibilities and thus re-establish the dominant heteronormative view. Much scholarly work could be done in this area.

Notes

Introduction

1 See Demata, "Italy and the Gothic," 1.
2 Churchill, *Italy and English Literature*, 5.
3 See Williams, "Horace in Italy," 27.
4 Sade, *Journey to Italy*, 39–40, 190.
5 Moore, *View of Society and Manners*, 1:123.
6 Perkins, "Gothic Vision of Italy," 38.
7 Perkins, "Gothic Vision of Italy," 42.
8 See Abbate Badin, "Discourse of Italy."
9 Dickens, *Pictures from Italy*, 140.
10 Botting, *Gothic*, 20.
11 Punter, *Literature of Terror*, 1:1–19.
12 Hogle, "Gothic in Western Culture," 4, 3.
13 Aloisi and Camilletti, "Introduction," 2. There were specific epochs (and styles) during which Italian culture and literature exceptionally celebrated what is excessive, bizarre, grotesque, and even monstrous; the most relevant example is the Italian baroque. In this respect, see, among many others, Hanak, "Emergence of Baroque Mentality."
14 Camilletti, "'Timore' e 'terrore,'" 244.
15 The article is quoted in Corradi, "Gothic and the Historical Novel," 30–1.
16 Despite his words of disdain, Manzoni was fascinated with the Gothic tradition. *I promessi sposi* (1827) is strongly imbued with elements typical of the Gothic novel, such as ruined castles, superhuman villains, unspeakable passions, forced monachizations, and secret murders. On Manzoni's debt to the Gothic tradition see, among others, Giannantonio, "Manzoni e il romanzo 'nero'"; Frangipani, *Motivi del romanzo nero*; Camilletti, "Il sorriso del conte zio"; Saggini, "Gothic in Nineteenth-Century Italy."

136 Notes to pages 5–11

17 Manzoni, *Lettere*, vol. 7, bk. 1, 344. All translations from Italian into English in this book, including translations of text from literary and scientific sources, are mine.
18 Aloisi and Camilletti, "Introduction," 4–5.
19 See Camilletti, "Gothic Beginnings."
20 See Camilletti, "Authorship and Authority," 315.
21 In this respect, see Foni, *Piccoli mostri crescono*, 48.
22 For an account of the centrality of the problem of violent crime in post-unification political discourses, see Davis, *Conflict and Control*, 2; Marchetti, "Le 'sentinelle del male,'" 1028; Garfinkel, *Criminal Law*, 55.
23 Garfinkel, *Criminal Law*, 27.
24 Gibson, *Born to Crime*, 13.
25 See Di Scala, *Italy*, 141.
26 Among the numerous studies devoted to Lombroso and positivist criminology, see Bulferetti, *Cesare Lombroso*; Villa, *Il deviante e i suoi segni*; Gibson, *Born to Crime*; Frigessi, *Cesare Lombroso*; Horn, *Criminal Body*; Montaldo and Tappero, *Cesare Lombroso cento anni dopo*; Montaldo, *Cesare Lombroso*; Baima Bollone, *Cesare Lombroso e la scoperta dell'uomo delinquente*; Ystehede and Knepper, *Cesare Lombroso Handbook*.
27 Lombroso initially called this emerging field of study "criminal anthropology" to underscore the shift in focus from the criminal deed to the criminal man, but one of his disciples, the criminologist Garofalo, called it simply "criminology" in his seminal *Criminologia* and the term gained acceptance afterwards. Like most scholars, I will use the general label "positivist criminology."
28 Patriarca, *Italian Vices*, 25.
29 Garfinkel, *Criminal Law*, 27.
30 Esposito, *Immunitas*, 137.
31 Horn, *Criminal Body*, 34.
32 Horn, *Criminal Body*, 37.
33 See Frigessi, *Cesare Lombroso*, 54–7.
34 For an overview see Davie, "In All but Name"; Davie, *Tracing the Criminal*.
35 Gibson, *Born to Crime*, 56.
36 Gibson, *Born to Crime*, 3.
37 Gibson, *Born to Crime*, 99.
38 Horn, *Social Bodies*, 28.
39 Foucault, "Concept of the 'Dangerous Individual,'" 17, 18.
40 Napoleone Colajanni (1847–1921) was a criminologist and sociologist. He was arguably the most ardent critic of the Lombrosian school, as well as one of Italy's leading theoretical writers on socialism. Trained in medicine, Colajanni does not completely rule out biology in the aetiology of crime but argues that the poor's more accentuated tendency to transgress the

law derived principally from the dreadful conditions in which they were forced to live rather than from congenital alterations.
41 Rafter, *Criminal Brain*, 85.
42 Kelly Hurley was among the first to note potential connections between positivist criminology and the Gothic: "The topics pursued by nineteenth-century science," she argued in 1996, "were often as 'gothic' as those found within any novel." Robert Mighall too suggests that positivist criminology "may be considered a 'gothic' science" due to its "rhetorical and thematic affinities with aspects of the Gothic fictional mode." Hurley, *Gothic Body*, 20; Mighall, *Geography of Victorian Gothic Fiction*, 132.
43 Smith, *Victorian Demons*, 6.
44 Darwin, *Descent of Man*, 57.
45 Karschay, *Degeneration*, 38.
46 The concept of degeneration was formally conceptualized by the French psychiatrist Bénédict Augustin Morel (1809–73) "comme une déviation maladive d'un type primitif" (as a pathological deviation from an original/normal type). Morel, *Traité des dégénérescences*, 5. Karschay explains that, in nineteenth-century criminological discourse, the concepts of atavism and degeneration were different in theoretical terms: "Degeneration signals a devolutionary development from a higher evolutionary standard," while "atavism signifies an individual's incapacity to reach a given level of evolutionary perfection." However, such distinction "between an innate process of arrested development and a regressive one triggered by external circumstances never caught hold in the popular imagination, and fictions of degeneration tended to collapse the theoretical differences between the two concepts." Karschay, *Degeneration*, 39, 235n.
47 See Hurley, *Gothic Body*.
48 The power of Lombroso's science also derived from its strong visual dimension. As Rafter argues, "no criminologist has ever drawn more heavily on the visual or revelled more in the imagery of crime." Rafter, "Introduction," 130. In particular, his last works – the fifth edition of *L'uomo delinquente* (1896–7) is emblematic – are filled with horrific images and illustrations of delinquents, as well as representations of the tattoos, handwriting, and art of prison inmates. Lombroso's Gothic collection of objects is now held at the Museum of Criminal Anthropology in Turin, which includes coloured wax death masks, skulls, skeletons, and drawings of criminals' tattoos.
49 Rafter and Ystehede, "Here Be Dragons," 276.
50 Horn, *Criminal Body*, 30.
51 See Violi, "Storie di fantasmi."
52 See Ystehede, "Demonizing Being."
53 See Botting, *Gothic*, 135–54.

54 Not surprisingly, the few works that explore Gothic manifestations in nineteenth-century Italy have been written in English. See Del Principe, *Rebellion, Death, and Aesthetics*; Billiani and Sulis, *Italian Gothic and Fantastic*.
55 Farnetti, "Patologie del romanticismo," 360.
56 Orlando, *Il soprannaturale letterario*.
57 For Todorov, the fantastic is a threshold genre that relies heavily on the tension between the real and the imaginary. The fantastic is created in between these two notions, when a story introduces an event that seems not to respect the natural laws of our world without providing a conclusive explanation. If the event were to be satisfactorily explained, the narrative would stop being fantastic and fall into one of two closely related genres: the uncanny or the marvellous. He thus defines the fantastic as "a hesitation common to reader and character, who must decide whether or not what they perceive derives from 'reality' as it exists in the common opinion." Todorov, *Fantastic*, 41.
58 Calvino, *Mondo scritto*, 210, 224.
59 Calvino, *Mondo scritto*, 224.
60 Ghidetti and Lattarulo, "Prefazione," xii.
61 Contini, "Prefazione."
62 Lo Castro, "Introduzione," 8.
63 Camilletti, *Italia lunare*, 9. See Foni, *Alla fiera dei mostri*.
64 Ceserani, "Boundaries of the Fantastic," 41. Remo Ceserani, in his influential study *Il fantastico* (1996), deliberately refuses to discuss popular fiction because it apparently contaminates the supposedly pure identity of the form. See Ceserani, *Il fantastico*, 10.
65 Lazzarin, "Trentacinque anni."
66 Mighall, *Geography of Victorian Gothic Fiction*, 167.

1. Gothic Cities

1 Garfinkel, *Criminal Law*, 55. Italy had not yet experienced the shift away from violent crime that had been achieved by other modern European nations.
2 In 1879, Lombroso affirmed that there had been a rapid, disproportionate, and exceptional increase in criminal activities the previous year. See Lombroso, *Sull'incremento del delitto*, 4. In 1899, he argued that, whereas 15 per cent of the prisoners in 1870 had criminal records, in 1893 and 1894 this had increased to 41 per cent. See Lombroso, "Review of Alfredo Niceforo." It was not only positivist criminologists that perceived this rise in crime. Colajanni, for instance, noted in 1889 that homeless and jobless individuals had multiplied from the 1870s to the present, with many having begun their criminal trajectory as vagrants: as he points out, "l'oziosità, il vagabondaggio, preparano, educano al delitto" (idleness and vagrancy lead to and teach crime). Colajanni, *La sociologia criminale*, 2:478.

3 Between 1861 and 1889, the 1859 Sardinian-Piedmontese criminal code applied everywhere in Italy except for Tuscany, which retained its own criminal code, and the territories of the former Kingdom of the Two Sicilies. Article 450 of the 1859 code specified a sentence of three to six months in prison for vagrancy. With the promulgation of the 1889 criminal code, a legal distinction between idlers (who did not have a profession but had a stable residence) and vagrants (who were homeless) was finally established. Idleness did not constitute a crime (although idlers could be sentenced to three to six months in prison followed by police surveillance if they proved incapable of complying with an official order to find a stable job), while vagrancy was treated as a crime, punishable with three to six months in prison. See Verona, *Oziosi e vagabondi*, 8; Davis, *Conflict and Control*, 219–20. In 1865, soon after unification, the passing of special legislation allowed prefects to prohibit idlers and vagrants from living in certain areas, while also increasing prison sentences from five to six months and authorizing the Minister of the Interior to send repeat offenders to penal colonies for up to five years. See Ashley, "Misfits," 113; Verona, *Oziosi e vagabondi*, 41.
4 Discussions of the dangerous classes began to appear in France and Great Britain in the first half of the nineteenth century, when journalists, novelists, travellers, and reformers, such as Honoré-Antoine Frégier (*Des classes dangereuses*), Thomas Beames (*Rookeries of London*), and Henry Mayhew (*London Labour*), started writing analytically about the lower classes and the underworld, identifying the inequalities that generated a hopelessly marginalized and self-replicating underclass and explaining why it produced crime. In Italy, theorizations on the dangerous classes began in the early 1870s. See Bolis, *La polizia*; Curcio, *Delle persone sospette*; Locatelli, *Sorveglianti e sorvegliati* and *Miseria e beneficenza*; Alongi, *La maffia nei suoi fattori* and *Polizia e delinquenza in Italia*.
5 Bolis, *La polizia*, 459–60.
6 Wong, *Race and the Nation*, 155–6n.
7 In this book, I refer to disciplines such as eugenics or positivist criminology as science rather than pseudoscience for two reasons; first, very banally, because these disciplines were treated as science at the time and were indeed leading fields of research. Second, because, as Kyla Schuller writes, referring to them "as pseudoscience positions science as a transcendent form of knowledge that is independent from its shifting means of knowledge production." Schuller, *Biopolitics of Feeling*, 219n.
8 Nani, *Ai confini della nazione*, 17.
9 Giuliani, *Race, Nation and Gender*, 34.
10 Lacchè, "La paura delle 'classi pericolose,'" 171.
11 Benigno, "Ripensare le 'classi pericolose' italiane," 62.
12 Foucault, "*Society Must Be Defended*," 62. Foucault's theorizations of biopower and biopolitics can be found in various lectures delivered

between the mid- and late 1970s. See Foucault, *"Society Must Be Defended"*; *Security, Territory, Population*; and *Birth of Biopolitics*.
13 Foucault, *"Society Must Be Defended,"* 254, 255.
14 Foucault, *"Society Must Be Defended,"* 255.
15 Foucault, *"Society Must Be Defended,"* 61.
16 Foucault, *"Society Must Be Defended,"* 257.
17 Curcio, *Delle persone sospette*, 41, 29.
18 Alongi, *Polizia e delinquenza in Italia*, 190.
19 Locatelli, *Sorveglianti e sorvegliati*, 123.
20 Alongi, *Polizia e delinquenza in Italia*, 195.
21 Locatelli, *Sorveglianti e sorvegliati*, 67, 62.
22 Lacchè, "La paura delle 'classi pericolose,'" 169 (emphasis in the original).
23 Francesco Mastriani (1819–91) was one of the most prolific Italian popular novelists of the nineteenth century. He undertook medical studies in Naples but then turned to literature. His work documents Neapolitan customs and attitudes and paints a remarkable picture of social structures and conflicts in the city. The novels *I vermi* and *I misteri di Napoli* belong to what Antonio Palermo calls Mastriani's "trilogia socialista" (socialist trilogy), from the second phase of his literary career, approximately between the 1860s and the 1870s. See Palermo, *Da Mastriani a Viviani*, 110.
24 Matilde Serao (1856–1927) was a journalist, novelist, and, more broadly, one of the key figures of Neapolitan culture at the turn of the twentieth century. *Il ventre di Napoli* is the result of a collection of journalistic pieces originally written for the Roman *Capitan Fracassa* paper in 1884.
25 Lodovico Corio (1847–1911) was a historian and journalist and is mainly remembered for the sociological enquiry *La plebe di Milano*. It initially appeared in instalments in the journal *La Vita Nuova* between 1876 (issue 15) and 1877 (issue 29). It was then published as a single volume in 1885 with the title *Milano in ombra: Abissi plebei*. I quote from this edition.
26 Paolo Valera (1850–1926) was an anarchist, journalist, and writer influenced by the literary tradition of *verismo*. His *Milano sconosciuta* originally appeared on the pages of *La plebe* in 1878 from 26 March (no. 12) to 30 September (no. 38). It was published as a single volume the following year and reprinted with additions in 1898, 1908, and 1922. I quote from the first edition from 1879: Valera, *Milano sconosciuta*.
27 Giulio Piccini (1849–1915) was a journalist and writer who published a variety of novels under the pen name Jarro. *Firenze sotterranea* (1884) collects a series of articles that appeared in the moderate newspaper *La nazione* and was reprinted in 1885 and 1900. I quote from the 1900 edition: Piccini, *Firenze sotterranea*.
28 I largely borrow themes and imagery from the urban Gothic mode, a literary form in which the Gothic is relocated to those alarming and

threatening cities that emerged in the nineteenth century. The term and concept of urban Gothic is foreshadowed in Fred Botting's widely disseminated *Gothic*, 74–87. The most relevant theorization of the urban Gothic is that of Mighall, *Geography of Victorian Gothic Fiction*, 27–77. For a summary of these ideas see Robert Mighall, "Gothic Cities." See also Ridenhour, *In Darkest London*.

29 In the early nineteenth century, capitals such as Paris, London, and New York became the theatres of some of the most famous Gothic novels of the period, which have been classified under the loose category of city mysteries or urban mysteries. The genre includes novels such as Victor Hugo's *Notre-Dame de Paris* (1831), Charles Dickens's *Oliver Twist* (1837–9), Eugène Sue's *Les Mystères de Paris* (1842–3), Paul Féval's *Les Mystères de Londres* (1843), Eugène-François Vidocq's *Les Vrais Mystères de Paris* (1844), G.M.W. Reynolds's *The Mysteries of London* (1844–8), George Lippard's *The Quaker City* (1845), and Edward Zane's *The Mysteries and Miseries of New York* (1848). For an overview of the genre, see Maxwell, *Mysteries of Paris and London*; Knight, *Mysteries of the Cities*.

30 Sue's *Les Mystères de Paris* was translated into Italian in 1834, while Féval's *Les Mystères de Londres* and Vidocq's *Les Vrais Mystères de Paris* appeared in 1844 and 1845. See Sue, *I misteri di Parigi*; Féval, *I misteri di Londra*; Vidocq, *I veri misteri parigini*. From approximately the late 1840s, a massive number of specifically Italian urban mysteries were published. Examples include Govean and Borella, *I misteri di Torino*; Sauli, *I misteri di Milano*; and Barrili, *I misteri di Genova*.

31 For Enrico Ghidetti, Sue's model was deeply trivialized and essentially deprived of its sociopolitical quality by Italian writers. According to Quinto Marini, who considers Francesco Mastriani's *I misteri di Napoli* (1869–70) the only clear example of the genre because of its depiction of an opulent, decadent aristocracy and a lowest class of criminals and outcasts, the Italian urban mysteries remained a literary phenomenon and did not contribute to fomenting political unrest in the same way as such novels did in France, where many of the workers on the barricades were ardent readers of Sue's works. Brian Moloney and Gillian Ania subsequently enlarged the canon of Italian mysteries, although they demonstrated that most of them, particularly those published in the 1840s and 1850s, when the cities were still largely rural and industrially underdeveloped, are simply love or adventure stories that used the term "mysteries" in their titles just to maximize sales. These novels rarely focused on problems related to the growth of the city, such as overpopulation and the rise in criminal activity, but rather mainly focused "sulle tensioni dell'unificazione … e sul conflitto tra liberali accanitamente anticlericali e ecclesiastici parimenti animati da forti sentimenti antisocialisti" (on

the tensions of unification ... and on the conflict between fiercely anticlerical liberals and ecclesiastics equally animated by strong anti-socialist sentiments). Ghidetti, "Per una storia," 97; Marini, *I "misteri" d'Italia*, 10; Moloney and Ania, "Analoghi vituperî," 196. A new study on nineteenth-century Italian mysteries was published while I completed this manuscript: a special issue of the journal *Transalpina*, called "Les mysterès urbains en Italie," edited by Stefano Lazzarin and Mariella Colin. The volume features, among other things, one of my essays that presents some of the ideas that I have further developed in this book. See Serafini, "Gotico e misteri."

32 The exclusion of Rome may be cause for surprise. However, the novels set in Rome, which was formally annexed to the Kingdom of Italy only in 1870, rarely dedicate attention to the city and its problems. On the one hand, as Maurizio Ascari claims, pre-unification novels such as Bonaiuto Del Vecchio's *I misteri di Roma contemporanea: Romanzo storico-politico* (1851) and Franco Mistrali's *I misteri del Vaticano, o La Roma dei Papi* (1861) appropriated the formula of the urban mysteries as a propaganda tool to convey a pro-unification and pro-liberal political message. On the other hand, post-unification texts such as Pier Francesco Paolo De Dominicis's *I misteri del chiostro romano e la presa di Roma* (1873) and the anonymous *I nuovi misteri della corte di Roma* (1875) became vehicles for the expression of anti-clerical and anti-papal ideas. See Ascari, "Mysteries of the Vatican," 111; Moloney and Ania, "Analoghi vituperî," 195.

33 Given its potentially intriguing connections with other major Western cities such as Paris, London, or even New York, Naples represents an excellent case study for the exploration of urban mysteries through a wider transnational lens.

34 Ghirelli, *Napoli italiana*, 17–21.

35 See Cresti and Fei, "Le vicende del 'risanamento'"; Fei, *Firenze 1881–1898*; Luccardini, *Firenze*, 88, 108; Pellegrino, "Firenze noir."

36 See Bigatti, *La città operosa*, 143; Del Panta, *Evoluzione demografica e popolamento*. From 1871 to 1890, the population of Milan grew by an average of 6,300 residents every year from both internal growth and immigration, with the great majority of new residents belonging to the second category. In the period 1872–1901, 16 per cent of the population growth in Milan was due to internal population growth and 84 per cent was due to immigration. See Gallo, *Senza attraversare le frontiere*, 60.

37 Mori, "Police," 277.

38 Bigatti, *La città operosa*, 174; Mori, "Police," 279.

39 Ashley, "Misfits," 4.

40 Ashley, "Misfits," 132.

41 Curcio, *Delle persone sospette*, 4.

42 Bolis, *La polizia*, 460.
43 Locatelli, *Sorveglianti e sorvegliati*, 103, 101.
44 Mastriani, "Prefazione alla prima edizione," in *I vermi*, 1:5.
45 Corio, *Milano in ombra*, 15.
46 Curcio, *Delle persone sospette*, 3; Alongi, *Polizia e delinquenza in Italia*, 68–9.
47 Corio, *Milano in ombra*, 16.
48 In *I vermi*, Mastriani inserts entire journal articles, includes excerpts from the Italian penal code, and relies on statistics when talking about homicides. Mastriani, *I vermi*, 2:22, 149. Corio relies heavily on statistics as well, especially when discussing the problem of prostitution. Corio, *Milano in ombra*, 18–29.
49 Mastriani, *I vermi*, 1:25.
50 Valera, *Milano sconosciuta*, 33–4.
51 Serao, *Il ventre di Napoli*, 63.
52 Piccini, *Firenze sotterranea*, xxx, 201. Florence experienced sudden and invasive urban development, as well as the growth of new industrial sectors, particularly engineering, between 1865 and 1871, when it was the capital of the Kingdom of Italy. See Luccardini, *Firenze*, 88.
53 Locatelli, *Sorveglianti e sorvegliati*, 279.
54 Corio, *Milano in ombra*, 60.
55 Curcio, *Delle persone sospette*, 4.
56 Piccini, *Firenze sotterranea*, x, xi.
57 Valera, *Milano sconosciuta*, 40.
58 Valera, *Milano sconosciuta*, 212.
59 Mastriani, *I vermi*, 4:65, 3:10.
60 Serao, *Il ventre di Napoli*, 9.
61 Piccini, *Firenze sotterranea*, 190.
62 Locatelli, *Sorveglianti e sorvegliati*, 65.
63 Curcio, *Delle persone sospette*, 11.
64 Curcio, *Delle persone sospette*, 40.
65 Arcangeli, "Una Firenze non proprio sotterranea," 86.
66 Palermo, *Da Mastriani a Viviani*, 124.
67 Rosa, *Identità di una metropoli*, 239; Rosa, *Il mito della capitale morale*, 66, 87–8.
68 Piccini, *Firenze sotterranea*, 36.
69 Conti, *Firenze vecchia*, 438–9.
70 Valera, *Gli scamiciati*, iii–iv.
71 The works of Mastriani and Serao have been investigated through the lens of the Gothic, although the role of the city has never been taken into consideration. See Scappaticci, *Tra orrore gotico*; Gallo, "I fabbricatori di storie"; Fanning, *Gender Meets Genre*; Noce Bottoni, *Il romanzo gotico*.
72 Ridenhour, *In Darkest London*, 10.
73 Mastriani, *I misteri di Napoli*, 2:489; Reynolds, *Mysteries of London*, 64.

74 Mastriani, *I misteri di Napoli*, 2:206.
75 Mastriani, *La cieca di Sorrento*, 1:5.
76 Mastriani, *La cieca di Sorrento*, 1:6.
77 Maxwell, *Mysteries of Paris and London*, 16.
78 Serao, *Il ventre di Napoli*, 11 (emphasis in the original).
79 Serao, *Il ventre di Napoli*, 10.
80 This passage is taken from the second edition of the book, published in 1906, in which Serao inserted a new chapter to show how little the city improved after the operations of urban renovation that started in 1885. Behind its new facade, the labyrinthine nature of the Neapolitan streets has not changed. Serao, *Il ventre di Napoli: Vent'anni fa*, 108.
81 Piccini, *Firenze sotterranea*, 182.
82 Piccini, *Firenze sotterranea*, 41.
83 Piccini, *L'assassinio*, 71.
84 Piccini, *L'assassinio*, 119.
85 Maxwell, *Mysteries of Paris and London*, 15.
86 Piccini, *L'assassinio*, 38.
87 Freud, "Uncanny," 237.
88 Freud, "Uncanny," 237.
89 Piccini, *L'assassinio*, 11.
90 Vidler, *Architectural Uncanny*, 6.
91 Piccini, *Firenze sotterranea*, 88.
92 Williams, *Art of Darkness*, 18.
93 Ashley, "Misfits," 125.
94 Lombroso, *Delitti vecchi e nuovi*, 101.
95 Locatelli, *Sorveglianti e sorvegliati*, 130.
96 Florian and Cavaglieri, *I vagabondi*. Cavaglieri (1871–1917) received a law degree from the University of Padua in 1892 and established a law practice in Rome. There, he founded the *Rivista Italiana di Sociologia* with others in 1897. Florian (1869–1945) was a major jurist and politician at the time and held a number of different university positions in the fields of law and criminal procedure.
97 Florian and Cavaglieri, *I vagabondi*, 2:15.
98 Florian and Cavaglieri, *I vagabondi*, 2:34.
99 Florian and Cavaglieri, *I vagabondi*, 2:14. Riccardi was the author of *Dati fondamentali di antropologia criminale*.
100 Florian and Cavaglieri, *I vagabondi*, 2:14.
101 Foucault, "Society Must Be Defended," 61.
102 Schuller, *Biopolitics of Feeling*, 58.
103 Schuller, *Biopolitics of Feeling*, 58.
104 Foucault, "Society Must Be Defended," 61.
105 Stoler, *Carnal Knowledge*, 159.

106 Mastriani, *I misteri di Napoli*, 2:338.
107 Mastriani, *I vermi*, 1:160–1.
108 Serao, *Il ventre di Napoli*, 15; Serao, *Il ventre di Napoli: Vent'anni fa*, 98.
109 Valera, *Milano sconosciuta*, 48, 107; Corio, *Milano in ombra*, 52.
110 Corio, *Milano in ombra*, 49.
111 Forgacs, "Imagined Bodies," 376.
112 See Forgacs, *Italy's Margins*.
113 Piccini, *I ladri di cadaveri*, 230.
114 Piccini, *I ladri di cadaveri*, 168.
115 Sighele, *Un paese di delinquenti nati*, 6. Scipio Sighele (1868–1913), who trained as a lawyer under the supervision of Enrico Ferri, was a sociologist, criminologist, jurist, journalist, and literary critic who extensively explored group behaviour and the power of suggestion in the context of collective crime. His most important text was *La folla delinquente: Saggio di psicologia collettiva* (1891). This was followed by numerous other explorations of the psychological mechanisms of collective behaviour and the power of social suggestion, including *La coppia criminale* (1892), *La delinquenza settaria* (1897), and *L'intelligenza della folla* (1903). He taught at the universities of Pisa and Rome and at the Istituto di Scienze Sociali in Florence, and he taught courses in criminal sociology and collective psychology at the Institut des Hautes Études in Brussels.
116 Piccini, *Firenze sotterranea*, xxi.
117 Corio, *Milano in ombra*, 11.
118 Foucault, *Discipline and Punish*, 286.
119 Vaccaro, *Genesi e funzioni*, 7. Michele Angelo Vaccaro (1854–1937) was a jurist, criminologist, and sociologist who straddled both the positivist and classical schools of criminology.
120 Vaccaro, *Genesi e funzioni*, 221, 222.
121 Vaccaro, *Genesi e funzioni*, 217.
122 Vaccaro, *Genesi e funzioni*, 224.
123 Vaccaro, *Genesi e funzioni*, 223.
124 Cassata, *Building the New Man*, 9–42.
125 Penta, *Pazzia e società*, 69.
126 Morselli, "La rivendicazione," 277–8. Enrico Morselli (1852–1929) was professor of psychiatry at the University of Turin and one of the key figures in the field of eugenics in early twentieth-century Italy. He also published extensively on topics such as mesmerism, hypnotism, and spiritualism.
127 Mighall, *Geography of Victorian Gothic*, 65.
128 Corbin, *Foul and the Fragrant*, 142, 3.
129 Miller, *Anatomy of Disgust*, 248–52.

130 Serao, *Il ventre di Napoli*, 11; Valera, *Milano sconosciuta*, 63.
131 Arrighi, *Il ventre di Milano*, 7. As Del Principe observes, the authors belonging to the *Scapigliatura*, a literary and artistic movement that began in Northern Italy in the 1860s, "lived in perpetual conflict with a prospering bourgeoisie, to whom they attributed an unmodulated thirst for Industrialization and Progress," and responded to decaying Risorgimento ideals with anarchy, protesting Catholicism, capitalism, and militarism. Del Principe, *Rebellion, Death, and Aesthetics*, 11.
132 Arrighi, *Il ventre di Milano*, 9.
133 Corbin, *Foul and the Fragrant*, 58.
134 Baldwin, *Contagion*, 128.
135 Baldwin, *Contagion*, 148. See also Barnes, *Making of a Social Disease*, 24; Barnes, *Great Stink of Paris*.
136 Hamlin, *Public Health*, 60.
137 Hamlin, *Public Health*, 61.
138 See Servitje, *Medicine Is War*, 10–11.
139 Rosenberg, *Cholera Years*, 30.
140 See Chen, *Victorian Contagion*, 28.
141 The breakthrough for germ theory was Robert Koch's discovery of *Mycobacterium tuberculosis* in 1882 and his publication two years later of the criteria for determining whether a microorganism causes a disease.
142 Jenner, "Follow Your Nose?," 346.
143 Nixon, *Kept from All Contagion*, 3.
144 Serao, *Il ventre di Napoli*, 10.
145 Piccini, *Firenze sotterranea*, 185.
146 Mastriani, *I vermi*, 1:27.
147 Mastriani, *I vermi*, 1:27.
148 Forgacs, "Imagined Bodies," 376.
149 Corio, *Milano in ombra*, 42.
150 Serao, *Il ventre di Napoli: vent'anni fa*, 99.
151 Corio, *Milano in ombra*, 95.
152 Piccini, *Firenze sotterranea*, 23.
153 Piccini, *Firenze sotterranea*, 79.
154 Botting, *Gothic*, 11.
155 Hogle, "Introduction," 11.
156 It must be remembered, though, that, perhaps coincidentally, Serao touches on the true cause of the spread of cholera in Naples: polluted water.
157 Piccini, *Firenze sotterranea*, 11.
158 Corio, *Milano in ombra*, 6.
159 Corio, for instance, admits, "Eppure con un po' di carità si potrebbero disarmare tanti odii, ammansare tante ire, cancellare tanti rancori tra … classi di cittadini" (even so, a little charity would defuse much hatred, assuage much anger, and erase much rancour between … classes of

citizens). Corio, *Milano in ombra*, 8. Valera is the only one who rejects what he sees as another form of begging: "Dite quello che volete. Magnificate pure la generosità di quegli uomini che lasciarono in loro patrimonio per dare uno sdraio alla plebe; ma noi preferiamo ucciderci piuttosto che ricorrere a questa beneficenza." (You can say what you wish. You can even exalt the generosity of those men who left a part of their estate to give some relief to plebeians; but we would rather kill ourselves than perform such acts of charity.) Valera, *Milano sconosciuta*, 215.

160 Valera, *Milano sconosciuta*, 225, 228.
161 Mastriani, *I misteri di Napoli*, 3:548.
162 The dominant assumption that most diseases could be prevented and curbed if the living environment were kept clean, healthy, and free of all materials that specialists saw as damaging to health fuelled various government initiatives for slum cleansing and urban rebuilding that culminated in the enactment and enforcement of a series of public health acts in numerous Italian cities; Florence and Naples are two notable examples.
163 Mastriani, *I vermi*, 3:143, 4:168.
164 Serao, *Il ventre di Napoli*, 12.
165 Piccini, *Firenze sotterranea*, 22. Piccini, in the preface to the 1900 edition of his book, underscores his crucial role in this initiative and stresses the positive effects of sanitization and urban renewal on the problem of criminality. Piccini, *Firenze sotterranea*, xxiii–xxix. Attempts to renovate the urban structure took place in Naples as well in 1885. As Serao acknowledges in a revised version of her *Il ventre di Napoli*, published in 1906, behind its new facade – which was larger and more spacious – very little had actually changed. Serao, *Il ventre di Napoli: Vent'anni fa*, 92–3.
166 Esposito, *Immunitas*, 139.
167 Esposito, *Immunitas*, 140.
168 Berkowitz, "Morality Plays," 79. For the full context, see Berkowitz, *Crime of My Very Existence*.
169 Berkowitz, "Morality Plays," 83.
170 Berkowitz, "Morality Plays," 83.
171 Loria, *Le basi economiche*, 150–1, 155.
172 Garofalo, *Criminologia*, 113.
173 Fornasari di Verce, "La criminalità," 370.
174 Colajanni, *La sociologia criminale*, 2:452.
175 Colajanni, *La sociologia criminale*, 2:453, 447, 455, 487.
176 Alfredo Niceforo (1876–1960) was a criminologist, anthropologist, racial thinker, statistician, and one of the key proponents of Italian eugenics. He was the theorist of the two Italies, as he applied statistics to demonstrate the backwardness of Southern Italy and the intrinsic difference between Italians from the North and Italians from the South in *Italiani del Nord e*

Italiani del Sud. He also categorized different social classes according to biological and anthropological features. He equated savages with the lower class on the basis of similar physical and psychological defects. See Niceforo, *Les classes pauvres*, 3–4.
177 See Caglioti, "Race, Statistics and Italian Eugenics," 467.
178 Niceforo and Sighele, *La mala vita*.
179 Niceforo and Sighele, *La mala vita*, 20, 215–16.
180 Niceforo and Sighele, *La mala vita*, 13.
181 Niceforo and Sighele, *La mala vita*, 15 (emphasis in the original).
182 Niceforo and Sighele, *La mala vita*, 12. Rome was not the Italian city with the highest level of crime, but, as the two authors claim, it had hitherto been completely overlooked by criminologists, social reformers, and novelists: "Mentre si è – con maggiore o minore ampiezza – analizzata la criminalità di Palermo e di Napoli, e almeno sfiorata quella di Milano e di Torino, si è del tutto trascurata quella di Roma." (While the problem of criminality in Palermo and Naples has, to a greater or lesser degree, been analysed, and that of Milan and Turin at least touched upon, Rome has been completely overlooked.) Niceforo and Sighele, *La mala vita*, 29.
183 Niceforo and Sighele, *La mala vita*, 34.

2. Gothic Minds

1 Ashley, "Misfits," 150.
2 Ferri, *I nuovi orizzonti*, 118. Enrico Ferri (1856–1929), trained in criminal law, became one of the most important members of the school of positivist criminology. His approach to the study of criminal behaviour slightly diverged from that of Lombroso, as Ferri softened his master's emphasis on biological factors and posited that the aetiology of crime lay in a combination of three different factors – anthropological, telluric, and social. Ferri's classification of offenders formed part of what he called "sociologia criminale" (criminal sociology), which differed from both the classical school of legal thought and, to a lesser extent, criminal anthropology as defined by Lombroso. For an overview of Ferri's work, see Gibson, *Born to Crime*, 30–5.
3 Ferri, *I nuovi orizzonti*, 14.
4 Colajanni, *La sociologia criminale*, 1:450–1n.
5 Colajanni, *La sociologia criminale*, 2:121, 2:122.
6 A pioneering contribution is Guarnieri, "Alienists on Trial."
7 See Gibson, *Born to Crime*, 9–52.
8 By this, I certainly do not mean that the body of the criminal man was not central in literary texts – quite the opposite. However, this chapter is more concerned with the mind of the (male) deviant and the gradual internalization of the monstrous in Italian culture.
9 Mori, *Becoming Policemen*, 114.

10 Stoker, *Dracula*, 293.
11 Botting, *Gothic*, 10.
12 See Spooner, "Crime and the Gothic," 245–7.
13 American and British crime fiction scholars generally agree that the psychological thriller flourished only from the second half of the twentieth century as a response to various social, political, and cultural circumstances, including the unprecedented disruptions caused by the two world wars and the rise of aggressive ideologies and racial conflicts. See Horsley, *Twentieth-Century Crime Fiction*, 117. See also Rubin, *Thrillers*; Horsley, *Noir Thriller*; Packer, *Movies and the Modern Psyche*; Simpson, "Noir and the Psycho-Thriller"; Mecholsky, "Psychological Thriller in Context." Following in the footsteps of American and British commentators, Italian critics have also situated the birth of the Italian psychological thriller in the late twentieth century. A typical example is Carlo Lucarelli's *Almost Blue* (1997), which is told from three different perspectives, one of which is that of the serial killer. See Crovi, *Tutti i colori del giallo*, 135–6; Guagnini, *Dal giallo*, 111–12.
14 Lombroso, "Il tipo criminale nella letteratura," 352–4.
15 Ferri, *I delinquenti nell'arte*, 175–83.
16 Svevo, "L'assassinio." Italo Svevo (1861–1928) was one of the pseudonyms of the writer and playwright Aaron Ettore Schmitz, one of the most influential Italian novelists of the time. He is best known for the classic modernist novel *La coscienza di Zeno* (1923).
17 Svevo, "L'assassinio," 6. On the concept of the "inept" in Svevo, see Ghidetti, *Per un ritratto*; Baldi, *Le maschere dell'inetto*.
18 Gabriele D'Annunzio (1863–1938) was a poet, journalist, and novelist generally associated with the Decadent movement. He occupies a prominent place in Italian literature and culture between the late nineteenth and early twentieth centuries.
19 Ferri, *I delinquenti nell'arte*, 153.
20 Emilio De Marchi (1851–1901) was a popular Milanese writer. He is generally considered a follower of Manzoni and French naturalism. He saw literature as a vehicle for moral and spiritual improvement. His novels exhibit several elements typical of the *Scapigliatura*, including denouncement of the status quo, dissatisfaction with the Italian literary scene, and depictions of the complexities of human existence. Luigi Capuana (1839–1915) was a writer and critic. Born in Sicily, he is recognized as one of the most active *veristi* writers of the period and the most instrumental in introducing the principles of French naturalism into Italian literary culture. He was also particularly interested in spiritualism and other occult practices. As well as a variety of stories dealing with the supernatural, he wrote essays specifically devoted to this topic, including *Spiritismo?* and *Mondo occulto*.
21 See Horsley, *Noir Thriller*, 10.

22 Horsley, *Noir Thriller*, 8.
23 *Il marchese di Roccaverdina* has occasionally been referred to as a crime story, while *Il cappello del prete* occupies a seminal position in the canon of Italian crime fiction. Folco Portinari has categorized the latter as a pure *giallo*, the Italian term defining crime or detective novels, while Luca Crovi, Loris Rambelli, and Barbara Pezzotti have identified it as one of the founding texts of what would become the Italian school of detective fiction. See Portinari, "De Marchi"; Rambelli, "Il presunto giallo italiano"; Crovi, *Tutti i colori del giallo*, 33; Pezzotti, *Importance of Place*, 57.
24 De Marchi, *Il cappello del prete*.
25 Lombroso and Ferri, *Su A. Faella*.
26 Curiously, *L'ora* published twenty-two instalments, which corresponded to twenty-two of the novel's twenty-four chapters. Capuana first refers to *Il marchese di Roccaverdina* in February 1881 in a letter to fellow Sicilian writer Giovanni Verga. See Perroni and Perroni, "Storia de *I Malavoglia*," 129–30.
27 Adamo, "Mondo giudiziario," 85.
28 Capuana's novel contains strongly autobiographical material. I am especially referring to his relationship with a former household servant. She was married off to another man after having borne several of the author's children, who were subsequently relegated to the orphanage at Caltagirone. In this respect, it could even be argued that Capuana locates deviance and monstrosity within himself.
29 De Marchi, *Il cappello del prete*, 112, 227.
30 Briganti, *Introduzione a De Marchi*, 110, 111. Likewise, for Rambelli, the novel is "una parabola, un apologo. Il tessuto moralistico è evidente; più che la storia di un delitto, è una storia di castigo e di espiazione." (A parable, an apologue. The moralistic texture is evident; more than the story of a murder, it is a story of punishment and atonement.) Rambelli, *Storia del giallo italiano*, 127.
31 Pierangeli, *Emilio De Marchi*, 217.
32 Caccia, "Luigi Capuana," 2908; Cappello, *Invito alla lettura*, 123.
33 Madrignani, *Capuana e il naturalismo*, 271.
34 Foucault, *Will to Knowledge*, 56.
35 Foucault, *Will to Knowledge*, 59.
36 Brooks, *Troubling Confessions*, 112.
37 De Marchi, *Il cappello del prete*, 81.
38 Brooks, *Troubling Confessions*, 46.
39 De Marchi, *Il cappello del prete*, 45.
40 De Marchi, *Il cappello del prete*, 200–1.
41 De Marchi, *Il cappello del prete*, 130.
42 De Marchi, *Il cappello del prete*, 192.
43 Capuana, *Il marchese di Roccaverdina*, 102.

44 Pagliaro, "Crisi etica o analisi positivistica," 114.
45 Capuana, *Il marchese di Roccaverdina*, 83.
46 Barnaby, "Myth, History, and Hagiography," 108.
47 Capuana, *Il marchese di Roccaverdina*, 78.
48 Capuana, *Il marchese di Roccaverdina*, 314–15.
49 Capuana, *Il marchese di Roccaverdina*, 255.
50 Capuana, *Il marchese di Roccaverdina*, 254–5.
51 James Cowles Prichard (1786–1848) defined moral insanity as a "madness consisting in a morbid perversion of the natural feelings, affections, inclinations, temper, habits, moral dispositions, and natural impulses, without any remarkable disorder or defect of the interest or knowing and reasoning faculties, and particularly without any insane illusion or hallucinations." Prichard, *Treatise on Insanity*, 12.
52 See Lombroso, "Identità dell'epilessia," 1.
53 Lombroso, "Identità dell'epilessia," 9–13.
54 Lombroso, *L'uomo delinquente in rapporto all'antropologia, alla giurisprudenza ed alle discipline carcerarie* (1889), 2:427. See also Lombroso, *L'uomo delinquente in rapporto all'antropologia, alla giurisprudenza ed alla psichiatria* (1897), 2:542–3.
55 See Lombroso, *L'uomo delinquente in rapporto all'antropologia, alla giurisprudenza ed alla psichiatria* (1897), 2:539n.
56 Lombroso, *L'uomo delinquente in rapporto all'antropologia, alla giurisprudenza ed alla psichiatria* (1897), 2:17.
57 Lombroso, *L'uomo delinquente in rapporto all'antropologia, alla giurisprudenza ed alla psichiatria* (1897), 2:318–19.
58 Stewart-Steinberg, *Pinocchio Effect*, 212.
59 De Marchi, *Il cappello del prete*, 135.
60 De Marchi, *Il cappello del prete*, 248.
61 De Marchi, *Il cappello del prete*, 258.
62 Lombroso, *L'uomo delinquente in rapporto all'antropologia, alla giurisprudenza ed alla psichiatria* (1897), 2:308.
63 Lombroso, *L'uomo delinquente in rapporto all'antropologia, alla giurisprudenza ed alla psichiatria* (1897), 2:549.
64 Lombroso, *L'uomo delinquente in rapporto all'antropologia, alla giurisprudenza ed alla psichiatria* (1897), 2:214.
65 Lombroso, *L'uomo delinquente in rapporto all'antropologia, giurisprudenza ed alle discipline carcerarie* (1878), 106. See also Lombroso, *L'uomo delinquente in rapporto all'antropologia, alla giurisprudenza ed alle discipline carcerarie* (1889), 2:126.
66 Lombroso, *L'uomo delinquente in rapporto all'antropologia, alla giurisprudenza ed alle discipline carcerarie* (1889), 2:222.
67 In 1884, Lombroso and Capuana began an association that was to endure for the remainder of Lombroso's life when the criminologist wrote two letters to the novelist commending him for *Spiritismo?*, which had just

appeared. The two soon became friends, frequently exchanging ideas on both science and literature. Capuana's 1907 volume *Un vampiro*, collecting the eponymous short story and "Fatale influsso," features a fervent dedication to Lombroso. For further information see Di Blasi, *Luigi Capuana originale e segreto*, 151.

68 Zangara, *Luigi Capuana*, 68. According to him, "il delitto è concepito dal Marchese come una reazione, eccessiva certo e riprovevole, dall'offesa subìta dal suo orgoglio che non sorge soltanto dallo spirito tortuoso e duro della gelosia ma da egoismo dispotico inerente al prestigio della casta." (The murder committed by the marquis is the result of a reaction, however excessive and reprehensible, to the offense suffered by his pride. This reaction stems not only from a strong and contorted spirit of jealousy, but also from the despotic egotism that is inherent in the standing of the caste to which the marquis belongs.) Zangara, *Luigi Capuana*, 61.
69 Cavalli Pasini, *La scienza del romanzo*, 119.
70 Capuana, *Il marchese di Roccaverdina*, 32, 186.
71 Davies, *Realism of Luigi Capuana*, 146.
72 Capuana, *Il marchese di Roccaverdina*, 90.
73 Capuana, *Il marchese di Roccaverdina*, 96.
74 Capuana, *Il marchese di Roccaverdina*, 370.
75 Capuana, *Il marchese di Roccaverdina*, 375.
76 Lombroso, *L'uomo delinquente in rapporto all'antropologia, alla giurisprudenza ed alle discipline carcerarie* (1889), 1:623, 619.
77 There is an obvious relationship in *Crime and Punishment* between free will, responsibility, and blame that Lombroso and Ferri deliberately and cunningly refuse to take into consideration in their own studies on the novel – in "Il tipo criminale nella letteratura" and *I delinquenti nell'arte*, respectively. As Jeanne Gaakeer points out, "it would seem that Lombroso and his followers usurped Dostoevsky and adapted him to their own purposes when they depicted him as the painter of atavism." Gaakeer, "Art," 2369.
78 Foucault, *Abnormal*, 62, 60.
79 Foucault, *"Society Must Be Defended,"* 252; Foucault, *Abnormal*, 168.
80 As is well known, "serial murder" is a new term, originally coined in the early 1980s when the FBI launched a large-scale initiative at its training academy in Quantico, Virginia, to document, study, and investigate repeat killers, classifying multiple homicides into mass, spree, and serial murders. In 2005, the FBI's renamed Behavioral Analysis Unit conducted a discussion of the definition of serial murder, which is now "the unlawful killing of two or more victims by the same offender(s) in separate events." Fox and Levin, *Extreme Killing*, 25.
81 The murders committed by Jack the Ripper resonated strongly in Italy. Various booklets focusing on this serial killer appeared during this period,

including *Jack l'assassino di Londra detto lo sventratore di donne* (1888), republished in 1901 as *Jack, lo sventratore di Londra: Racconto storico*, and *Jack lo sventratore di donne a Londra* (1891). Daniele Oberto Marrama's "Il compagno di viaggio," a short story that appeared in issue 29 of the journal *La Domenica del Corriere* of 1905, is an enjoyable parody of Jack the Ripper's murders that testifies to the long-lasting fascination with this historical figure. Marrama (1874–1912) was a Neapolitan journalist and writer who collaborated with journals such as *Il Mattino*, *La Settimana*, and *Il Giorno*. He wrote several short stories for *La Domenica del Corriere* that combine crime with supernatural and detective elements. Some of these texts were then collected in the volume *Il ritratto del morto*, which appeared with a preface by Matilde Serao.

82 Lee Six and Thompson, "From Hideous to Hedonist," 248.
83 The novel was first rediscovered as a Gothic/fantastic text in 2009 by Claudio Gallo and Fabrizio Foni, who inserted a significant excerpt of it in their volume *Ottocento nero italiano*, 425–45.
84 De Amicis, *La moralità del male*, 5. Ugo De Amicis (1879–1962) was the son of the better-known Edmondo and produced a variety of texts, including novels, short stories, and anecdotes. *La moralità del male*, an insightful enquiry into the terrain of the psyche, is arguably his most intriguing novel.
85 Bevione, "L'ossessione rossa." First printed in *La Lettura* 6, no. 2 (1906): 118–25. Giuseppe Bevione (1879–1976) was an important figure in the political and journalistic climate of twentieth-century Italy. In 1923, after having converted to Fascism, he became director of the newspaper *Il Secolo* and was then nominated senator. This short story is one of his few incursions into the territory of literary fiction. A brief analysis of "L'ossessione rossa," which also refers to the figure of Vincenzo Verzeni, is contained in Foni, *Alla fiera dei mostri*, 84–95.
86 Bevione, "L'ossessione rossa," 401.
87 See Beccalossi, "'Italian Vice.'"
88 See Pozzo, "Male Homosexuality."
89 Benadusi, *Enemy of the New Man*, 91–6.
90 Guaiana and Seymour, "From Giarre to Civil Unions," 168.
91 Duncan, *Reading and Writing Italian Homosexuality*, 20.
92 Richard von Krafft-Ebing (1840–1902) was a dominant figure in nineteenth-century psychiatry and a founder of the study of human sexuality. His seminal *Psychopathia Sexualis: Eine klinische-forensische Studie* (1886), which went through twelve editions after its initial publication, investigates the relationship of various sex crimes to insanity and had a significant influence on subsequent understandings of sexual deviancy. Havelock Ellis (1859–1939) was an English physician and social reformer

who extensively studied human sexuality. His *The Criminal* (1890) served to spread Lombrosian ideas in Great Britain. The first volume of his *Studies in the Psychology of Sex*, which was originally published in 1897, was also devoted to homosexuality.
93 See Ashley, "Misfits," 190.
94 Krafft-Ebing, *Psychopathia Sexualis*, 326. Lombroso sponsored the highly respected medical publishing house Bocca's publication of the Italian translation of the book in 1889, and he wrote the introduction. Krafft-Ebing developed the idea of homosexuality as a form of degeneration in an article originally published in 1877. Krafft-Ebing, "Über gewisse Anomalies."
95 Krafft-Ebing, *Psychopathia Sexualis*, 328.
96 Tamassia, "Sull'inversione dell'istinto sessuale." Arrigo Tamassia (1848–1917) graduated in medicine from the University of Pavia in 1873 and became Lombroso's assistant. After completing his training in legal medicine in Berlin, Paris, and Vienna, he was appointed professor of legal medicine at the University of Pavia in 1876. In 1875, he translated Henry Maudsley's seminal *Responsibility in Mental Disease* (1874). He coined and popularized the concept of "inversione dell'istinto sessuale" (sexual inversion), which was subsequently used in France, Great Britain, and the United States by the most important specialists of the time. For an overview of Tamassia's life and work, see Beccalossi, "Arrigo Tamassia."
97 Tamassia, "Sull'inversione dell'istinto sessuale," 97.
98 Tamassia, "Sull'inversione dell'istinto sessuale," 101–2.
99 Tamassia, "Sull'inversione dell'istinto sessuale," 115, 117.
100 Tamassia, "Sull'inversione dell'istinto sessuale," 117. Tamassia would later stress anew the close relationship between "sexual inversion" and criminality in an article that appeared in 1906, the year Bevione's short story was published. See Tamassia, *L'inversione dell'istinto sessuale*.
101 Beccalossi, "Sexual Deviancies."
102 Lombroso, "L'amore nei pazzi."
103 Lombroso, "L'amore nei pazzi," 24–7.
104 Beccalossi, "Madness and Sexual Psychopathies," 316.
105 Lombroso, *L'uomo delinquente in rapporto all'antropologia, alla giurisprudenza ed alle discipline carcerarie* (1889), 1:593.
106 The journal remained in print for only one year, but it was received very favourably by the international scientific community, as shown by the contribution of several influential specialists, including Ellis and Krafft-Ebing.
107 See Beccalossi, "Madness and Sexual Psychopathies," 319.
108 Lombroso, *L'uomo delinquente in rapporto all'antropologia, alla giurisprudenza ed alle discipline carcerarie* (1889), 1:120.
109 See Beccalossi, "Madness and Sexual Psychopathies," 322.

110 Tanzi, *Trattato delle malattie mentali*, 2:672. Eugenio Tanzi (1856–1934) was one of the most important and influential Italian psychiatrists of his time. He studied medicine at the Universities of Padua and Graz and became professor of psychiatry at the University of Cagliari in 1893 and at the University of Florence in 1895. He remained at the University of Florence for the rest of his career. He was a pioneer in experiments on neurology and neuropsychology.
111 Tanzi, *Trattato delle malattie mentali*, 2:673.
112 Bevione, "L'ossessione rossa," 402.
113 Bevione, "L'ossessione rossa," 403.
114 Bevione, "L'ossessione rossa," 402.
115 See Jung, "Hereditary Tendency in Insanity," 106.
116 Esquirol, *Mental Maladies*, 49.
117 Beccalossi, *Female Sexual Inversion*, 61.
118 Binet, "Le fétichisme," 153, 166–7. For an analysis of the topic, see Nye, "Medical Origins of Sexual Fetishism."
119 Krafft-Ebing, *Psychopathia Sexualis*, 211.
120 Bevione, "L'ossessione rossa," 403.
121 Bevione, "L'ossessione rossa," 406.
122 Bevione, "L'ossessione rossa," 406 (emphasis in the original).
123 Bevione, "L'ossessione rossa," 408.
124 Bevione, "L'ossessione rossa," 407.
125 Bevione, "L'ossessione rossa," 412, 413.
126 Bevione, "L'ossessione rossa," 412.
127 Krafft-Ebing, *Psychopathia Sexualis*, 327–8.
128 Ellis, "Note sulle facoltà artistiche," 243.
129 Lombroso, "Du parallélisme."
130 Ashley, "*Misfits*," 193.
131 Krafft-Ebing, *Psychopathia Sexualis*, 326.
132 Lombroso, "L'amore nei pazzi," 27.
133 In the 1889 edition of *L'uomo delinquente*, Lombroso includes a long chapter on the concept of epilepsy and the figure of the epileptic criminal, a variation of the born criminal, with whom several traits are shared. See Lombroso, *L'uomo delinquente in rapporto all'antropologia, alla giurisprudenza ed alle discipline carcerarie* (1889), 2:1–116.
134 Chevalier, *L'inversion sexuelle*, 354–6.
135 Bevione, "L'ossessione rossa," 411.
136 Lombroso, *L'uomo delinquente in rapporto all'antropologia, alla giurisprudenza ed alle discipline carcerarie* (1889), 2:21.
137 Bevione, "L'ossessione rossa," 413.
138 Lombroso, *L'uomo delinquente in rapporto all'antropologia, alla giurisprudenza ed alle discipline carcerarie* (1889), 2:21.
139 See Beccalossi, *Female Sexual Inversion*, 159.

140 Bevione, "L'ossessione rossa," 412.
141 Homosexuality was "antithetical to the regime's project of transforming Italians into a race of virile warriors who would lead the military expansion of the new Fascist empire, one of Mussolini's fundamental goals." Ebner, "Persecution of Homosexual Men," 140. Even without reintroducing anti-homosexual laws, a hostile regime still had many tools at its disposal to prosecute homosexual men. See Benadusi, *Enemy of the New Man*.
142 A partial exception is represented by one of the very first Italian novels centred on a vampiric figure, Franco Mistrali's *Il vampiro* (1869). This novel owes more to Eastern European folklore than the British Gothic but is nonetheless centred on the power of blood. See Mistrali, *Il vampiro*.
143 Waltje, *Blood Obsession*, 2. See also Picart and Greek, "Compulsions."
144 See Centini, *Il vampiro della Padania*, 52.
145 Krafft-Ebing, *Psychopathia Sexualis*, 86.
146 See Lombroso, *Verzeni e Agnoletti*; Lombroso, "L'amore nei pazzi," 11–12.
147 For an account of the trial, see "Vincenzo Verzeni lo sventratore di donne."
148 Krafft-Ebing, *Psychopathia Sexualis*, 87–8.
149 Krafft-Ebing, *Psychopathia Sexualis*, 88, 89.
150 Penta, *I pervertimenti sessuali*, 153.
151 Penta, *I pervertimenti sessuali*, 46.
152 See Lombroso, "L'amore nei pazzi," 11–12.
153 Lombroso, *L'uomo delinquente in rapporto all'antropologia, alla giurisprudenza ed alle discipline carcerarie* (1889), 2:74.
154 Krafft-Ebing, *Psychopathia Sexualis*, 90.
155 Krafft-Ebing, *Psychopathia Sexualis*, 89–90.
156 The process of killing, Penta explicitly claims, is a substitute for sex. See Penta, *I pervertimenti sessuali*, 69.
157 Cusson and Proulx, "Motivation and Criminal Career," 144.
158 Tamassia, "Sull'inversione dell'istinto sessuale," 117.
159 Penta, *I pervertimenti sessuali*, 50, 43. Among these anomalies, already identified by Lombroso, Penta mentions the following: "La volta del frontale e la maggior parte del parietale destro sono abbassate ... il seno frontale destro invece e la porzione interna dell'arcata orbitaria omonima, sono molto sviluppati" (the frontal skull bones and most of the right parietal bones are depressed ... the right frontal sinus, on the other hand, and the internal portions of the brow ridge of the same are well developed). Penta, *I pervertimenti sessuali*, 50.
160 See "Vincenzo Verzeni lo sventratore di donne," 89. At the end of the trial, Lombroso admitted that he could not find any abnormalities; to the Court of Assizes in Bergamo, he gave the verdict that, in general, Verzeni

acted normally, except of course when committing his crimes, though he managed to regain the shroud of normalcy afterwards.
161 Most contemporary Italian books on serial killers, whether academic or popular, deal extensively with Verzeni's case. See Fornari and Birkhoff, *Serial Killer*, 5–26; Lucarelli and Picozzi, *Serial Killer*, 9–23; Vronsky, *Serial Killer*, 58–61; Lupi, *Serial killer italiani*, 45–50.

3. Gothic Bodies

1 During this period, crime journals started to offer a larger variety of contributions on women, while the number of books devoted to the subject increased. Examples include Lombroso and Ottolenghi, *La donna delinquente*; Gurrieri, *Sensibilità e anomalie fisiche*; Lombroso and Ferrero, *La donna delinquente*; Sergi, "La donna normale"; Moraglia, "Nuove ricerche su criminali"; De Blasio, *Anomalie multiple*. For an overview of the development of theories of crime about women in fin de siècle Italy, see Gibson, *Born to Crime*, 53–95. See also Babini, "Il lato femminile."
2 See Gibson, *Born to Crime*, 55; and Gibson, *Prostitution and the State*.
3 Lombroso and Ferrero define the normal woman as a "semi-criminaloide innocua" (innocuous quasi-criminaloid). Lombroso and Ferrero, *La donna delinquente*, 434.
4 Mazzoni, "Impressive Cravings, Impressionable Bodies," 153.
5 Sergi, "Sensibilità femminile."
6 Gibson and Rafter, "Editors' Introduction," 3. For an analysis of the legacy of Lombroso's theories on criminal women in Italian society, see Azara and Tedesco, *La donna delinquente*.
7 Lombroso and Ferrero, *La donna delinquente*, 467.
8 Lombroso and Ferrero, *La donna delinquente*, 319–20, 467.
9 Lombroso and Ferrero, *La donna delinquente*, 434.
10 Amoia, *No Mothers We!*, 67.
11 Neera and Mantegazza, *Dizionario d'igiene*, 221, 102, 225.
12 See Gibson, *Born to Crime*, 53–95.
13 Carrino, *Luride, agitate, criminali*, 75.
14 Horn, *Criminal Body*, 142 (emphasis in the original).
15 Foucault, "Concept of the 'Dangerous Individual,'" 14.
16 Horn, *Social Bodies*, 15.
17 See Foucault, *History of Sexuality*, vol. 1, *Introduction*, 104.
18 Ward, "Legislating for Human Nature," 69.
19 See Canonico, *Introduzione*, 304; Scarlata, *La imputabilità*, 49; Vignoli, "Note intorno."
20 Scarfoglio, *Il processo di Frine*. Edoardo Scarfoglio (1860–1917) was a writer, particularly a practitioner of realism, and a journalist. He is now

mainly remembered as the husband of Matilde Serao, one of the most important writers of the time, and the couple founded the Neapolitan newspaper *Il Mattino*, which remains to this day the largest daily newspaper in the city.

21 Scarfoglio, *Il processo di Frine*, 68–9.
22 Scarfoglio, *Il processo di Frine*, 70.
23 Fusaro, *La nevrosi*, 217.
24 Verga, *La lupa*.
25 For an interesting examination of this short story and its relation to the cultural, mythical, and anthropological heritage of the symbol of the she-wolf, see Klein, "When Good Girls Go Bad."
26 Lombroso and Ferrero, *La donna delinquente*, 467.
27 Examples include Ida in Alfredo Oriani's *No* (1881), the Countess Livia in Camillo Boito's *Senso* (1883), Irene in Gaetano Chelli's *L'eredità Ferramonti* (1883), Lavinia in Enrico Annibale Butti's *L'automa* (1892), and Ginevra in D'Annunzio's *Giovanni Episcopo* (1892).
28 For more information on the femme fatale, see Allen, *Femme Fatale*; Dijkstra, *Idols of Perversity*; Dijkstra, *Evil Sisters*; Craciun, *Fatal Women of Romanticism*; Menon, *Evil by Design*.
29 Allen, *Femme Fatale*, vii.
30 D'Annunzio, *Trionfo della morte*.
31 D'Annunzio, *Trionfo della morte*, 30, 184.
32 Doane, *Femmes Fatales*, 2 (emphasis in the original).
33 Doane, *Femmes Fatales*, 2–3.
34 Stott, *Fabrication*, 54.
35 D'Annunzio, *Trionfo della morte*, 80.
36 D'Annunzio, *Trionfo della morte*, 280.
37 D'Annunzio, *Trionfo della morte*, 280.
38 D'Annunzio, *Trionfo della morte*, 274.
39 D'Annunzio, *Trionfo della morte*, 274.
40 D'Annunzio, *Trionfo della morte*, 314.
41 D'Annunzio, *Trionfo della morte*, 376.
42 D'Annunzio, *Trionfo della morte*, 376.
43 Barisonzi, "Motherhood, Sexuality and Beauty," 516.
44 Kristeva, *Powers of Horror*, 54.
45 McAfee, "Abjection," 46.
46 D'Annunzio, *Trionfo della morte*, 376.
47 Moraglia, "Nuove ricerche su criminali," 323.
48 D'Annunzio, *Trionfo della morte*, 370.
49 Bronfen, "Femme Fatale," 106.
50 Carolina Invernizio (1851–1916) was arguably the most popular Italian writer from the late nineteenth and the early twentieth centuries. She

made her debut in 1876 and wrote more than a hundred novels that blend the Gothic, crime, sensationalism, and melodrama. In her stories, which pivot on guilty secrets and in which coincidences multiply, she depicts deeply contrasting psychological types, staging an inexorable duel between the incompatible principles of good and evil. Among the few studies devoted to her writing, see Eco, *Carolina Invernizio*; Bonino and Ioli, *Carolina Invernizio*; Cantelmo, *Carolina Invernizio*.

51 Mitchell, *Italian Women Writers*, 6.
52 Invernizio, "Le operaie italiane."
53 Lepschy, "Popular Novel," 177.
54 Invernizio, *Peccatrice moderna*, 14.
55 Invernizio, *Peccatrice moderna*, 330.
56 Invernizio, *Peccatrice moderna*, 21.
57 Invernizio, *Peccatrice moderna*, 118.
58 Lombroso and Ferrero, *La donna delinquente*, 568.
59 Lombroso and Ferrero, *La donna delinquente*, 569.
60 Invernizio, *Peccatrice moderna*, 130.
61 Invernizio, *Peccatrice moderna*, 194.
62 Invernizio, *Peccatrice moderna*, 343.
63 Lombroso and Ferrero, *La donna delinquente*, 437, 435.
64 Gibson, *Born to Crime*, 56.
65 Scholarly texts that examine the problem of infanticide in late nineteenth- and early twentieth-century Italy at the intersection of medicine and criminal law include Selmini, *Profili*; Guarnieri, *L'ammazzabambini*; Guarnieri, "Madri che uccidono"; Stewart-Steinberg, *Pinocchio Effect*, 184–228; Guarnieri, "Men Committing Female Crimes"; Chiletti, "Infanticide and the Prostitute."
66 Chiletti, "Infanticide and the Prostitute," 144. Further information on the phenomenon of the abandonment of children can be found in De Rosa, *Il baule di Giovanna*; Rampinelli, *Storie di abbandoni*; Tapaninen, "Motherhood through the Wheel."
67 Modifications to the 1859 code include changes to article 525, which defined infanticide as the killing of a child recently born and not yet baptized, and to article 532, which made compulsory the extenuating circumstances for the infanticidal mother when the offspring is illegitimate.
68 The Tuscan Penal Code of 1853, in force in that region until 1889, does not explicitly make provision for the element of honour, although it laid down a maximum sentence of twenty years' imprisonment for infanticide. The Sardinian-Piedmontese Code of 1859, although it made provision for the justification of *causa d'onore*, nonetheless allowed the death penalty for such crimes.
69 Stewart-Steinberg, *Pinocchio Effect*, 190.

70 Carrara, *Programma del corso*, 293–352. Francesco Carrara (1805–88) was a jurist and politician and one of the leading exponents of the so-called classical school of legal thought, which was rooted in Beccaria's theorizations. He taught criminal law at the University of Lucca, where he gained his doctorate, and the University of Pisa. He became one of the most important European experts in criminal law in the 1860s and 1870s, and his theses had a major impact on the 1889 criminal code.
71 Carrara, *Programma del corso*, 302.
72 Carrara, *Programma del corso*, 341.
73 Ferriani, *La infanticida*, 110–11 (emphasis in the original).
74 Ferriani, *La infanticida*, 111.
75 Sighele, "Sull'infanticidio," 190.
76 Shapiro, *Breaking the Codes*, 133. See also Goc, *Women, Infanticide, and the Press*.
77 Puerperal mania was documented as early as 1820 in the Anglophone world. However, there was little consensus regarding its symptoms and how and by whom they should be treated. See Marland, "Getting Away with Murder?," 174.
78 See Guarnieri, "Madri che uccidono," 147; Gentilomo, Burgazzi, and Bertolini, "L'infanticidio"; Chiletti, "Infanticide and Mental Illness."
79 See Stewart-Steinberg, *Pinocchio Effect*, 184–228.
80 Chiletti, "Infanticide and the Prostitute," 145.
81 Chiletti, "Infanticide and the Prostitute," 153–5. See Stoppato, *Infanticidio e procurato aborto*; Arena, *L'infanticidio*.
82 Lombroso and Ferrero, *La donna delinquente*, 495.
83 Lombroso and Ferrero, *La donna delinquente*, 495–7.
84 Lombroso and Ferrero, *La donna delinquente*, 492–3.
85 Lombroso and Ferrero, *La donna delinquente*, 509.
86 Impallomeni, *L'omicidio nel diritto penale*, 551.
87 Chiletti, "Infanticide and the Prostitute," 157–8.
88 See, among others, Groppi, "Il teatro della giustizia"; Simpson, *Murder and Media*.
89 See "Infanticide assolte"; "Un processo per infanticidio"; "Una domestica infanticida"; "Infanticidio," *Gazzetta Piemontese*; "Condanna di un'infanticida."
90 "Un atroce infanticidio."
91 "Processo per infanticidio."
92 "Infanticidio," *Il Corriere della Sera*. The woman was eventually sentenced to two years and six months in prison.
93 "Solita storia."
94 "Per infanticidio."

95 Mastriani, *La Medea di Porta Medina*. As is clear from the title, the reference to the Greek myth of Medea frames Mastriani's novel as a case of infanticide. In Euripides's tragedy, Medea murders her children as an act of revenge against her unfaithful husband. The crime has historically crystallized the image of Medea as the infanticidal mother. For further information, see Pedrazzini, *Medea*.
96 See *Dizionario delle leggi*.
97 Invernizio, *Storia d'una sartina*. The novel is also analysed in Truglio, *Beyond the Family Romance*, 86. Chapter 3 (83–106) contains references to the writings of, among others, Lombroso, Capuana, and D'Annunzio on infanticide.
98 Invernizio, *Storia d'una sartina*, 63.
99 Guarnieri, "Forzate analogie," 51.
100 Mastriani, *La Medea di Porta Medina*, 18.
101 Mastriani, *La Medea di Porta Medina*, 19.
102 Mastriani, *La Medea di Porta Medina*, 260.
103 Invernizio, *Storia d'una sartina*, 47.
104 Mastriani, *La Medea di Porta Medina*, 93.
105 Mastriani, *La Medea di Porta Medina*, 277.
106 MacPike, "Fallen Woman's Sexuality," 57.
107 Mastriani, *La Medea di Porta Medina*, 233.
108 Mastriani, *La Medea di Porta Medina*, 167, 188.
109 Invernizio, *Storia d'una sartina*, 64.
110 Invernizio, *Storia d'una sartina*, 64.
111 Invernizio, *Storia d'una sartina*, 15.
112 Invernizio, *Storia d'una sartina*, 33.
113 Mulvey-Roberts, *Dangerous Bodies*, 3.
114 Mastriani, *La Medea di Porta Medina*, 262.
115 Invernizio, *Storia d'una sartina*, 14–15.
116 Mastriani, *La Medea di Porta Medina*, 278.
117 Mastriani, *La Medea di Porta Medina*, 261.
118 Mastriani, *La Medea di Porta Medina*, 260.
119 Mastriani, *La Medea di Porta Medina*, 63.
120 Mastriani, *La Medea di Porta Medina*, 64.
121 Invernizio, *Storia d'una sartina*, 15.
122 Invernizio, *Storia d'una sartina*, 47.
123 Invernizio, *Storia d'una sartina*, 52.
124 For a general overview, see Oppenheim, *Other World*; Winter, *Mesmerized*; Thurschwell, *Literature, Technology, and Magical Thinking*; Luckhurst, *Invention of Telepathy*; Kontou and Willburn, *Ashgate Research Companion*. With regard to the Italian context, see Gallini, *La sonnambula meravigliosa*; Cigliana, *Futurismo esoterico*; Cigliana, *La seduta spiritica*; Corradi, *Spettri d'Italia*, 41–82.

125 McCorristine, "Introduction," xiii (emphasis in the original).
126 Bown, Burdett, and Thurschwell, "Introduction," 8.
127 Jarvis, "Weird," 1138.
128 See Tardiola, *Il vampiro*, 33.
129 Camilletti, *Italia lunare*, 51.
130 See Gottlieb, "European Vampire," 42; Melton and Hornick, *Vampire in Folklore*, 39; Beresford, *From Demons to Dracula*, 100.
131 Capuana, "Un vampiro"; Marrama, "Il dottor Nero." The storyline of Marrama's short story can also be found in Appiani's "Il segreto della morta," in which a recently deceased man returns from the grave in the form of a ghost to kill his adulteress wife.
132 Marrama, "Il dottor Nero," 11.
133 Marrama, "Il dottor Nero," 11 (emphasis in the original).
134 Tardiola, *Il vampiro*, 37; Loria, "Un vampiro," 404.
135 Lombroso, *La donna delinquente*, 44.
136 Lombroso, *La donna delinquente*, 571.
137 See Seymour, "Keystone of the Patriarchal Family?," 302.
138 "La donna degradata."
139 Seymour, "Keystone of the Patriarchal Family?," 300.
140 Capuana, "Un vampiro," 297.
141 Capuana, "Un vampiro," 295.
142 Capuana, "Un vampiro," 306.
143 McLaren, *Impotence*, xii; Patriarca, *Italian Vices*, 15; Seymour, "Contesting Masculinity," 254. Patriarca remarks that, since the Risorgimento, "debating national character in Italy has meant debating a uniqueness fraught with liabilities. It has meant to impute some special virtues to the Italian people ... but also, at the same time, to denounce their numerous 'vices.'" Patriarca, *Italian Vices*, 7.
144 Stewart-Steinberg, *Pinocchio Effect*, 4.
145 Duncan, *Reading and Writing Italian Homosexuality*, 19.
146 Capuana, "Un vampiro," 295.
147 Capuana, "Un vampiro," 299 (emphasis in the original).
148 Curiously, the politician and social thinker Dino Carina (1836–72) argued in his treatise on idlers that Italy's centuries-long subjugation to foreign powers resulted in lack of a work ethic and a sense of civic responsibility that promoted antisocial behaviour. See Carina, *Dell'ozio in Italia*, 14.
149 Stewart-Steinberg, *Pinocchio Effect*, 2.
150 Patriarca, *Italian Vices*, 15.
151 D'Annunzio, *L'innocente*, 129.
152 Welch, *Vital Subjects*, 156.

153 Welch, *Vital Subjects*, 157.
154 D'Annunzio, *L'innocente*, 152–3.
155 Welch, *Vital Subjects*, 158.
156 Stephanou, *Reading Vampire Gothic*, 99.
157 Stevenson, "Vampire in the Mirror," 144.
158 D'Annunzio, *L'innocente*, 14.
159 Grosz, *Volatile Bodies*, 206.
160 D'Annunzio, *L'innocente*, 20.
161 D'Annunzio, *L'innocente*, 12.
162 D'Annunzio, *L'innocente*, 110–11.
163 D'Annunzio, *L'innocente*, 125.
164 D'Annunzio, *L'innocente*, 127.
165 D'Annunzio, *L'innocente*, 127.
166 D'Annunzio, *L'innocente*, 185.
167 D'Annunzio, *L'innocente*, 200.
168 Wolf, *Misconceptions*, 25.
169 D'Annunzio, *L'innocente*, 208.
170 D'Annunzio, *L'innocente*, 175.
171 D'Annunzio, *L'innocente*, 176.
172 D'Annunzio, *L'innocente*, 214–15.
173 D'Annunzio, *L'innocente*, 217.
174 D'Annunzio, *L'innocente*, 215, 217.
175 D'Annunzio, *L'innocente*, 216.
176 D'Annunzio, *L'innocente*, 216.
177 D'Annunzio, *L'innocente*, 223, 232.
178 D'Annunzio, *L'innocente*, 241.
179 Foucault, "*Society Must Be Defended*," 138.
180 Foucault, "*Society Must Be Defended*," 125.
181 D'Annunzio, *L'innocente*, 217–18.
182 D'Annunzio, *L'innocente*, 219; Welch, *Vital Subjects*, 160.
183 Jones, *On the Nightmare*, 119.
184 Francesco Ernesto Morando (1858–1935) was a writer, journalist, and literary scholar. *Studi di letteratura e storia* (1937) is probably his most famous work. The short story "Vampiro innocente" was originally published in the magazine *Fanfulla della Domenica* in 1885. It was rediscovered and republished in 2009 by Gallo and Foni in *Ottocento nero italiano* (197–207).
185 This was also related to Italy's failure to emulate the apparently effortless colonial successes of the British and French empires, a failure most famously symbolized by Italy's military defeat at the hands of the "barbarian" Ethiopians at Adwa on 1 March 1896.
186 D'Annunzio, *L'innocente*, 268.

Conclusion

1. Examples of studies that address the interaction between culture and racial concerns in the interwar period include Aguirre, "La difesa della razza"; Fabbri, "Queer Neorealism"; Giuliani, *Race, Nation and Gender*; Carrieri and Capristo, *Italian Jewish Musicians*.
2. Spackman, *Fascist Virilities*, xii.
3. Curiously, at the time of writing, Andrew Smith's new monograph has just been published. In this book, Smith looks at a wide array of texts, from novels to poems and memoirs, that employ the ghostly figures of soldiers to make sense of war trauma and reflect on feelings of loss and despair. See Smith, *Gothic Fiction*.
4. Mulvey-Roberts, "Female Gothic Body," 117.
5. Examples include Carrino, *Luride, agitate, criminali*; Azara and Tedesco, *La donna delinquente*.
6. See Giovannini, *Il libro dei vampiri*; Giovannoli, *Il vampiro innominato*; Foni, *Fantastico Salgari*, 74–93; Pautasso, *Vampiro futurista*; Camilletti, *Italia lunare*, 27–69.
7. See Gibson, *Born to Crime*, 127–74; Horn, *Social Bodies*, 28–34; Dunnage, "Legacy of Cesare Lombroso."
8. Garfinkel, *Criminal Law*.
9. Article 1, Royal Decree 1743 of 14 September 1919.
10. Horn, *Social Bodies*, 32.
11. Royal Decree 1848 of 6 November 1926.
12. Gibson, *Born to Crime*, 220.
13. Friedlander, *Origins of Nazi Genocide*, 3.
14. Weikart, *From Darwin to Hitler*, 203.
15. Crawford, *Gothic Fiction*, 160.
16. Caglioti, "Race, Statistics and Italian Eugenics," 463.
17. For an analysis of the convergences of science, race, and politics in Fascist Italy, see Gillette, *Racial Theories in Fascist Italy*; Maiocchi, *Scienza e Fascismo*; De Napoli, *La prova della razza*; and Israel, *Il fascismo e la razza*.
18. On neurocriminology, see Raine, Buchsbaum, and LaCasse, "Brain Abnormalities"; Raine et al., "Reduced Prefrontal"; Hodgins, Viding, and Plodowski, *Neurobiological Basis of Violence*; Glenn and Raine, "Neurocriminology." On molecular genetics, see Ferguson and Beaver, "Natural Born Killers."
19. For a history of scientific constructions of the homosexual body, see Terry, *American Obsession*. See Williams et al., "Finger-Length Ratios"; LeVay, "Evidence for Anatomical Differences"; Hamer et al., "Linkage between DNA Markers."

20 See Romano, "DNA Profiles."
21 See Rafter, *Criminal Brain*; Merzagora, *Colpevoli si nasce?*; Musumeci, *Cesare Lombroso e le neuroscienze*.
22 See Feresin, "Lighter Sentence." And see Barras, "Controversial Debut."

Bibliography

Abbate Badin, Donatella. "The Discourse of Italy in Nineteenth Century Irish Gothic: Maturin's *Fatal Revenge*, Le Fanu's Exotic Tales, and *The Castle of Savina*." In *Dracula: An International Perspective*, edited by Marius-Mircea Crişan, 39–52. Cham: Palgrave Macmillan, 2017. https://doi.org/10.1007/978-3-319-63366-4_3.

Adamo, Sergia. "Mondo giudiziario e riscrittura narrativa in Italia dopo l'Unità." *Problemi* 113 (1999): 70–98.

Aguirre, Mariana. "*La difesa della razza* (1938–1943): Primitivism and Classicism in Fascist Italy." *Politics, Religion & Ideology* 16, no. 4 (2015): 370–90. https://doi.org/10.1080/21567689.2015.1132412.

Allen, Virginia. *The Femme Fatale: Erotic Icon*. Troy, NY: Whitston Publishers, 1983.

Aloisi, Alessandra, and Fabio Camilletti. "Introduction." In *Archaeology of the Unconscious: Italian Perspectives*, edited by Alessandra Aloisi and Fabio Camilletti, 1–12. New York: Routledge, 2019. https://doi.org/10.4324/9780429293047.

Alongi, Giuseppe. *La maffia nei suoi fattori e nelle sue manifestazioni: Studio sulle classi pericolose della Sicilia*. Turin: Bocca, 1887.

– *Polizia e delinquenza in Italia*. Rome: Cecchini, 1887.

Amoia, Alba. *No Mothers We! Italian Women Writers and Their Revolt Against Maternity*. Lanham, MD: University Press of America, 2000.

Appiani, Virginio. "Il segreto della morta." *La Domenica del Corriere* 42 (1901): 10–12.

Arcangeli, Massimo. "Una Firenze non proprio sotterranea: Sulla lingua di Giulio Piccini." In *Giulio Piccini (Jarro) tra Risorgimento e Grande Guerra (1849–1915)*, edited by Francesco Lucioli, 67–86. Pisa: ETS, 2016.

Arena, Pasquale. *L'infanticidio per ragion d'onore: Studio giuridico-sociologico*. Naples: De Angelis and Bellisario, 1896.

Arrighi, Cletto. *Il ventre di Milano*. 1888. Reprint, Milan: Longanesi, 1977.

Ascari, Maurizio. "The Mysteries of the Vatican: From Nineteenth-Century Anti-Clerical Propaganda to Dan Brown's Religious Thriller." In *Crime Fiction in the City: Capital Crimes*, edited by Lucy Andrew and Catherine Phelps, 107–25. Cardiff: University of Wales Press, 2013.

Ashley, Susan A. *"Misfits" in Fin-de-Siècle France and Italy: Anatomies of Difference*. London: Bloomsbury, 2017. https://doi.org/10.5040/9781350013421.

Azara, Liliosa, and Luca Tedesco, eds. *La donna delinquente e la prostituta: L'eredità di Lombroso nella cultura e nella società italiane*. Rome: Viella, 2019.

Babini, Valeria Paola. "Il lato femminile della criminalità." In *La donna nelle scienze dell'uomo: Immagini del femminile nella cultura scientifica italiana*, edited by Valeria Paola Babini, Fernanda Minuz, and Annamaria Tagliavini, 27–77. Milan: FrancoAngeli, 1989. https://doi.org/10.1057/9781137396990.

Babini, Valeria, Chiara Beccalossi, and Lucy Riall, eds. *Italian Sexualities Uncovered, 1789–1914*. Basingstoke: Palgrave Macmillan, 2015.

Baima Bollone, Pierluigi. *Cesare Lombroso e la scoperta dell'uomo delinquente*. Scarmagno, Italy: Priuli e Verlucca, 2009.

Baldi, Guido. *Le maschere dell'inetto: Lettura di Senilità*. Turin: Paravia Scriptorium, 1998.

Baldwin, Peter. *Contagion and the State in Europe, 1830–1930*. Cambridge: Cambridge University Press, 1999. https://doi.org/10.1017/CBO9780511497544.

Barisonzi, Michela. "Motherhood, Sexuality and Beauty in Gabriele D'Annunzio's Trilogy *I romanzi della Rosa*." *Forum Italicum* 51, no. 2 (August 2017): 505–24. https://doi.org/10.1177/0014585817698412.

Barnaby, Paul. "*Il marchese di Roccaverdina*: Myth, History, and Hagiography in Post-Risorgimento Sicily." *Italian Studies* 55, no. 1 (2000): 99–120. https://doi.org/10.1179/its.2000.55.1.99.

Barnes, David S. *The Great Stink of Paris and the Nineteenth-Century Struggle Against Filth and Germs*. Baltimore, MD: Johns Hopkins University Press, 2006.

– *The Making of a Social Disease: Tuberculosis in Nineteenth-Century France*. Oakland: University of California Press, 1995. https://doi.org/10.1525/9780520915176.

Barras, Colin. "The Controversial Debut of Genes in Criminal Cases." *BBC*, 30 May 2018. https://www.bbc.com/future/article/20180530-the-controversial-debut-of-genes-in-criminal-cases.

Barrili, Anton Giulio. *I misteri di Genova: Cronache contemporanee*. 2 vols. Genoa: Andrea Moretti, 1867–70.

Beames, Thomas. *The Rookeries of London: Past, Present and Prospective*. London: Thomas Bosworth, 1850.

Beccalossi, Chiara. "Arrigo Tamassia, l'inversione sessuale e la sessuologia di fine Ottocento." *Rivista sperimentale di freniatria* 138, no. 2 (July 2014): 27–42. https://doi.org/10.3280/RSF2014-002004.

- *Female Sexual Inversion: Same-Sex Desires in Italian and British Sexology, 1870–1920*. Basingstoke: Palgrave Macmillan, 2012. https://doi.org/10.1057/9780230354111.
- "The 'Italian Vice': Male Homosexuality and British Tourism in Southern Italy." In Babini, Beccalossi, and Riall, *Italian Sexualities Uncovered*, 185–206. https://doi.org/10.1057/9781137396990_10.
- "Madness and Sexual Psychopathies as the Magnifying Glass of the Normal: Italian Psychiatry and Sexuality c.1880–1910." *Social History of Medicine* 27, no. 2 (May 2014): 303–25. https://doi.org/10.1093/shm/hkt077.
- "Sexual Deviancies, Disease, and Crime in Cesare Lombroso and the 'Italian School' of Criminal Anthropology." In Peckham, *Disease and Crime*, 40–55.

Benadusi, Lorenzo. *The Enemy of the New Man: Homosexuality in Fascist Italy*. Madison: University of Wisconsin Press, 2012.

Benigno, Francesco. "Ripensare le 'classi pericolose' italiane: Letteratura, politica e crimine nel XIX secolo." In *Questione criminale e identità nazionale in Italia tra Otto e Novecento*, edited by Luigi Lacchè and Monica Stronati, 57–77. Macerata, Italy: EUM, 2014.

Beresford, Matthew. *From Demons to Dracula: The Creation of the Modern Vampire Myth*. London: Reaktion, 2008.

Berkowitz, Michael. *The Crime of My Very Existence: Nazism and the Myth of Jewish Criminality*. Berkeley: University of California Press, 2007. https://doi.org/10.1525/9780520940680.

- "Morality Plays: Presentation of Criminality and Disease in Nazi Ghettoes and Concentration Camps." In Peckham, *Disease and Crime*, 79–92.

Bevione, Giuseppe. "L'ossessione rossa" [1906]. In Gallo and Foni, *Ottocento nero italiano*, 401–14.

Bigatti, Giorgio. *La città operosa: Milano nell'Ottocento*. Milan: Franco Angeli, 2000.

Billiani, Francesca, and Gigliola Sulis, eds. *The Italian Gothic and Fantastic: Encounters and Rewritings of Narrative Traditions*. Madison, WI: Fairleigh Dickinson University Press, 2007.

Binet, Alfred. "Le fétichisme dans l'amour." *Revue Philosophique* 24 (1887): 143–67, 252–74.

Bolis, Giovanni. *La polizia e le classi pericolose della società*. Bologna: Zanichelli, 1871.

Bonino, Guido Davico, and Giovanna Ioli. *Carolina Invernizio: Il romanzo d'appendice*. Turin: Gruppo Editoriale Forma, 1983.

Botting, Fred. *Gothic*. London: Routledge, 1996.

Bown, Nicola, Carolyn Burdett, and Pamela Thurschwell. "Introduction." In *The Victorian Supernatural*, edited by Nicola Bown, Carolyn Burdett, and Pamela Thurschwell, 1–19. Cambridge: Cambridge University Press, 2004.

Briganti, Alessandra. *Introduzione a De Marchi*. Rome: Laterza, 1992.

Bronfen, Elisabeth. "Femme Fatale: Negotiations of Tragic Desire." *New Literary History* 35, no. 1 (Winter 2004): 103–16. https://doi.org/10.1353/NLH.2004.0014.

Brooks, Peter. *Troubling Confessions: Speaking Guilt in Law and Literature.* Chicago: University of Chicago Press, 2000.
Bulferetti, Luigi. *Cesare Lombroso.* Turin: UTET, 1975.
Caccia, Ettore. "Luigi Capuana." In *Letteratura italiana: I Minori*, vol. 4, 2908. Milan: Marzorati, 1962.
Caglioti, Angelo Matteo. "Race, Statistics and Italian Eugenics: Alfredo Niceforo's Trajectory from Lombroso to Fascism (1876–1960)." *European History Quarterly* 47, no. 3 (July 2017): 461–89. https://doi.org/10.1177/0265691417707164.
Calvino, Italo. *Mondo scritto e mondo non scritto.* Milan: Mondadori, 2002.
Camilletti, Fabio. "Authorship and Authority in the Classicist/Romantic Quarrel." *Forum for Modern Language Studies* 54, no. 3 (July 2018): 307–19. https://doi.org/10.1093/fmls/cqy020.
– "Gothic Beginnings, 1764–1827." In Malvestio and Serafini, *Italian Gothic*, 19–29.
– "Il sorriso del conte zio: Manzoni, Sade e l'omaggio alla Vergine." *Enthymema* 14 (July 2016): 231–46. https://doi.org/10.13130/2037-2426/6959.
– *Italia lunare: Gli anni Sessanta e l'occulto.* Oxford: Peter Lang, 2018.
– "'Timore' e 'terrore' nella polemica classico-romantica: L'Italia e il ripudio del gotico." *Italian Studies* 69, no. 2 (2014): 231–45. https://doi.org/10.1179/0075163414Z.00000000069.
Canonico, Tancredi. *Introduzione allo studio del diritto penale: Del reato e della pena in genere.* Turin: UTET, 1866.
Cantelmo, Andrea. *Carolina Invernizio e il romanzo d'appendice.* Florence: Atheneum, 1992.
Cappello, Angelo Piero. *Invito alla lettura di Luigi Capuana.* Milan: Mursia, 1994.
Capuana, Luigi. *Il marchese di Roccaverdina.* Milan: Treves, 1901.
– *Mondo occulto.* Naples: Pierro, 1896.
– *Spiritismo?* Catania, Italy: Giannotta, 1884.
– "Un vampiro" [1904]. In *Fantastico italiano: Racconti fantastici dell'Ottocento e del primo Novecento italiano*, edited by Costanza Melani, 290–308. Milan: Rizzoli, 2009.
Carina, Dino. *Dell'ozio in Italia.* Lucca: Canovetti, 1870.
Carrara, Francesco. *Programma del corso di diritto criminale: Parte speciale*, vol. 1. 1863. Reprint, Lucca: Tipografia Giusti, 1872.
Carrieri, Alessandro, and Annalisa Capristo, eds. *Italian Jewish Musicians and Composers under Fascism: Let Our Music Be Played.* Basingstoke: Palgrave Macmillan, 2021. https://doi.org/10.1007/978-3-030-52931-4.
Carrino, Candida. *Luride, agitate, criminali: Un secolo di internamento femminile, 1850–1950.* Rome: Carocci, 2018.
Cassata, Francesco. *Building the New Man: Eugenics, Racial Science, and Genetics in Twentieth-Century Italy.* Budapest: Central European University Press, 2011. https://doi.org/10.1515/9789639776890.

Cavalli Pasini, Annamaria. *La scienza del romanzo: Romanzo e cultura scientifica tra Otto e Novecento*. Bologna: Pàtron, 1982.

Centini, Massimo. *Il vampiro della Padania: Le indagini ed il processo a Vincenzo Verzeni, lo "strangolatore di donne."* Turin: Ananke, 2009.

Ceserani, Remo. "The Boundaries of the Fantastic." In Billiani and Sulis, *Italian Gothic and Fantastic*, 37–45.

– *Il fantastico*. Bologna: Il Mulino, 1996.

Chen, Chung-jen. *Victorian Contagion: Risk and Social Control in the Victorian Literary Imagination*. London: Routledge, 2019. https://doi.org/10.4324/9780429343643.

Chevalier, Julien. *L'inversion sexuelle : Une maladie de la personnalité*. Paris: G. Masson, 1893.

Chiletti, Silvia. "Infanticide and Mental Illness: Theories and Practices Involving Psychiatry and Justice (Italy, 19th–20th Century)." *Histoire, médecine et santé* 6 (Autumn 2015): 17–31. https://doi.org/10.4000/hms.691.

– "Infanticide and the Prostitute: Honour, Sentiment and Deviancy Between Human Sciences and the Law." In Babini, Beccalossi, and Riall, *Italian Sexualities Uncovered*, 143–61. https://doi.org/10.1057/9781137396990_8.

Churchill, Kenneth. *Italy and English Literature: 1764–1930*. Totowa, NJ: Barnes and Noble, 1980. https://doi.org/10.1007/978-1-349-04642-3.

Cigliana, Simona. *Futurismo esoterico: Contributi per una storia dell'irrazionalismo italiano tra Otto e Novecento*. Naples: Liguori, 2002.

– *La seduta spiritica: Dove si racconta come e perché i fantasmi hanno invaso la modernità*. Rome: Fazi, 2007.

Colajanni, Napoleone. *La sociologia criminale*. 2 vols. Catania: Tropea, 1889.

"Condanna di un'infanticida." *Il Corriere della Sera*, 22–3 December 1892, p. 2.

Conti, Giuseppe. *Firenze vecchia: Storia, cronaca aneddotica, costumi, 1799–1859*. Florence: Bemporad, 1899.

Contini, Gianfranco. "Prefazione." In *Italia magica*, edited by Gianfranco Contini, 1. 1946. Reprint, Turin: Einaudi, 1988.

Corbin, Alain. *The Foul and the Fragrant: Odour and the French Social Imagination*. Leamington Spa, UK: Berg, 1986.

Corio, Lodovico. *Milano in ombra: Abissi plebei*. Milan: Civelli, 1885.

Corradi, Morena. "The Gothic and the Historical Novel, 1828–1860." In Malvestio and Serafini, *Italian Gothic*, 30–47. https://doi.org/10.3366/edinburgh/9781474490160.003.0003.

– *Spettri d'Italia: Scenari del fantastico nella pubblicistica postunitaria milanese*. Ravenna: Longo Editore, 2016.

Craciun, Adriana. *Fatal Women of Romanticism*. Cambridge: Cambridge University Press, 2003. https://doi.org/10.1017/CBO9780511484155.

Crawford, Joseph. *Gothic Fiction and the Invention of Terrorism: The Politics and Aesthetics of Fear in the Age of the Reign of Terror*. London: Bloomsbury, 2013.

Cresti, Carlo, and Silvano Fei. "Le vicende del 'risanamento' di Mercato Vecchio." *Storia Urbana* 1, no. 1 (1977): 99–126.
Crovi, Luca. *Tutti i colori del giallo: Il giallo italiano da De Marchi a Scerbanenco a Camilleri*. Venice: Marsilio, 2002.
Curcio, Giorgio. *Delle persone sospette in Italia*. Milan: Tip. ed. Lombarda, 1874.
Cusson, Maurice, and Jean Proulx. "The Motivation and Criminal Career of Sexual Murderers." In *Sexual Murderers: A Comparative Analysis and New Perspectives*, edited by Jean Proulx, Éric Beauregard, Maurice Cusson, and Alexandre Nicole, 143–55. Chichester: John Wiley and Sons, 2007.
D'Annunzio, Gabriele. *L'innocente*. 1892. Reprint, Milan: Mondadori, 1976.
– *Trionfo della morte*. 1894. Reprint, Milan: Mondadori, 1995.
Darwin, Charles. *The Descent of Man and Selection in Relation to Sex*. 1871. Reprint, London: Penguin, 2004. https://doi.org/10.5962/bhl.title.110063.
Davie, Neil. "A 'Criminal Type' in All but Name: British Prison Medical Officers and the 'Anthropological' Approach to the Study of Crime (c.1865–1895)." *Victorian Review* 29, no. 1 (2003): 1–30. https://doi.org/10.1353/vcr.2003.0007.
– *Tracing the Criminal: The Rise of Scientific Criminology in Britain, 1860–1918*. Oxford: Bardwell Press, 2005.
Davies, Judith. *The Realism of Luigi Capuana: Theory and Practice in the Development of Late Nineteenth-Century Italian Narrative*. Cambridge: Modern Humanities Research Association, 1979. https://doi.org/10.59860/td.b493b1a.
Davis, John. *Conflict and Control: Law and Order in Nineteenth-Century Italy*. Basingstoke: Macmillan Education, 1988. https://doi.org/10.1007/978-1-349-19277-9.
De Amicis, Ugo. *La moralità del male*. Turin: Renzo Streglio, 1906.
De Blasio, Abele. *Anomalie multiple in un cranio di prostituta*. Naples: Pesole, 1900.
De Marchi, Emilio. *Il cappello del prete*. 1888. Reprint, Cava de' Tirreni, Italy: Avagliano, 2000.
De Napoli, Olindo. *La prova della razza*. Florence: Le Monnier, 2009.
De Rosa, Diana. *Il baule di Giovanna: Storie di abbandoni e infanticidi*. Palermo: Sellerio, 1995.
Del Panta, Lorenzo. *Evoluzione demografica e popolamento nell'Italia dell'Ottocento: 1796–1914*. Bologna: CLUEB, 1984.
Del Principe, David. *Rebellion, Death, and Aesthetics in Italy: The Demons of Scapigliatura*. Madison, WI: Fairleigh Dickinson University Press, 1996.
D'Elia, Antonio, Alberico Guarnieri, Monica Lanzillotta, and Giuseppe Lo Castro, eds. *La tentazione del fantastico: Racconti italiani da Gualdo a Svevo*. Cosenza, Italy: Pellegrini, 2007.
Demata, Massimiliano. "Italy and the Gothic." *Gothic Studies* 8, no. 1 (May 2006): 1–8. https://doi.org/10.7227/GS.8.1.2.
Di Blasi, Corrado. *Luigi Capuana originale e segreto*. Catania: Giannotta, 1968.

Di Scala, Spencer. *Italy: From Revolution to Republic, 1700 to the Present*. Boulder, CO: Westview, 1995.
Dickens, Charles. *Pictures from Italy*. 1846. Reprint, London: Penguin, 1998.
Dijkstra, Bram. *Evil Sisters: The Threat of Female Sexuality and the Cult of Manhood*. New York: Alfred A. Knopf, 1996.
– *Idols of Perversity: Fantasies of Feminine Evil in Fin-de-Siècle Culture*. Oxford: Oxford University Press, 1986.
Dizionario delle leggi del Regno di Napoli. 4 vols. Naples: Vincenzo Manfredi, 1788.
Doane, Mary Ann. *Femmes Fatales: Feminism, Film Theory, Psychoanalysis*. London: Routledge, 1991.
Duncan, Derek. *Reading and Writing Italian Homosexuality: A Case of Possible Difference*. Aldershot: Ashgate, 2006.
Dunnage, Jonathan. "The Legacy of Cesare Lombroso and Criminal Anthropology in the Post-War Italian Police: A Study of the Culture, Narrative and Memory of a Post-Fascist Institution." *Journal of Modern Italian Studies* 22, no. 3 (2017): 365–84. https://doi.org/10.1080/1354571X.2017.1321934.
Ebner, Michael R. "The Persecution of Homosexual Men under Fascism." In *Gender, Family and Sexuality: The Private Sphere in Italy, 1860–1945*, edited by Perry Wilson, 139–56. Basingstoke: Palgrave Macmillan, 2004.
Eco, Umberto, ed. *Carolina Invernizio, Matilde Serao, Liala*. Florence: La Nuova Italia, 1979.
Ellis, Havelock. "Note sulle facoltà artistiche degli invertiti." *Archivio delle psicopatie sessuali* 1 (1896): 243–5.
Esposito, Roberto. *Immunitas: The Protection and Negation of Life*. Cambridge: Polity Press, 2011.
Esquirol, Jean-Étienne-Dominique. *Mental Maladies: A Treatise on Insanity*. 1838. Reprint, Philadelphia: Lea and Blanchard, 1845.
Fabbri, Lorenzo. "Queer Neorealism: Luchino Visconti's *Ossessione* and the Cinema of Conspiracy Against Fascism." *Screen* 60, no. 1 (Spring 2019): 1–24. https://doi.org/10.1093/screen/hjy062.
Fanning, Ursula. *Gender Meets Genre: Woman as Subject in the Fictional Universe of Matilde Serao*. Ballsbridge: Irish Academic Press, 1997.
Farnetti, Monica. "Patologie del romanticismo: Il gotico e il fantastico fra Italia ed Europa." In *Mappe della letteratura europea e mediterranea: Dal Barocco all'Ottocento*, edited by Gian Mario Anselmi, vol. 2, 340–66. Milan: Bruno Mondadori, 2000.
Fei, Silvano. *Firenze 1881–1898: La grande operazione urbanistica*. Rome: Officina Edizioni, 1977.
Feresin, Emiliano. "Lighter Sentence for Murderer with 'Bad Genes.'" *Scientific American*, 30 October 2009, https://www.scientificamerican.com/article/lighter-sentence-for-murderer-/.

Ferguson, Christopher, and Kevin Beaver. "Natural Born Killers: The Genetic Origins of Extreme Violence." *Aggression and Violent Behavior* 14, no. 5 (September–October 2009): 286–94. https://doi.org/10.1016/j.avb.2009.03.005.

Ferri, Enrico. *I delinquenti nell'arte*. Genoa: Libreria Editrice Ligure, 1896.

– *I nuovi orizzonti del diritto e della procedura penale*. Bologna: Zanichelli, 1881.

Ferriani, Lino. *La infanticida nel codice penale e nella vita sociale*. Milan: Dumolard, 1886.

Féval, Paul. *I misteri di Londra*. Translated by Angiolo Orvieto, 4 vols. Livorno: Vannini, 1844–5.

Florian, Eugenio, and Guido Cavaglieri. *I vagabondi: Studio sociologico-giuridico*. 2 vols. Turin: Bocca, 1897–1900.

Foni, Fabrizio. *Alla fiera dei mostri: Racconti "pulp," orrori e arcane fantasticherie nelle riviste italiane, 1899–1932*. Latina, Italy: Tunué, 2007.

– *Fantastico Salgari: Dal "vampiro" Sandokan al "Giornale illustrato dei viaggi."* Cuneo, Italy: Nerosubianco, 2011.

– *Piccoli mostri crescono: Nero, fantastico e bizzarrie varie nella prima annata de "La Domenica del Corriere."* 1899. Reprint, Ozzano dell'Emilia: Perdisa Pop, 2010.

Forgacs, David. "Imagined Bodies: Rhetorics in Social Investigation in Late Nineteenth-Century Italy and France." *Journal of the Institute of Romance Studies* 1 (1992): 375–94.

– *Italy's Margins: Social Exclusion and Nation Formation Since 1861*. Cambridge: Cambridge University Press, 2014. https://doi.org/10.1017/CBO9781107280441.

Fornari, Ugo, and Jutta Birkhoff. *Serial Killer: Tre mostri infelici del passato a confronto*. Turin: Centro scientifico, 1996.

Fornasari di Verce, Ettore. "La criminalità e le vicende economiche d'Italia dal 1873 al 1890." *Archivio di psichiatria, scienze penali ed antropologia criminale* 14 (1893): 365–405, 536–55.

Foucault, Michel. *Abnormal: Lectures at the Collège de France 1974–1975*. Translated by Graham Burchell. London: Verso, 2016.

– "About the Concept of the 'Dangerous Individual' in 19th-Century Legal Psychiatry." Translated by Alain Baudot and Jane Couchman. *International Journal of Law and Psychiatry* 1, no. 1 (February 1978): 1–18. https://doi.org/10.1016/0160-2527(78)90020-1.

– *The Birth of Biopolitics*. Translated by Graham Burchell. 1978. Reprint, Basingstoke: Palgrave Macmillan, 2008.

– *Discipline and Punish: The Birth of the Prison*. Translated by Alan Sheridan. 1975. Reprint, Harmondsworth: Penguin, 1979.

– *The History of Sexuality*. Vol. 1, *An Introduction*. Translated by Robert Hurley. 1976. Reprint, New York: Pantheon Books, 1978.

– *Security, Territory, Population: Lectures at the Collège de France 1977–1978*. Translated by Kenneth A. Loparo. Basingstoke: Palgrave Macmillan, 2009.

- "*Society Must Be Defended*": *Lectures at the Collège de France 1975–1976*. Translated by David Macey. New York: Picador, 2003.
- *The Will to Knowledge*. Vol. 1 of *The History of Sexuality*. Translated by Robert Hurley. 1976. Reprint, London: Penguin, 1998.

Fox, James Alan, and Jack Levin. *Extreme Killing: Understanding Serial and Mass Murder*. Los Angeles: SAGE, 2015.

Frangipani, Maria Antonietta. *Motivi del romanzo nero nella letteratura lombarda*. Rome: Elia, 1981.

Frégier, Honoré-Antoine. *Des classes dangereuses de la population dans les grandes villes, et des moyens de les rendre meilleures*. 2 vols. Paris: J.-B. Baillière, 1840.

Freud, Sigmund. "The Uncanny." In *The Standard Edition of the Complete Psychological Works of Sigmund Freud*, vol. 17, translated by James Strachey, 217–52. London: Vintage, 2001.

Friedlander, Henry. *The Origins of Nazi Genocide: From Euthanasia to the Final Solution*. Chapel Hill: University of North Carolina Press, 1995.

Frigessi, Delia. *Cesare Lombroso*. Turin: Einaudi, 2003.

Fusaro, Edwige Comoy. *La nevrosi tra medicina e letteratura: Approccio epistemologico alle malattie nervose nella narrativa italiana (1865–1922)*. Florence: Polistampa, 2007.

Gaakeer, Jeanne. "The Art to Find the Mind's Construction in the Face: Lombroso's Criminal Anthropology and Literature; The Examples of Zola, Dostoevsky, and Tolstoy." *Cardozo Law Review* 26, no. 6 (May 2005): 2345–77.

Gallini, Clara. *La sonnambula meravigliosa: Magnetismo e ipnotismo nell'Ottocento italiano*. Milan: Feltrinelli, 1983.

Gallo, Claudio. "I fabbricatori di storie che trafficavano con le anime dei morti: Paura ed orrore tra appendice, Scapigliatura e spiritismo; Da Francesco Mastriani a Carolina Invernizio." In *Paure ovvero: Di come le apparizioni degli spiriti, dei vampiri o redivivi, etc., gli esseri, i personaggi, i fatti, le cose mostruose, orrorifiche o demoniache, nonché gli assassinii e le morti apparenti furono trattati nei libri e nelle immagini; e in particolare in "Dylan Dog,"* edited by Claudio Gallo, 79–119. Verona: Colpo di fulmine, 1998.

Gallo, Claudio, and Fabrizio Foni, eds. *Ottocento nero italiano: Narrativa fantastica e crudele*. Milan: Nino Aragno Editore, 2009.

Gallo, Stefano. *Senza attraversare le frontiere: Le migrazioni interne dall'Unità a oggi*. Rome: Laterza, 2012.

Garfinkel, Paul. *Criminal Law in Liberal and Fascist Italy*. Cambridge: Cambridge University Press, 2016. https://doi.org/10.1017/9781316266151.

Garofalo, Raffaele. *Criminologia: Studio sul delitto, sulle sue cause e sui mezzi di repressione*. 1885. Reprint, Turin: Bocca, 1891.

Gentilomo, Andrea, Eleonora Burgazzi, and Lia Bertolini. "L'infanticidio a Milano tra 1862 e 1930: Analisi di 65 dispositivi di sentenza." *Rassegna italiana di Criminologia* 4 (November 2012): 234–48.

Ghidetti, Enrico. *Per un ritratto di Italo Svevo: Ipotesi sull'inetto e sull'ebreo.* Florence: Sansoni, 1980.

– "Per una storia del romanzo popolare in Italia: I 'misteri' di Toscana." In Enrico Ghidetti, *Il sogno della ragione: Dal racconto fantastico al romanzo popolare,* 85–117. Rome: Editori Riuniti, 1987.

Ghidetti, Enrico, and Leonardo Lattarulo. "Prefazione." In *Notturno Italiano: Racconti fantastici del Novecento,* edited by Enrico Ghidetti and Leonardo Lattarulo, vii–xii. Rome: Editori Riuniti, 1984.

Ghirelli, Antonio. *Napoli italiana: Storia della città dopo il 1860.* Turin: Einaudi, 1977.

Giannantonio, Pompeo. "Manzoni e il romanzo 'nero.'" *Otto/Novecento* 3, no. 2 (March–April 1979): 5–37.

Gibson, Mary. *Born to Crime: Cesare Lombroso and the Origins of Biological Criminology.* Westport, CT: Praeger, 2002.

– *Prostitution and the State in Italy, 1860–1915.* New Brunswick, NJ: Rutgers University Press, 1986.

Gibson, Mary, and Nicole Rafter. "Editors' Introduction." In Cesare Lombroso and Guglielmo Ferrero, *Criminal Woman, the Prostitute, and the Normal Woman,* 3–33. Durham, NC: Duke University Press, 2004. https://doi.org/10.1215/9780822385592-001.

Gillette, Aaron. *Racial Theories in Fascist Italy.* London: Routledge, 2002. https://doi.org/10.4324/9780203164891.

Giovannini, Fabio. *Il libro dei vampiri.* 1985. Reprint, Bari: Dedalo, 1997.

Giovannoli, Renato. *Il vampiro innominato: Il "caso Manzoni-Dracula" e altri casi di vampirismo letterario.* Milan: Medusa, 2008.

Giuliani, Gaia. *Race, Nation and Gender in Modern Italy: Intersectional Representations in Visual Culture.* Basingstoke: Palgrave Macmillan, 2018.

Glenn, Andrea, and Adrian Raine. "Neurocriminology: Implications for the Punishment, Prediction and Prevention of Criminal Behavior." *Nature Reviews Neuroscience* 15 (January 2014): 54–63. https://doi.org/10.1038/nrn3640.

Goc, Nicolá. *Women, Infanticide, and the Press, 1822–1922: News Narratives in England and Australia.* Farnham: Ashgate, 2013.

Gottlieb, Richard M. "The European Vampire: Applied Psychoanalysis and Applied Legend." *Folklore Forum* 24, no. 2 (1991): 39–58.

Govean, Felice, and Alessandro Borella. *I misteri di Torino scritti da una penna a quattro mani.* Turin: Claudio Perrin Editore, 1849.

Groppi, Angela. "Il teatro della giustizia: Donne colpevoli nell'opinione pubblica dell'Italia liberale." *Quaderni storici* 3, no. 111 (December 2002): 649–80. https://doi.org/10.1408/8028.

Grosz, Elizabeth. *Volatile Bodies: Toward a Corporeal Feminism.* Bloomington: Indiana University Press, 1994.

Guagnini, Elvio. *Dal giallo al noir e oltre: Declinazioni del poliziesco italiano.* Formia, Italy: Ghenomena, 2010.

Guaiana, Yuri, and Mark Seymour. "From Giarre to Civil Unions: The 'Long March' for Same-Sex Relationships in Italy." In *From Sodomy Laws to Same-Sex Marriage: International Perspectives since 1789*, edited by Sean Brady and Mark Seymour, 161–81. London: Bloomsbury, 2019.

Guarnieri, Patrizia. "Alienists on Trial: Conflict and Convergence Between Psychiatry and Law (1876–1913)." *History of Science* 29, no. 4 (December 1991): 393–410. https://doi.org/10.1177/007327539102900403.

– "Forzate analogie: L'infanticidio nel discorso giuridico." In *In scienza e coscienza: Maternità, nascite e aborti tra esperienze e bioetica*, edited by Patrizia Guarnieri, 47–61. Rome: Carocci, 2010.

– *L'ammazzabambini: Legge e scienza in un processo toscano di fine Ottocento*. Turin: Einaudi, 1988.

– "Madri che uccidono: Diritto, psicologia e mentalità sull'infanticidio dal 1810 ad oggi." In *Sapere e narrare: Figure della follia*, edited by Mimma Bresciani Califano, 145–74. Florence: Olschki, 2005.

– "Men Committing Female Crimes: Infanticide, Family and Honor in Italy, 1890–1981." *Crime, History and Society* 13, no. 2 (2009): 41–54. https://doi.org/10.4000/chs.1108.

Gurrieri, Raffaele. *Sensibilità e anomalie fisiche e psichiche nella donna normale e nella prostituta*. Turin: Bocca, 1892.

Hamer, Dean, Stella Hu, Victoria L. Magnuson, Nan Hu, and Angela M.L. Pattatucci. "A Linkage Between DNA Markers on the X Chromosome and Male Sexual Orientation." *Science* 361, no. 5119 (16 July 1993): 321–7. https://doi.org/10.1126/science.8332896.

Hamlin, Christopher. *Public Health and Social Justice in the Age of Chadwick: Britain, 1800–1854*. Cambridge: Cambridge University Press, 1998.

Hanak, Miroslav John. "The Emergence of Baroque Mentality and Its Cultural Impact on Western Europe after 1550." *Journal of Aesthetics and Art Criticism* 28, no. 3 (Spring 1970): 315–26. https://doi.org/10.2307/429498.

Hodgins, Sheilagh, Essi Viding, and Anna Plodowski, eds. *Neurobiological Basis of Violence: Science and Rehabilitation*. New York: Oxford University Press, 2009. https://doi.org/10.1093/oso/9780199543533.001.0001.

Hogle, Jerrold E. "Introduction: The Gothic in Western Culture." In *The Cambridge Companion to Gothic Fiction*, edited by Jerrold E. Hogle, 1–20. Cambridge: Cambridge University Press, 2002. https://doi.org/10.1017/CCOL0521791243.001.

Horn, David G. *The Criminal Body: Lombroso and the Anatomy of Deviance*. London: Routledge, 2003.

– *Social Bodies: Science, Reproduction, and Italian Modernity*. Chichester: Princeton University Press, 1994. https://doi.org/10.1515/9781400821457.

Horsley, Lee. *The Noir Thriller*. Basingstoke: Palgrave Macmillan, 2001.

- *Twentieth-Century Crime Fiction*. Oxford: Oxford University Press, 2005. https://doi.org/10.1093/oso/9780199283453.001.0001.
Hurley, Kelly. *The Gothic Body: Sexuality, Materialism, and Degeneration at the Fin de Siècle*. Cambridge: Cambridge University Press, 1996. https://doi.org/10.1017/CBO9780511519161.
Impallomeni, Giovanni Battista. *L'omicidio nel diritto penale*. Turin: Unione Tipografico-Editrice, 1900.
"Infanticide assolte." *Il Corriere della Sera*, 19–20 November 1884, p. 3.
"Infanticidio." *Il Corriere della Sera*, 18–19 April 1891, p. 3.
"Infanticidio." *Gazzetta Piemontese*, 26 June 1891, p. 3.
Invernizio, Carolina. "Le operaie italiane." In *Nero per signora*, edited by Riccardo Reim, 257–75. Rome: Editori riuniti, 1986.
- *Peccatrice moderna*. 1915. Reprint, Rome: Avagliano, 2011.
- *Storia d'una sartina*. Florence: Salani, 1892.
Israel, Giorgio. *Il fascismo e la razza: La scienza italiana e le politiche razziali del regime*. Bologna: Il Mulino, 2010.
Jack l'assassino di Londra detto lo sventratore di donne. Florence: Salani, 1888.
Jack lo sventratore di donne a Londra. Codogno, Italy: Cairo, 1891.
Jack, lo sventratore di Londra: Racconto storico. Florence: Salani, 1901.
Jackson, Mark, ed. *Infanticide: Historical Perspectives on Child Murder and Concealment, 1550–2000*. Aldershot: Ashgate, 2002.
Jarvis, Timothy. "The Weird, the Posthuman, and the Abjected World-in-Itself: Fidelity to the 'Lovecraft Event' in the Work of Caitlín R. Kiernan and Laird Barron." *Textual Practice* 31, no. 6 (2017): 1133–48. https://doi.org/10.1080/0950236X.2017.1358693.
Jenner, Mark S.R. "Follow Your Nose? Smell, Smelling, and Their Histories." *American Historical Review* 116, no. 2 (April 2011): 335–51. https://doi.org/10.1086/ahr.116.2.335.
Jones, Ernest. *On the Nightmare*. London: Hogarth Press, 1931.
Jung, W. "Hereditary Tendency in Insanity." *Journal of Mental Science* 25 (1867): 106–7.
Karschay, Stephan. *Degeneration, Normativity, and the Gothic at the Fin-de-Siècle*. New York: Palgrave Macmillan, 2015. https://doi.org/10.1057/9781137450333.
Klein, Ilona. "When Good Girls Go Bad (Or Do They?): Nymphomania and Lycanthropy in Verga's 'La Lupa.'" *Modern Languages Notes* 134, no. 6 (September 2019): 272–85. https://doi.org/10.1353/mln.2019.0072.
Knight, Stephen. *The Mysteries of the Cities: Urban Crime Fiction in the Nineteenth Century*. Jefferson, NC: McFarland, 2012.
Kontou, Tatiana, and Sarah Willburn, eds. *The Ashgate Research Companion to Nineteenth-Century Spiritualism and the Occult*. Farnham: Ashgate, 2012.
Krafft-Ebing, Richard von. *Psychopathia Sexualis*. Translated by Francis J. Rebman. 1886. Reprint, London: Aberdeen University Press and Rebman, 1899.

- "Über gewisse Anomalies des Geschlechtstriebs und dieklinisch-forensich Verwertung derselben als eines wahrscheinlich funktionellen Degenerationszeichens des centralen Nervensystems." *Archiv für Psychiatrie und Nervenkrankheiten* 7, no. 2 (June 1877): 291–312. https://doi.org/10.1007/BF01969552.
Kristeva, Julia. *Powers of Horror: An Essay on Abjection*. New York: Columbia University Press, 1982.
Lacchè, Luigi. "La paura delle 'classi pericolose': Ritorno al futuro?" *Quaderno di storia del penale e della giustizia* 1 (2019): 159–78.
"La donna degradata." *L'Osservatore Romano*, 1 July 1879, p. 1.
Lazzarin, Stefano. "Trentacinque anni di teoria e critica del fantastico italiano (dal 1980 a oggi)." In *Il fantastico italiano: Bilancio critico e bibliografia commentata (dal 1980 a oggi)*, edited by Stefano Lazzarin, Felice Italo Beneduce, Eleonora Conti, Fabrizio Foni, Rita Fresu, and Claudia Zudini, 1–58. Florence: Le Monnier, 2016.
Lee Six, Abigail, and Hannah Thompson. "From Hideous to Hedonist: The Changing Face of the Nineteenth-Century Monster." In *The Ashgate Research Companion to Monsters and the Monstrous*, edited by Asa Simon Mittman and Peter J. Dendle, 237–55. Farnham: Ashgate, 2012.
Lepschy, Anna Laura. "The Popular Novel 1850–1920." In *A History of Women's Writing in Italy*, edited by Sharon Wood and Letizia Panizza, 177–89. Cambridge: Cambridge University Press, 2000.
LeVay, Simon. "Evidence for Anatomical Differences in the Brains of Homosexual Men." *Science* 253, no. 5023 (30 August 1991): 1034–7. https://doi.org/10.1126/science.1887219.
Lo Castro, Giuseppe. "Introduzione." In D'Elia et al., *La tentazione del fantastico*, 5–18.
Locatelli, Paolo. *Miseria e beneficenza: Ricordi di un funzionario di pubblica sicurezza*. Milan: Dumolard, 1878.
- *Sorveglianti e sorvegliati: Appunti di fisiologia sociale presi dal vero*. Milan: Brigola, 1876.
Lombroso, Cesare. *Delitti vecchi e nuovi*. Turin: Bocca, 1902.
- "Du parallélisme entre l'homosexualité et la criminalité innée." *Archivio di psichiatria* 27 (1906): 378–81.
- "Identità dell'epilessia colla pazzia morale e delinquenza congenita." *Archivio di psichiatria, scienze penali ed antropologia criminale* 6 (1885): 1–28.
- "Il tipo criminale nella letteratura." In Cesare Lombroso, *Le più recenti scoperte ed applicazioni della psichiatria ed antropologia criminale*, 339–63. Turin: Bocca, 1893.
- "L'amore nei pazzi." *Archivio di psichiatria, scienze penali ed antropologia criminale* 2 (1881): 1–32.
- *L'uomo delinquente in rapporto all'antropologia, alla giurisprudenza ed alle discipline carcerarie*. 2 vols. 4th ed. Turin: Bocca, 1889.

- *L'uomo delinquente in rapporto all'antropologia, alla giurisprudenza ed alla psichiatria*. 3 vols. 5th ed. Turin: Bocca, 1896–7.
- *L'uomo delinquente in rapporto all'antropologia, giurisprudenza ed alle discipline carcerarie*. 2nd ed. Turin: Bocca, 1878.
- *L'uomo delinquente in rapporto all'antropologia, giurisprudenza ed alle discipline carcerarie*. 3rd ed. Turin: Bocca, 1884.
- *L'uomo delinquente studiato in rapporto alla antropologia, alla medicina legale ed alle discipline carcerarie*. 1st ed. Milan: Hoepli, 1876.
- "Review of Alfredo Niceforo, Sull'aumento della delinquenza." *Archivio di psichiatria, scienze penali ed antropologia criminale* 2 (1899): 646.
- *Sull'incremento del delitto in Italia e sui mezzi per arrestarlo*. Turin: Bocca, 1879.
- *Verzeni e Agnoletti*. Rome: Artero, 1873.

Lombroso, Cesare, and Guglielmo Ferrero. *La donna delinquente: La prostituta e la donna normale*. Rome: Roux and Co., 1893.

Lombroso, Cesare, and Enrico Ferri. *Su A. Faella e sugli osteomi e le cardiopatie negli alienati*. Turin: Loescher, 1882.

Lombroso, Cesare, and Salvatore Ottolenghi. *La donna delinquente e la prostituta: Studio*. Turin: Unione tipografico-editrice, 1891.

Loria, Achille. *Le basi economiche della costituzione sociale*. 1886. Reprint, Turin: Bocca, 1902.

Loria, Annamaria. "Luigi Capuana: *Un vampiro*; Fra racconto fantastico e racconto spiritico." In D'Elia et al., *La tentazione del fantastico*, 395–412.

Lucarelli, Carlo, and Massimo Picozzi. *Serial killer: Storie di ossessione omicida*. Milan: Mondolibri, 2003.

Luccardini, Rinaldo. *Firenze: L'ingrandimento della città nell'Ottocento*. Genoa: Sagep, 2016.

Luckhurst, Roger. *The Invention of Telepathy 1870–1901*. Oxford: Oxford University Press, 2002. https://doi.org/10.1093/oso/9780199249626.001.0001.

Lupi, Giordano. *Serial killer italiani: Cento casi agghiaccianti da Vincenzo Verzeni a Donato Bilancia*. Florence: Olimpia, 2005.

MacPike, Loralee. "The Fallen Woman's Sexuality: Childbirth and Censure." In *Sexuality and Victorian Literature*, edited by Don Richard Cox, 54–71. Knoxville: University of Tennessee Press, 1984.

Madrignani, Carlo. *Capuana e il naturalismo*. Bari: Laterza, 1970.

Maiocchi, Roberto. *Scienza e Fascismo*. Rome: Carocci, 2004.

Malvestio, Marco, and Stefano Serafini, eds. *Italian Gothic: An Edinburgh Companion*. Edinburgh: Edinburgh University Press, 2023. https://doi.org/10.3366/edinburgh/9781474490160.001.0001.

Manzoni, Alessandro. *Lettere*. Edited by Cesare Arieti. In *Tutte le opere di Alessandro Manzoni*, edited by Alberto Chiari and Fausto Ghisalberti, 7 vols. Milan: Mondadori, 1970.

Marchetti, Paolo. "Le 'sentinelle del male': L'invenzione ottocentesca del criminale nemico della società tra naturalismo giuridico e normativismo psichiatrico." *Quaderni fiorentini per la storia del pensiero giuridico moderno* 38 (2009): 1009–80.

Marini, Quinto. *I "misteri" d'Italia*. Pisa: ETS, 1993.

Marland, Hilary. "Getting Away with Murder? Puerperal Insanity, Infanticide and the Defence Plea." In Jackson, *Infanticide*, 168–92. https://doi.org/10.4324/9781315252308-9.

Marrama, Daniele Oberto. "Il dottor Nero." *La Domenica del Corriere* 33 (1904): 10–12.

– *Il ritratto del morto: Racconti bizzarri*. Naples: Perrella, 1907.

Mastriani, Francesco. *I misteri di Napoli*: Studi storico sociali. 2 vols. Naples: G. Nobile, 1870.

– *I vermi: Studi storici su le classi pericolose in Napoli*. 5 vols. 1863. Reprint, Naples: Gabriele Regina Editore, 1877.

– *La cieca di Sorrento*. 2 vols. Naples: Tramater, 1852.

– *La Medea di Porta Medina*. 1882. Reprint, Naples: Attività bibliografica editoriale, 1977.

Maxwell, Richard. *The Mysteries of Paris and London*. Charlottesville: University Press of Virginia, 1992.

Mayhew, Henry. *London Labour and the London Poor*. London: George Woodfall and Son and Griffin, 1851.

Mazzoni, Cristina. "Impressive Cravings, Impressionable Bodies: Pregnancy and Desire from Cesare Lombroso to Ada Negri." *Annali d'Italianistica* 15 (1997): 137–58.

McAfee, Noëlle. "Abjection." In *Julia Kristeva*, 45–57. New York: Routledge, 2004. https://doi.org/10.4324/9780203634349.

McCorristine, Shane. "Introduction." In *Spiritualism, Mesmerism and the Occult, 1800–1920*, 5 vols., edited by Shane McCorristine, 3:v–xxiv. London: Pickering and Chatto, 2012.

McLaren, Angus. *Impotence: A Cultural History*. Chicago: University of Chicago Press, 2007. https://doi.org/10.7208/chicago/9780226500935.001.0001.

Mecholsky, Kristopher. "The Psychological Thriller in Context." In *The American Thriller*, edited by Gary Hoppenstand, 48–70. Hackensack, NJ: Salem Press, 2014.

Melton, Gordon, and Alysa Hornick, eds. *The Vampire in Folklore: History, Literature, Film and Television: A Comprehensive Bibliography*. Jefferson, NC: McFarland, 2015.

Menon, Elizabeth K. *Evil by Design: The Creation and Marketing of the Femme Fatale*. Urbana: University of Illinois Press, 2006.

Merzagora, Isabella. *Colpevoli si nasce? Criminologia, determinismo, neuroscienze*. Milan: Raffaello Cortina, 2012.

Mighall, Robert. *A Geography of Victorian Gothic Fiction: Mapping History's Nightmares.* Oxford: Oxford University Press, 1999.
– "Gothic Cities." In *The Routledge Companion to Gothic*, edited by Catherine Spooner and Emma McEvoy, 54–62. London: Routledge, 2007.
Miller, William Ian. *The Anatomy of Disgust.* London: Harvard University Press, 1997. https://doi.org/10.4159/9780674041066.
Mistrali, Franco. *Il vampiro: Storia vera.* Bologna: Società Tipografica dei Compositori, 1869.
Mitchell, Katharine. *Italian Women Writers: Gender and Everyday Life in Fiction and Journalism 1870–1910.* Toronto: University of Toronto Press, 2014. https://doi.org/10.3138/9781442665637.
Moloney, Brian, and Gillian Ania. "Analoghi vituperî: La bibliografia del romanzo dei misteri in Italia." *La bibliofilia* 106, no. 2 (2004): 173–213.
Montaldo, Silvano, ed. *Cesare Lombroso: Gli scienziati e la nuova Italia.* Bologna: Il Mulino, 2011.
Montaldo, Silvano, and Paolo Tappero, eds. *Cesare Lombroso cento anni dopo.* Turin: UTET, 2009.
Moore, John. *View of Society and Manners in Italy.* 3 vols. Dublin: Price, Watson, et al., 1781.
Moraglia, Giovan Battista. "Nuove ricerche su criminali, prostitute e psicopatiche." *Archivio di psichiatria, scienze penali ed antropologia criminale* 16 (1895): 305–27, 501–23.
Morando, Francesco Ernesto. "Vampiro innocente." *Fanfulla della Domenica* 33 (16 August 1885): 3–4.
Morel, Bénédict Augustin. *Traité des dégénérescences physiques, intellectuelles et morales de l'espèce humaine.* Paris: J.B. Baillière, 1867.
Mori, Simona. "Becoming Policemen in Nineteenth-Century Italy: Police Gender Culture through the Lens of Professional Manuals." In *A History of Police and Masculinities, 1700–2010*, edited by David G. Barrie and Susan Broomhall, 102–22. New York: Routledge, 2012.
– "The Police and the Urban 'Dangerous Classes': The Culture and Practice of Public Law and Order in Milan after National Unity." *Urban History* 43, no. 2 (May 2016): 266–84. https://doi.org/10.1017/S0963926815000280.
Morselli, Enrico. "La rivendicazione delle leggi di Morel." *Quaderni di Psichiatria* 3, nos. 11–12 (1916): 272–8.
Mulvey-Roberts, Marie. *Dangerous Bodies: Historicising the Gothic Corporeal.* Manchester: Manchester University Press, 2016. https://doi.org/10.7228/manchester/9780719085413.001.0001.
– "The Female Gothic Body." In *Women and the Gothic: An Edinburgh Companion*, edited by Avril Horner and Sue Zlosnik, 106–19. Edinburgh: Edinburgh University Press, 2016. https://doi.org/10.1515/9780748699131-009.
Musumeci, Emilia. *Cesare Lombroso e le neuroscienze: Un parricidio mancato.* Milan: FrancoAngeli, 2012.

Nani, Michele. *Ai confini della nazione: Stampa e razzismo nell'Italia di fine Ottocento*. Rome: Carocci, 2006.
Neera and Paolo Mantegazza. *Dizionario d'igiene per le famiglie*. Milan: Brigola, 1881.
Niceforo, Alfredo. *Italiani del Nord e Italiani del Sud*. Florence: Tip. Cooperativa, 1899.
— *Les classes pauvres : Recherches anthropologiques et sociales*. Paris: Giard and Brière, 1905.
Niceforo, Alfredo, and Scipio Sighele. *La mala vita a Roma*. Turin: Roux Frassati e C. editori, 1898.
Nixon, Kari. *Kept from All Contagion: Germ Theory, Disease, and the Dilemma of Human Contact in Late Nineteenth-Century Literature*. Albany: State University of New York Press, 2021. https://doi.org/10.1353/book76827.
Noce Bottoni, Patrizia. *Il romanzo gotico di Francesco Mastriani*. Florence: Franco Cesati, 2015.
Nye, Robert A. "The Medical Origins of Sexual Fetishism." In *Fetishism as Cultural Discourse*, edited by Emily Apter and William Pietz, 13–30. Ithaca, NY: Cornell University Press, 1993.
Oppenheim, Janet. *The Other World: Spiritual and Psychical Research in England 1850–1914*. Cambridge: Cambridge University Press, 1985.
Orlando, Francesco. *Il soprannaturale letterario: Storia, logica, forme*. Turin: Einaudi, 2017.
Packer, Sharon. *Movies and the Modern Psyche*. London: Praeger, 2007. https://doi.org/10.5040/9798400687914.
Pagliaro, Annamaria. "Il marchese di Roccaverdina di Luigi Capuana: Crisi etica o analisi positivistica?" *Italian Studies* 52, no. 1 (1997): 111–30. https://doi.org/10.1179/its.1997.52.1.111.
Pagnier, Armand. *Le vagabond : Ses origines, sa psychologie, ses formes*. Paris: Vigot Frères, 1910.
Palermo, Antonio. *Da Mastriani a Viviani: Per una storia della letteratura a Napoli fra Otto e Novecento*. Naples: Liguori, 1972.
Patriarca, Silvana. *Italian Vices: Nation and Character from the Risorgimento to the Republic*. Cambridge: Cambridge University Press, 2010.
Pautasso, Guido Andrea. *Vampiro futurista: I futuristi e l'esoterismo*. Albissola Marina, Italy: Vanillaedizioni, 2018.
Peckham, Robert, ed. *Disease and Crime: A History of Social Pathologies and the New Politics of Health*. New York: Routledge, 2014.
Pedrazzini, Paola. *Medea fra tipo e arche-tipo: La ferita dell'amore fatale nelle diagnosi del teatro*. Rome: Carocci, 2007.
Pellegrino, Anna. "Firenze noir: Criminalità e marginalità a Firenze tra Otto e Novecento." *Diacronie: Studi di Storia Contemporanea* 21, no. 1 (2015): 1–21. https://doi.org/10.4000/diacronie.1845.
Penta, Pasquale. *I pervertimenti sessuali nell'uomo e Vincenzo Verzeni strangolatore di donne: Studio biologico*. Naples: Luigi Pierro Editore, 1893.

- *Pazzia e società*. Milan: Vallardi, 1893.
"Per infanticidio." *Gazzetta Piemontese*, 9 May 1891, p. 3.
Perkins, Pam. "John Moore, Ann Radcliffe and the Gothic Vision of Italy." *Gothic Studies* 8, no. 1 (May 2006): 35–51. https://doi.org/10.7227/GS.8.1.5.
Perroni, Lina, and Vito Perroni. "Storia de *I Malavoglia*." *Nuova Antologia* 408 (1940): 105–31, 237–51.
Pezzotti, Barbara. *The Importance of Place in Contemporary Italian Crime Fiction*. Madison, WI: Fairleigh Dickinson University Press, 2012.
Picart, Caroline Joan, and Cecil Greek. "The Compulsions of Real/Reel Serial Killers and Vampires: Toward a Gothic Criminology." In *Monsters In and Among Us: Toward a Gothic Criminology*, edited by Caroline Joan Picart and Cecil Greek, 227–55. Madison, WI: Fairleigh Dickinson University Press, 2007.
Piccini, Giulio. *Firenze sotterranea: Appunti, ricordi, descrizioni, bozzetti*. 1884. Reprint, Florence: Bemporad, 1900.
- *I ladri di cadaveri*. 1884. Reprint, Reggio Emilia: Aliberti, 2004.
- *L'assassinio nel vicolo della luna*. Milan: Treves, 1883.
Pierangeli, Fabio. *Emilio De Marchi: Condanna e perdono*. Naples: Paolo Loffredo Editore, 2018.
Portinari, Folco. "De Marchi." In *Dizionario critico della letteratura italiana*, edited by Vittore Branca, 146–51. Turin: UTET, 1992.
Pozzo, Barbara. "Male Homosexuality in Nineteenth-Century Italy." In *Homosexuality in Italian Literature, Society, and Culture, 1789–1919*, edited by Lorenzo Benadusi, Paolo L. Bernardini, Elisa Bianco, and Paola Guazzo, 103–28. Newcastle: Cambridge Scholars Publishing, 2017.
Prichard, James Cowles. *A Treatise on Insanity and Other Disorders Affecting the Mind*. London: Sherwood Gilbert, 1835. https://doi.org/10.1037/10551-000.
"Processo per infanticidio." *Il Corriere della Sera*, 7–8 May 1892, p. 2.
Punter, David. *The Literature of Terror: A History of Gothic Fictions from 1765 to the Present Day*. 2 vols. 1980. Reprint, London: Longman, 1996.
Rafter, Nicole. *The Criminal Brain: Understanding Biological Theories of Crime*. New York: New York University Press, 2008.
- "Introduction to special issue on Visual Culture and the Iconography on Crime and Punishment." *Theoretical Criminology* 18, no. 2 (May 2014): 128–33. https://doi.org/10.1177/1362480613510547.
Rafter, Nicole, and Per Ystehede. "Here Be Dragons: Lombroso, the Gothic, and Social Control." In *Popular Culture, Crime, and Social Control*, edited by Mathieu Deflem, 263–84. Bingley, UK: Emerald, 2010. https://doi.org/10.1108/S1521-6136(2010)0000014015.
Raine, Adrian, Monet Buchsbaum, and Lori LaCasse. "Brain Abnormalities in Murderers Indicated by Positron Emission Tomography." *Biological Psychiatry* 42, no. 6 (September 1997): 495–508. https://doi.org/10.1016/S0006-3223(96)00362-9.

Raine, Adrian, J. Reid Meloy, Susan Bihrle, Jackie Stoddard, Lori Lacasse, and Monte S. Buchsbaum. "Reduced Prefrontal and Increased Subcortical Brain Functioning Assessed Using Positron Emission Tomography in Predatory and Affective Murderers." *Behavioral Sciences and the Law* 16, no. 3 (Summer 1998): 319–32. https://doi.org/10.1002/(sici)1099-0798(199822)16:3<319::AID-BSL311>3.0.CO;2-G.

Rambelli, Loris. "Il presunto giallo italiano: Dalla preistoria alla storia." *Problemi* 86 (1989): 233–56.

– *Storia del giallo italiano*. Milan: Garzanti, 1979.

Rampinelli, Francesca. *Storie di abbandoni: I processi per esposizione d'infante a Firenze dal 1870 al 1900*. Florence: Le lettere, 2000.

Reynolds, G.W. *The Mysteries of London*. 1844–8. Reprint, Keele, UK: Keele University Press, 1996.

Riccardi, Paolo. *Dati fondamentali di antropologia criminale e principi antropologici sulla teoria dell'imputabilità*. Milan: Vallardi, 1889.

Ridenhour, Jamieson. *In Darkest London: The Gothic Cityscape in Victorian Literature*. Lanham, MD: Scarecrow Press, 2013.

Romano, Aja. "DNA Profiles from Ancestry Websites Helped Identify the Golden State Killer Suspect." *Vox*, 27 April 2018. https://www.vox.com/2018/4/27/17290288/golden-state-killer-joseph-james-deangelo-dna-profile-match.

Rosa, Giovanna. *Identità di una metropoli: La letteratura della Milano moderna*. Turin: N. Aragno, 2004.

– *Il mito della capitale morale: Letteratura e pubblicistica a Milano fra Otto e Novecento*. Milan: Edizioni di comunità, 1982.

Rosenberg, Charles E. *The Cholera Years: The United States in 1832, 1849, and 1866*. 1962. Reprint, Chicago: University of Chicago Press, 1987. https://doi.org/10.7208/chicago/9780226726762.001.0001.

Rubin, Martin. *Thrillers*. Cambridge: Cambridge University Press, 1999. https://doi.org/10.1017/CBO9780511624414.

Rzepka, Charles J., and Lee Horsley, eds. *A Companion to Crime Fiction*. Chichester: Wiley-Blackwell, 2010. https://doi.org/10.1002/9781444317916.

Sade, Marquis de. *Journey to Italy*. Toronto: University of Toronto Press, 2020.

Saggini, Francesca. "The Gothic in Nineteenth-Century Italy." In *The Cambridge History of the Gothic*, vol. 2, *The Gothic in the Nineteenth Century*, edited by Angela Wright and Dale Townshend, 303–27. Cambridge: Cambridge University Press, 2020. https://doi.org/10.1017/9781108561082.015.

Sauli, Alessandro. *I misteri di Milano: Storia contemporanea*. 2 vols. Milan: Libreria di Francesco Sanvito succ. alla ditta Borroni e Scotti, 1857–9.

Scappaticci, Tommaso. *Tra orrore gotico e impegno sociale: La narrativa di Francesco Mastriani*. Cassino, Italy: Garigliano, 1992.

Scarfoglio, Edoardo. *Il processo di Frine*. 1884. Reprint, Rome: Armando, 2002.

Scarlata, Francesco. *La imputabilità e le cause che la escludono o la diminuiscono.* Messina: Tipografia Fratelli Messina, 1891.

Schuller, Kyla. *The Biopolitics of Feeling: Race, Sex, and Science in the Nineteenth Century.* Durham, NC: Duke University Press, 2018. https://doi.org/10.1215/9780822372356.

Selmini, Rossella. *Profili di uno studio storico sull'infanticidio.* Milan: Giuffré, 1987.

Serafini, Stefano. "Gotico e misteri nell'Italia postunitaria." *Transalpina* 25 (2022): 87–100. https://doi.org/10.4000/transalpina.3773.

Serao, Matilde. *Il ventre di Napoli.* 1884. Reprint, Pisa: ETS, 1995.

– *Il ventre di Napoli: Vent'anni fa, adesso, l'anima di Napoli.* Naples: Perrella, 1906.

Sergi, Giuseppe. "La donna normale e la degenerata." *Nuova antologia* 130 (1893): 152–62.

– "Sensibilità femminile." *Archivio di psichiatria, scienze penali ed antropologia criminale* 13, no. 1 (1892): 1–8.

Servitje, Lorenzo. *Medicine Is War: The Martial Metaphor in Victorian Literature and Culture.* Albany: State University of New York Press, 2021. https://doi.org/10.1515/9781438481692.

Seymour, Mark. "Contesting Masculinity in Post-Unification Italy: The Murder of Captain Giovanni Fadda." *Gender & History* 25, no. 2 (August 2013): 252–69. https://doi.org/10.1111/1468-0424.12021.

– "Keystone of the Patriarchal Family? Indissoluble Marriage, Masculinity and Divorce in Liberal Italy." *Italian Studies* 10, no. 3 (2005): 297–313. https://doi.org/10.1080/13545710500188247.

Shapiro, Ann-Louise. *Breaking the Codes: Female Criminality in Fin-de-Siècle Paris.* Stanford, CA: Stanford University Press, 1996. https://doi.org/10.1515/9780804764834.

Sighele, Scipio. "Sull'infanticidio." *Archivio giuridico* 42 (1889): 177–209.

– *Un paese di delinquenti nati.* Turin: Bocca, 1890.

Simpson, Philip. "Noir and the Psycho-Thriller." In Rzepka and Horsley, *Companion to Crime Fiction*, 187–97. https://doi.org/10.1002/9781444317916.ch14.

Simpson, Thomas. *Murder and Media in the New Rome: The Fadda Affair.* New York: Palgrave Macmillan, 2010. https://doi.org/10.1057/9780230116535.

Smith, Andrew. *Gothic Fiction and the Writing of Trauma, 1914–1934.* Edinburgh: Edinburgh University Press, 2022. https://doi.org/10.3366/edinburgh/9781474443432.001.0001.

– *Victorian Demons: Medicine, Masculinity and the Gothic at the Fin-de-Siècle.* Manchester: Manchester University Press, 2004.

"Solita storia." *Gazzetta Piemontese*, 27 May 1883, p. 3.

Spackman, Barbara. *Fascist Virilities: Rhetoric, Ideology and Social Fantasy in Italy.* Minneapolis: University of Minnesota Press, 1996.

Spooner, Catherine. "Crime and the Gothic." In Rzepka and Horsley, *Companion to Crime Fiction*, 245–57. https://doi.org/10.1002/9781444317916.ch19.
Stephanou, Aspasia. *Reading Vampire Gothic Through Blood: Bloodlines*. Basingstoke: Palgrave Macmillan, 2014. https://doi.org/10.1057/9781137349231.
Stevenson, John Allen. "A Vampire in the Mirror: The Sexuality of *Dracula*." *PMLA* 103, no. 2 (March 1988): 139–49. https://doi.org/10.2307/462430.
Stewart-Steinberg, Suzanne. *The Pinocchio Effect: On Making Italians, 1860–1920*. Chicago: University of Chicago Press, 2007.
Stoker, Bram. *Dracula*. 1897. Reprint, New York: Cosimo, 2009.
Stoler, Ann Laura. *Carnal Knowledge and Imperial Power: Race and the Intimate in Colonial Rule*. Berkeley: University of California Press, 2002.
Stoppato, Alessandro. *Infanticidio e procurato aborto*. Verona: Drucker e Tedeschi, 1887.
Stott, Rebecca. *Fabrication of the Late-Victorian Femme Fatale: Kiss of Death*. Basingstoke: Macmillan, 1992.
Sue, Eugène. *I misteri di Parigi*. Translated by Filippo Berti, 7 vols. Florence: Tipografia Pezzati, 1843–4.
Svevo, Italo. "L'assassinio di via Belpoggio" (1890). In *L'assassinio di via Belpoggio e altri racconti*, 5–29. Milan: Guide Moizzi, 2011.
Tamassia, Arrigo. *L'inversione dell'istinto sessuale come causa di impulsività criminosa*. Padua: Randi, 1906.
– "Sull'inversione dell'istinto sessuale." *Rivista sperimentale di freniatria e medicina legale delle alienazioni mentali* 4 (1878): 97–117.
Tanzi, Eugenio. *Trattato delle malattie mentali*. 2 vols. Milan: Società editrice libraria, 1905.
Tapaninen, Anna Maria. "Motherhood Through the Wheel: The Care of Foundlings in Late Nineteenth-Century Naples." In *Gender, Family and Sexuality: The Private Sphere in Italy, 1860–1945*, edited by Perry Willson, 51–70. Basingstoke: Palgrave Macmillan, 2004.
Tardiola, Giuseppe. *Il vampiro nella letteratura italiana*. Anzio: De Rubeis, 1991.
Terry, Jennifer. *An American Obsession: Science, Medicine, and Homosexuality in America*. Chicago: University of Chicago Press, 1999. https://doi.org/10.7208/chicago/9780226793689.001.0001.
Thurschwell, Pamela. *Literature, Technology, and Magical Thinking, 1880–1920*. Cambridge: Cambridge University Press, 2001. https://doi.org/10.1017/CBO9780511484537.
Todorov, Tzvetan. *The Fantastic: A Structural Approach to a Literary Genre*. Ithaca, NY: Cornell University Press, 1975.
Truglio, Maria. *Beyond the Family Romance: The Legend of Pascoli*. Toronto: University of Toronto Press, 2007. https://doi.org/10.3138/9781442684065.
"Un atroce infanticidio." *Gazzetta Piemontese*, 19 March 1884, p. 1.

"Un processo per infanticidio." *Il Corriere della Sera*, 22–3 June 1888, p. 2.
"Una domestica infanticida." *Il Corriere della Sera*, 10–11 August 1890, p. 3.
Vaccaro, Michele Angelo. *Genesi e funzioni delle leggi penali: Ricerche sociologiche*. Turin: Bocca, 1889.
Valera, Paolo. *Gli scamiciati: Seguito alla Milano sconosciuta*. 1881. Reprint, Milan: Lampi di Stampa, 2004.
– *Milano sconosciuta*. Milan: Bignami, 1879.
Verga, Giovanni. *La lupa*. Turin: Einaudi, 1982.
Verona, Flavio. *Oziosi e vagabondi nella legislazione penale dell'Italia liberale*. Pisa: ETS, 1984.
Vidler, Anthony. *Architectural Uncanny: Essays in the Modern Unhomely*. London: MIT Press, 1992.
Vidocq, Eugène-François. *I veri misteri parigini*. Translated by Angiolo Orvieto, 3 vols. Florence: Casoni, 1845.
Vignoli, Tito. "Note intorno ad una psicologia sessuale." *Rivista di filosofia scientifica* 6 (1887): 420–34, 472–87, 532–47.
Villa, Renzo. *Il deviante e i suoi segni: Lombroso e la nascita dell'antropologia criminale*. Milan: FrancoAngeli, 1985.
"Vincenzo Verzeni lo sventratore di donne." In *Processi celebri contemporanei italiani e stranieri*, edited by Oscar Pio and Nicola Argenti, 45–117. Naples: Anfossi, 1889.
Violi, Alessandra. "Storie di fantasmi per adulti: Lombroso e le tecnologie dello spettrale." In *Lombroso e la fotografia*, edited by Silvana Turzio, 43–69. Milan: Mondadori, 2005.
Vronsky, Peter. *Serial Killer: The Method and Madness of Monsters*. New York: Berkley Groups, 2004.
Waltje, Jörg. *Blood Obsession: Vampires, Serial Murder, and the Popular Imagination*. New York: Peter Lang, 2005.
Ward, Tony. "Legislating for Human Nature: Legal Responses to Infanticide, 1860–1938." In Jackson, *Infanticide*, 24–69.
Weikart, Richard. *From Darwin to Hitler: Evolutionary Ethics, Eugenics, and Racism in Germany*. Basingstoke: Palgrave Macmillan, 2004. https://doi.org/10.1007/978-1-137-10986-6.
Welch, Rhiannon Noel. *Vital Subjects: Race and Biopolitics in Italy, 1860–1920*. Liverpool: Liverpool University Press, 2016. https://doi.org/10.26530/OAPEN_608318.
Williams, Anne. *Art of Darkness: A Poetics of Gothic*. Chicago: University of Chicago Press, 1995. https://doi.org/10.7208/chicago/9780226899039.001.0001.
– "Horace in Italy: Discovering a Gothic Imagination." *Gothic Studies* 8, no. 1 (May 2006): 22–34. https://doi.org/10.7227/GS.8.1.4.
Williams, Terrance J., Michelle E. Pepitone, Scott E. Christensen, Bradley M. Cooke, Andrew D. Huberman, Nicholas J. Breedlove, Tessa J. Breedlove, Cynthia L. Jordan, and S. Marc Breedlove. "Finger-Length Ratios and

Sexual Orientation." *Nature* 404, no. 6777 (30 March 2000): 455–6. https://doi.org/10.1038/35006555.

Winter, Alison. *Mesmerized: Powers of Mind in Victorian Britain*. Chicago: University of Chicago Press, 1998.

Wolf, Naomi. *Misconceptions: Truth, Lies, and the Unexpected on the Journey to Motherhood*. London: Vintage, 2002.

Wong, Aliza. *Race and the Nation in Liberal Italy, 1861–1911: Meridionalism, Empire, and Diaspora*. Basingstoke: Palgrave Macmillan, 2006.

Ystehede, Per. "Demonizing Being, Lombroso and the Ghosts of Criminology." In Ystehede and Knepper, *Cesare Lombroso Handbook*, 72–97.

Ystehede, Per, and Paul Knepper, eds. *The Cesare Lombroso Handbook*. London: Routledge, 2013.

Zangara, Mario. *Luigi Capuana*. Catania: La Navicella, 1964.

Index

Adamo, Sergia, 63
Allen, Virginia, 95
Almost Blue (Lucarelli), 149n13
Aloisi, Alessandra, 5
Alongi, Giuseppe, 23, 24, 28
Amoia, Alba, 91
"L'amore nei pazzi" (Lombroso), 77, 83–4
Ania, Gillian, 141–2n31
anthropology of lower classes, 53–6
anticontagionism (miasma theory), 46–9
Antropologia delle classi povere (Niceforo), 55
Appiani, Virginio, 162n131
Arcangeli, Massimo, 32
L'archivio delle psicopatie sessuali (journal), 78, 82, 84
Archivio di psichiatria, scienze penali ed antropologia criminale (journal), 11, 44
Arena, Pasquale, 104
Argenti, Nicola, 105
Arrighi, Cletto, 46
Artena, 42
Ascari, Maurizio, 142n32
Ashley, Susan, 27–8, 57
"L'assassinio di via Belpoggio" (Svevo), 60–1, 62
L'assassinio nel vicolo della luna (Piccini), 35–6, 37
atavism, 8–15, 57–8, 104, 118
L'automa (Butti), 158n27
Le avventure di Pinocchio (Collodi), 16
d'Azeglio, Massimo, 5

bacteriology, 47
Baldwin, Peter, 46
Baraldi, Barbara, 133
Beames, Thomas, 141n4
Beccalossi, Chiara, 77, 80
Beccaria, Cesare, 10
Benadusi, Lorenzo, 75–6
Benigno, Francesco, 22
Berkowitz, Michael, 52–3
Bevione, Giuseppe, 74–5, 78–85, 86–9, 128
Bianchi, Leonardo, 78
Billiani, Francesca, 16–17
Binet, Alfred, 80, 87
biopolitics, 8–9, 22–3
biopower, 22–3, 39, 120, 123
blood: in *L'innocente* (D'Annunzio), 119, 122–4; in "L'ossessione rossa" (Bevione), 80–2, 85, 87–8; vampires and, 85–6, 114, 119; Verzeni and, 87–8
body trade, 34

Index

Boito, Camillo, 158n27
Bolis, Giovanni, 21
Boni, Enrico, 114
"Borrhomeo the Astrologer: A Monkish Tale" (Le Fanu), 4
Botting, Fred, 4, 49, 59, 140–1n28
Bown, Nicola, 113
brigandage, 7
Briganti, Alessandra, 64
Bronfen, Elisabeth, 98
Brooks, Peter, 65–6
Burdett, Carolyn, 113
Butti, Enrico Annibale, 158n27

Caccia, Ettore, 64–5
Calvino, Italo, 15–16
Camilletti, Fabio, 5, 16, 114
Canonico, Tancredi, 92
Capitan Fracassa (newspaper), 140n24
Cappello, Angelo Piero, 64–5
Il cappello del prete (De Marchi), 61–6, 69–71, 73–4
Capuana, Luigi: crime-confession nexus and, 61–2, 63–8, 71–4; female sexuality and, 116–18; impact and popularity of, 14–15; vampires and, 114, 124. *See also specific works*
Carina, Dino, 162n148
Carmignani, Giovanni, 75–6
Carrara, Francesco, 11, 92, 102
Carrara, Mario, 131
Carrino, Candida, 92
Carrisi, Donato, 133
Cassata, Francesco, 44
Castle of Otranto, The (Walpole), 3
Castle of Savina, or the Irishman in Italy: A Tale, The (Anon.), 4
castration, 44
Catholic Church, 3, 85, 110–11, 116
Cavaglieri, Guido, 38
Cavalli Pasini, Annamaria, 72

Ceserani, Remo, 16–17
Chadwick, Edwin, 46
Chelli, Gaetano, 158n27
Chevalier, Julien, 83
childbearing. *See* motherhood
Chiletti, Silvia, 101–2, 104
cholera, 29, 31, 47, 52, 146n156
Churchill, Kenneth, 3
La cieca di Sorrento (Mastriani), 34
cities: crime in, 20–6; Gothicization of Italy and, 3–4. *See also* Florence; Milan; Naples; urban mysteries (city mysteries)
Les classes pauvres (Niceforo), 55
Classicist-Romantic quarrel, 5–6
Colajanni, Napoleone, 11, 54, 57–8, 92, 139n2
Colin, Mariella, 142n31
Collodi, Carlo, 16
"Il compagno di viaggio" (Marrama), 153n81
Il conciliatore (literary journal), 5
confession. *See* crime-confession nexus
confino di polizia, 130
contagionism, 46–9
Conti, Giuseppe, 32
Conti, Ugo, 58
Contini, Gianfranco, 15, 16
La coppia criminale (Ferri), 145n115
Corbin, Alain, 45
Corio, Lodovico: on dangerous classes, 24–5, 26, 28–30, 32; infection and, 48; nation-building process and, 49–50; otherness and, 40–1, 42; on prostitution, 143n48. See also *Milano in ombra* (Corio)
Corradi, Morena, 5
Correnti, Dario, 133
Corriere della Sera (newspaper), 105
Corriere di Napoli (newspaper), 62
La coscienza di Zeno (Svevo), 149n16

Crawford, Joseph, 131
crime and criminality: class and, 27–31; debate on, 11–12, 57–8; as infection, 48–53; masculinity and, 58–9; nation-building process and, 6–9, 20–5; Nazi Germany and, 52–3, 131; poverty and, 45, 48–53, 54; in urban areas, 20–6; women and, 58–9, 90–4. *See also* dangerous classes; sexual monsters
Crime and Punishment (Dostoevsky), 60, 65, 152n77
crime-confession nexus: in "L'assassinio di via Belpoggio" (Svevo), 60–1; in *Il cappello del prete* (De Marchi), 61–6, 69–71; in *Crime and Punishment* (Dostoevsky), 60; in *Giovanni Episcopo* (D'Annunzio), 61; in *Il marchese di Roccaverdina* (Capuana), 61–2, 63–8, 71–4; paradigm of, 59
Criminal, The (Ellis), 154n92
criminal code (1859), 75, 102
criminal code (1889), 12, 75–6, 85, 102–3
criminal code (1930), 103
criminal law, 12, 130–2. *See also* specific criminal codes
Criminal Law in Liberal and Fascist Italy (Garfinkel), 58
Crovi, Luca, 150n23
Curcio, Giorgio, 23, 28, 30, 31
Cusson, Maurice, 87–8

dangerous classes: anthropology of lower classes and, 53–6; as infection, 25, 45–53, 127–8; medical and sociocultural construction of, 21–5, 27–31; *Les Mystères de Paris* (Sue) and, 25–6; otherness and, 25, 37–44; poverty and, 25–33; women and, 92, 103. *See also* femmes fatales

D'Annunzio, Gabriele: crime-confession nexus and, 61; on female sexuality, 96–8, 119–23; femmes fatales and, 95–8, 158n27; impact and popularity of, 14–15; on monstrosity, 96–8, 120–5; vampires and, 118–25. *See also Giovanni Episcopo* (D'Annunzio); *L'innocente* (D'Annunzio); *Trionfo della morte* (D'Annunzio)
Darwin, Charles, 9, 10, 12
Davies, Judith, 72
De Amicis, Edmondo, 153n84
De Amicis, Ugo, 74
De Dominicis, Pier Francesco Paolo, 142n32
De Marchi, Emilio, 61–6, 69–71, 73–4
De Sanctis, Francesco, 6
degeneration: concept of, 12–13; homosexuality and, 76–8; infanticidal mothers and, 101; in *L'innocente* (D'Annunzio), 118–25; in "L'ossessione rossa" (Bevione), 82–3, 84, 86–7; poverty and, 43–4; vampires and, 118–25; Verzeni and, 86–7
Dei delitti e delle pene (Beccaria), 10
Del Principe, David, 146n131
Del Vecchio, Bonaiuto, 142n32
I delinquenti nell'arte (Ferri), 60, 61, 152n77
La delinquenza settaria (Sighele), 145n115
Delle persone sospette in Italia (Curcio), 23, 28, 30, 31
democracy, 45
Depretis, Agostino, 31, 51
Descent of Man, The (Darwin), 12
Di Tullio, Benigno, 131
Dickens, Charles, 4
divine retribution, 66–8
divorce, 116, 129

194 Index

Dizionario di criminologia (Florian et al.), 131
Dizionario d'igiene per le famiglie (Neera and Mantegazza), 91–2
Doane, Ann, 95–6
La Domenica del Corriere (journal), 153n81
domicilio coatto, 130
La donna delinquente (Lombroso and Ferrero), 91, 94–5, 100
Dostoevsky, Fyodor, 60, 61, 64, 152n77
"Il dottor Nero" (Marrama), 114–15, 118, 124
Dracula (Stoker), 59, 85
Duncan, Derek, 76, 117–18
Dunnage, Jonathan, 130

Ellero, Pietro, 11, 92
Ellis, Havelock, 76, 82, 154n106
epilepsy, 13, 38, 69, 83–4, 87
L'eredità Ferramonti (Chelli), 158n27
Esposito, Roberto, 8–9, 51–2
Esquirol, Jean-Étienne-Dominique, 80
ethnocentrism, 21
eugenics, 43–4, 52, 55, 128, 131–2

Faella, Alessandro, 62
Il Fanfulla (journal), 11
fantastico, 15–16
Il fantastico (Ceserani), 138n64
Farnetti, Monica, 15
Fascist Italy: criminal law and, 130–2; the persecution of homosexual men in, 76, 79, 85, 128–9
Fatal Revenge or the Family of Montorio, The (Maturin), 4
FBI (Federal Bureau of Investigation), 152n80
La felicità nel delitto (Invernizio), 99
female sexuality: criminology on, 97; in *L'innocente* (D'Annunzio), 119–23; medical perspective on, 90–4; nation-building process and, 116–18; in *Peccatrice moderna* (Invernizio), 100–1; in *Trionfo della morte* (D'Annunzio), 96–8
feminism, 115–16
femmes fatales, 94–101
Ferrero, Guglielmo, 91, 94–5, 100, 101, 104, 131
Ferri, Enrico: career of, 145n115; on *Crime and Punishment* (Dostoevsky), 60, 152n77; debate on criminogenic factors and, 57; on Faella, 62; on *L'innocente* (D'Annunzio), 61; revision of criminal code and, 130
Ferriani, Lino, 102–3
fetishism, 80, 84, 87
Féval, Paul, 141n30
Firenze sotterranea (Piccini): dangerous classes in, 29–30, 31, 32; labyrinth metaphor in, 35, 37; nation-building process and, 26; *La nazione* (newspaper) and, 140n27; smells and infection in, 47, 49
Firenze vecchia (Conti), 32
Florence, 25, 26–7, 143n52. See also *Firenze sotterranea* (Piccini)
Florian, Eugenio, 38, 131
La folla delinquente (Sighele), 145n115
Foni, Fabrizio, 16, 153n83
Forgacs, David, 41, 47–8
Fornasari di Verce, Ettore, 54
Forza e ricchezza (Niceforo), 55
Foucault, Michel: on abnormality, 74; on biopolitics and biopower, 22–3, 39, 123; on dangerousness, 11, 92; on medicalization of society, 51–2; on otherness, 42
Foul and the Fragrant, The (Corbin), 45
Frégier, Honoré-Antoine, 141n4
Freud, Sigmund, 36
Fusaro, Edwige Comoy, 93–4

Gallo, Claudio, 153n83
Gamma, Andrea, 132–3
Garfinkel, Paul, 7, 20, 58, 130
Garofalo, Raffaele, 54, 136n27
Gazzetta Letteraria (journal), 11
Gazzetta Piemontese (newspaper), 105
Genesi e funzioni delle leggi penali (Vaccaro), 43–4
genetics, 132–3
Geography of Victorian Gothic Fiction, A (Mighall), 17
germ theory, 46–9
Ghidetti, Enrico, 15, 16, 141n31
Giacinta (Capuana), 116
Gibson, Mary: on crime in modern Italy, 7–8; on illegitimate children, 101; on the nineteenth-century woman question, 90; on positivist criminology, 10, 58, 130, 131
Giovanni Episcopo (D'Annunzio), 61, 98, 158n27
Giuliani, Gaia, 21–2
Gothic: concept of, 4–6; in contemporary fiction and cinema, 133; female body and, 90–4 (*see also* femmes fatales; infanticidal mothers); future research on, 127–33; infection and, 25, 45–53; in Italian literature, 15–18, 126–7 (*see also specific authors and works*); Italy as, 3–4, 6–7; labyrinth metaphor and, 25, 33–7; the mind and (*see* crime-confession nexus; mental illness; sexual monsters); otherness and, 25, 37–44; positivist criminology and, 12–15. *See also* vampires
I Grandi Processi Illustrati (magazine), 105
Gray, Thomas, 3
great unwashed, the, 45
Grimaldi, Laura, 133

Grosz, Elizabeth, 120
Guaiana, Yuri, 76
Guarnieri, Patrizia, 107–8
guilt. *See* crime-confession nexus

Haeckel, Ernst, 9
Hamlin, Christopher, 46–7
heredity: dangerous classes and, 22; homosexuality and, 76; in "L'ossessione rossa" (Bevione), 84, 86–7; Verzeni and, 86–7. *See also* atavism
heteronormativity, 45
Hogle, Jerrold E., 4, 49
homosexuality: repression of, 79, 85, 128–9; legal culture and medical research on, 59, 75–9, 82–5, 88–9, 117–18; in "L'ossessione rossa" (Bevione), 78–85, 128
honour, 102–4, 105, 107–8
Horn, David, 9, 13, 92, 130
Hurley, Kelly, 12, 137n42
hysteria, 109

illegitimate children, 101–4
illness. *See* infection
Impallomeni, Giovanni Battista, 104
impotence, 117
L'Indipendente (newspaper), 60–1
infanticidal mothers: in *L'innocente* (D'Annunzio), 106–7; legal, medical, and popular views of, 101–6; in *La Medea di Porta Medina* (Mastriani), 107–13; in *Storia d'una sartina* (Invernizio), 107–13
infection, 25, 45–53, 127–8
L'innocente (D'Annunzio), 61, 98, 106–7, 118–25
L'intelligenza della folla (Sighele), 145n115
internal migration, 20, 26–7

Introduction à la littérature fantastique (Todorov), 15
Invernizio, Carolina, 14–15, 98–101, 107–13
L'Italia del popolo (newspaper), 62
Italia magica (Contini), 16
Italian Gothic (Malvestio and Serafini), 17
Italian Gothic and Fantastic, The (Billiani and Sulis), 16–17

Jack the Ripper, 74
Jarvis, Timothy, 113–14
Jenner, Mark, 47
Jones, Ernest, 124
Journey to Italy (Sade), 3

Karschay, Stephan, 12, 137n46
Koch, Robert, 47
Krafft-Ebing, Richard von: *L'archivio delle psicopatie sessuali* (journal) and, 154n106; on fetishism, 80; on homosexuality, 76–7, 82, 83; on Verzeni, 86, 87
Kristeva, Julia, 97

labyrinths, 25, 33–7
Lacassagne, Alexandre, 83
Lacchè, Luigi, 21, 22, 24
I ladri dell'onore (Invernizio), 99
I ladri di cadaveri (Piccini), 41–2
Lattarulo, Leonardo, 16
Lazzarin, Stefano, 17, 142n31
Le Fanu, Joseph Sheridan, 4
Lee Six, Abigail, 74
Leopardi, Giacomo, 16
Lepschy, Anna Laura, 99
La Lettura (journal), 11, 74–5
Lister, Joseph, 47
Lo Castro, Giuseppe, 16
Locatelli, Paolo, 23, 24, 28, 30, 38
Lombroso, Cesare: on atavism, 8–15; on *Crime and Punishment* (Dostoevsky), 60, 152n77; D'Annunzio and, 96; *Dracula* (Stoker) and, 85; on Faella, 62; Gothic and, 12–15; legacy of, 131–2; on moral insanity, 69–73; Niceforo and, 54–5; on rise in crime, 139n2; on sexual deviance and homosexuality, 77, 78, 82–3, 86, 87, 117–18; on vagrancy, 37–40; on women as criminals, 91, 94–5, 100, 101, 104
Loria, Achille, 54
Loria, Annamaria, 115
Lucarelli, Carlo, 133, 149n13
Lucchini, Luigi, 11
"La lupa" (Verga), 94–5

MacPike, Loralee, 109
Madrignani, Carlo, 65
La mala vita a Roma (Niceforo), 55–6
Malvestio, Marco, 17
Mantegazza, Paolo, 9, 91–2
Manuale di semejotica delle malattie mentali (Morselli), 77
Manzoni, Alessandro, 5, 149n20
Marchesa Colombi (Maria Antonietta Torriani), 98–9
Il marchese di Roccaverdina (Capuana), 61–2, 63–8, 71–4
Marini, Quinto, 141n31
Marrama, Daniele Oberto, 114–15, 118, 124, 153n81
marriage, 116, 129
Martella, Vittorio, 114
masculinity: criminality and, 58–9; repression of homosexuality and, 128–9; in *L'innocente* (D'Annunzio), 124; nation-building process and, 116–18; in *Trionfo della morte* (D'Annunzio), 95, 98; vampires and, 118–20
Mastriani, Francesco: on dangerous classes, 24–5, 28, 29–31, 32; impact

and popularity of, 14–15; labyrinth metaphor and, 33–4, 37; nation-building process and, 26, 50–1; otherness and, 39–40; on smells and infection, 47–8, 51. See also *La Medea di Porta Medina* (Mastriani); *I misteri di Napoli* (Mastriani); *I vermi* (Mastriani)
Maturin, Charles, 4
Maudsley, Henry, 9, 154n96
Maxwell, Richard, 34, 36
Mayhew, Henry, 141n4
Mazzoni, Cristina, 90–1
McAfee, Noëlle, 97
McCorristine, Shane, 113
McLaren, Angus, 117
La Medea di Porta Medina (Mastriani), 107–13
medical science: body trade and, 34; homosexuality and, 76–8; infection and, 25, 45–53, 127–8; nation-building process and, 7–9; otherness and, 37–44; police writing and, 24; on women, 90–4
mental illness: crime-confession nexus and, 65–6, 68–73; as hereditary, 79–80; homosexuality as, 76–8, 83; infanticidal mothers and, 109–10; in "L'ossessione rossa" (Bevione), 86–7, 88–9; in *Il processo di Frine* (Scarfoglio), 93; Verzeni and, 86–7
miasma theory (anticontagionism), 46–9
Mighall, Robert, 17, 45, 137n42
Milan, 25, 26–7, 142n36. See also *Milano in ombra* (Corio); *Milano sconosciuta* (Valera)
Milano in ombra (Corio): dangerous classes in, 26, 28–30, 32; infection in, 48; nation-building process and, 49–50; otherness in, 40–1, 42;

on prostitution, 143n48; *La Vita Nuova* (journal) and, 140n25
Milano sconosciuta (Valera): dangerous classes in, 26, 29–30; nation-building process and, 147n159; smells and infection in, 46
Miller, William Ian, 45
I misteri del chiostro romano e la presa di Roma (De Dominicis), 142n32
I misteri del Vaticano (Mistrali), 142n32
I misteri di Napoli (Mastriani): dangerous classes in, 32; labyrinth metaphor in, 33–4, 37; Marini on, 141n31; nation-building process and, 26; otherness in, 40; "trilogia socialista" (socialist trilogy) and, 140n23
I misteri di Roma contemporanea (Del Vecchio), 142n32
Mistrali, Franco, 142n32, 156n142
Mitchell, Katharine, 98–9
Moll, Albert, 82
Moloney, Brian, 141–2n31
monstrosity, 41, 96–8, 110–12, 120–5. See also sexual monsters
Moore, John, 3–4
Moraglia, Giovan Battista, 97
moral insanity, 69–73
La moralità del male (De Amicis), 74
Morando, Francesco, 114, 124
Morel, Bénédict Augustin, 137n42
Mori, Simona, 27, 58
Morselli, Enrico, 44, 77
motherhood, 90–1, 100. See also infanticidal mothers
Mulvey-Roberts, Marie, 110, 129
Mycobacterium tuberculosis, 146n141
Les Mystères de Londres (Féval), 141n30
Les Mystères de Paris (Sue), 25–6, 42
Mysteries of London, The (Reynolds), 33–4

Nani, Michele, 21–2
Naples, 25, 26–7. See also *I misteri di Napoli* (Mastriani); *Il ventre di Napoli* (Serao)
Naspini, Sacha, 133
nation-building process: crime and, 6–9, 20–5; female sexuality and, 116–18; urban mysteries and, 26, 41–2, 49–52
Nazi Germany, 52–3, 131
La nazione (newspaper), 140n27
necrophilia, 87
Neera (Anna Maria Radius Zuccari), 91–2, 98–9
Nerozzi, Gianfranco, 133
neurocriminology, 132–3
New Woman, 115–16
Niceforo, Alfredo, 54–6, 131
Nicolson, David, 9
Nightingale, Florence, 46
Nixon, Kari, 47
No (Oriani), 158n27
Nostalgia del sangue (Correnti), 133
I nuovi misteri della corte di Roma (Anon.), 142n32

occultism, 113–14. *See also* vampires
On the Nightmare (Jones), 124
Operette morali (Leopardi), 16
L'ora (journal), 63
Oriani, Alfredo, 158n27
Origin of Species, The (Darwin), 10
Orlando, Francesco, 15
L'Osservatore Romano (newspaper), 116
"L'ossessione rossa" (Bevione), 74–5, 78–85, 86–9, 128
otherness, 25, 37–44

Pagliaro, Annamaria, 67
Palermo, Antonio, 32, 140n23
Paris, 46
Pasteur, Louis, 47

Patriarca, Silvana, 8, 117, 118
Pazzia e società (Penta), 44
Peccatrice moderna (Invernizio), 98, 99–101
Pende, Nicola, 131
Penta, Pasquale, 44, 78, 80, 84, 86, 87
Perkins, Pam, 3–4
I pervertimenti sessuali (Penta), 86
Pessina, Enrico, 11
Pezzotti, Barbara, 150n23
Piccini, Giulio: on dangerous classes, 24–5, 29–30, 31, 32; impact and popularity of, 14–15; labyrinth metaphor and, 35–6, 37; nation-building process and, 26, 49–50; otherness and, 41–2; on smells and infection, 47, 49. *See also L'assassinio nel vicolo della luna* (Piccini); *Firenze sotterranea* (Piccini); *I ladri di cadaveri* (Piccini)
Picozzi, Massimo, 133
Pictures from Italy (Dickens), 4
Pierangeli, Fabio, 64
Pio, Oscar, 105
La plebe di Milano (Corio). See *Milano in ombra* (Corio)
police writing, 23–4, 28, 30, 31, 38
Polizia e delinquenza in Italia (Alongi), 23, 24, 28
La polizia e le classi pericolose della società (Bolis), 21
Portinari, Folco, 150n23
positivism and positivist criminology: anthropology of lower classes and, 54–5; dangerous classes and, 27–8; D'Annunzio and, 61; debate on criminogenic factors and, 11–12, 57–8; Fascist Italy and, 130–2; as Gothic, 12–15; nation-building process and, 7–9, 116; on sexual deviance, 76–8; spiritism and, 113–14; on vagrancy,

37–40; on women as criminals, 91. *See also* atavism; heredity; Lombroso, Cesare
poverty: crime and, 45, 48–53, 54; dangerous classes and, 25–33; degeneration and, 43–4; as infection, 45, 48–53, 127–8
Prichard, James Cowles, 69
prison system, 20–1
Processi celebri contemporanei italiani e stranieri (Pio and Argenti), 105
I processi celebri di tutti i popoli (1868), 105
Il processo di Frine (Scarfoglio), 92–3
Profumo (Capuana), 116–17
I promessi sposi (Manzoni), 135n16
prostitution: as crime, 90; in *Giovanni Episcopo* (D'Annunzio), 61; infanticide and, 102–3; Lombroso and Ferrero on, 104; otherness and, 38–9, 40; as source of infection, 47–8; in *I vermi* (Mastriani), 40. *See also* dangerous classes
Proulx, Jean, 87–8
psychological thrillers, 59, 62, 68–9, 75
Psychopathia Sexualis (Krafft-Ebing), 153n92
Punter, David, 4

race and scientific racism, 21–3, 39–44, 119–20, 123–4
Radcliffe, Ann, 3, 15
Rafter, Nicole, 12, 13, 137n48
Rambelli, Loris, 150n23, 150n30
recidivism, 20–1
Responsibility in Mental Disease (Maudsley), 154n96
Reynolds, G.W., 33–4
Riccardi, Paolo, 38–9
Ridenhour, Jamieson, 33
Il ritratto del morto (Marrama), 153n81

Rivista Italiana di Sociologia (journal), 144n96
Rocco, Alfredo, 130
Roma (journal), 107
Romanticism, 5
Rome, 142n32, 148n182
Rosa, Giovanna, 32
Rosenberg, Charles, 47

Sade, Donatien Alphonse François, Marquis de, 3
Gli scamiciati (Valera), 32–3
Scapigliatura, 46, 149n20
Scarfoglio, Edoardo, 92–3
Scarlata, Francesco, 92
Schiff, Moritz, 9
Schiff, Wilhelm, 74
Schuller, Kyla, 39, 141n4
scientism, 113–14
"Il segreto della morta" (Appiani), 162n131
Semmelweis, Ignaz, 47
Senso (Boito), 158n27
Serao, Matilde: on dangerous classes, 24–5, 29–30, 31; impact and popularity of, 14–15; labyrinth metaphor and, 34–5; Marrama and, 153n81; nation-building process and, 26, 51; otherness and, 40; Scarfoglio and, 157–8n20; on smells and infection, 46, 47, 48, 51; on women's role in society, 98–9. *See also Il ventre di Napoli* (Serao)
Sergi, Giuseppe, 91
serial killing, 74
sexology, 59, 74, 75, 76–8, 80, 82–4
sexual monsters: figure of, 59, 73–8; in *La moralità del male* (De Amicis), 74; in "L'ossessione rossa" (Bevione), 74–5, 78–85, 86–9; Verzeni as, 74, 85–8
Seymour, Mark, 76, 116, 117

Shapiro, Ann-Louise, 103
Sighele, Scipio, 42, 55–6, 103
smells, 25, 45–9
Smith, Andrew, 12
Smith, Thomas Southwood, 46
social reforms, 30–1
Società italiana di antropologia e di etnologia, 9
Società operaia di Napoli, 99
Sociologia criminale (Colajanni), 54
Il soprannaturale letterario (Orlando), 15
Sorveglianti e sorvegliati (Locatelli), 23, 24, 28, 30, 38
Spain, 118
"Spalatro: From the Notes of Fra Giacomo" (Le Fanu), 4
Spencer, Herbert, 9
Spiritismo? (Capuana), 151–2n67
spiritualism, 113–14. See also vampires
La stampa (newspaper), 105
Stephanou, Aspasia, 119
sterilization, 44
Stevenson, John Allen, 119
Stewart-Steinberg, Suzanne, 70, 102, 117, 118
Stoker, Bram, 59, 85
Stoler, Ann Laura, 39
Stoppato, Alessandro, 104
Storia d'una sartina (Invernizio), 107–13
Stott, Rebecca, 96
Studi di letteratura e storia (Morando), 163n184
Sue, Eugène, 25–6, 42
"Sul romanticismo" (Manzoni), 5
Sulis, Gigliola, 16–17
Sull'incremento del delitto (Lombroso), 139n2
supernatural phenomena, 6, 12, 14, 66–8, 113. See also vampires
Svevo, Italo, 60–1, 62

Tamassia, Arrigo, 76–7, 88
Tanzi, Eugenio, 78
Tardiola, Giuseppe, 115
Thompson, Hannah, 74
Thomson, James Bruce, 9
Thurschwell, Pamela, 113
Todorov, Tzvetan, 15
Tonsi, Giuseppe, 114
Transalpina (journal), 142n31
Trattato delle malattie mentali (Tanzi), 78
La Tribuna Giudiziaria (journal), 86
Trionfo della morte (D'Annunzio), 95–8, 119
tuberculosis, 47, 146n141
Tuscan Penal Code (1853), 160n68

uncanny, 36
L'uomo delinquente (Lombroso), 10, 13, 78, 87, 155n133
urban mysteries (city mysteries): anthropology of lower classes and, 53–6; dangerous classes in, 25–33; infection in, 25, 45–53, 127–8; labyrinth metaphor in, 25, 33–7; origins and characteristics of, 25–6; otherness in, 25, 37–44; Rome and, 142n32

Vaccaro, Michele Angelo, 43–4
Vacher, Joseph Gleydson, 37–8
vagrancy, 37–40, 43, 49, 141n3. See also dangerous classes
Valera, Paolo: on dangerous classes, 24–5, 26, 29–30, 32–3; nation-building process and, 50; otherness and, 40–1; on smells and infection, 46. See also *Milano sconosciuta* (Valera); *Gli scamiciati* (Valera)
vampires: blood and, 85–6, 114, 119; female sexuality and, 129; figure of, 85–6; in Italian literature, 114–16, 117–25

"Un vampiro" (Boni), 114
"Un vampiro" (Capuana), 114, 115, 117–18, 124, 151–2n67
"Il vampiro" (Martella), 114
Il vampiro (Mistrali), 156n142
"Il vampiro" (Tonsi), 114
"Vampiro innocente" (Morando), 114, 124
venereal disease, 47–8
Il ventre di Milano (Arrighi), 46
Il ventre di Napoli (Serao): dangerous classes in, 29–30, 31; labyrinth metaphor in, 34–5; nation-building process and, 26; revised version of, 147n165; smells and infection in, 46, 47, 48, 51
Verga, Giovanni, 94–5, 150n26
verismo, 140n26
I vermi (Mastriani): dangerous classes in, 28, 29–31; journal articles and statistics in, 143n48; nation-building process and, 26; otherness in, 40; smells and infection in, 47–8, 51; "trilogia socialista" (socialist trilogy) and, 140n23
Verzeni, Vincenzo, 74, 85–8, 133
Vidler, Anthony, 37
Vidocq, Eugène-François, 141n29, 141n30
Vidoni, Giuseppe, 131

Vignoli, Tito, 92
virility. *See* masculinity
Vita dei campi (Verga), 94–5
La Vita Nuova (journal), 140n25
Volatile Bodies (Grosz), 120
Les Vrais Mystères de Paris (Vidocq), 141n30

Walpole, Horace, 3
Ward, Tony, 92
Weikart, Richard, 131
Welch, Rhiannon Noel, 119
Westphal, Carl, 76–7
Williams, Ann, 37
women: criminality and, 58–9, 90–4, 129; emergence of feminism and, 115–16; as femmes fatales, 94–101; legal culture and medical research on, 90–4; mental illness and, 79–80; motherhood and, 90–1, 100; as source of infection, 47–8. *See also* infanticidal mothers; prostitution
Wong, Aliza, 21

Ystehede, Per, 13

Zanardelli, Giuseppe, 75–6
Zangara, Mario, 72
Zannetti, Arturo, 9